First published in the United Kingdom in 2024 by
Thames & Hudson Ltd, 181A High Holborn, London WC1V 7QX

First published in the United States of America in 2024 by
Thames & Hudson Inc., 500 Fifth Avenue, New York, New York 10110

Edited by Simon Hilton
Publisher: Tristan de Lancey
Designer: Nick Jakins
Managing Editor: Jane Laing

British Library Cataloguing-in-Publication Data
A catalogue record for this book is available from the British Library

Library of Congress Control Number 2024935635

ISBN 978-0-500-02778-3

Printed by GPS Group, Bosnia and Herzegovina

FSC
www.fsc.org
MIX
Paper | Supporting
responsible forestry
FSC® C118234

Find out more about John Lennon at johnlennon.com
Find out more about Yoko Ono at imaginepeace.com
Join us at citizenofnutopia.com

Be the first to know about our new releases,
exclusive content and author events by visiting
thamesandhudson.com
thamesandhudsonusa.com
thamesandhudson.com.au

MIND GAMES

JOHN LENNON & YOKO ONO

With contributions from
the people who were there

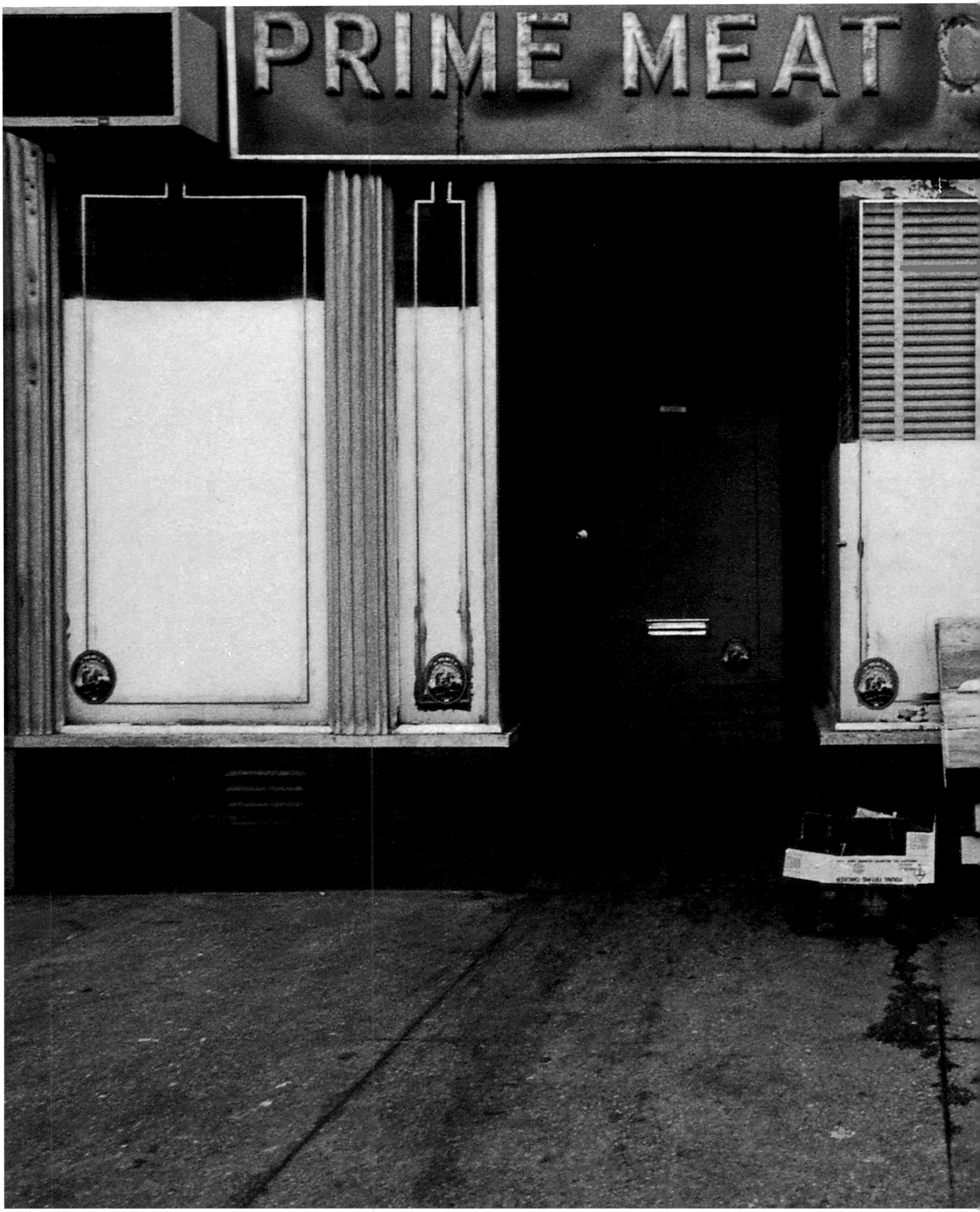
PRIME MEAT

mix out man down to F#

break Sax solo?

steel

intuition   (Moreover darlin) chorus

Solo   You are here (8b   (Sax perc) Harps   (1)?
2:55   Saxs)   wooden Xphone
                                                   Hawaiian steel drum
na   Great City Tamb   Saxs)
     Kay Electric bass
3:12 only People (stereoside   Tamb   + Sax solo
                  guitar?)   midd 8 clap chorus.   bird
4:13 Minder Save in Tamb   x chorus 8 + (Steel (mellotron)
K's solo (2 min)   peace + /clap   clap hands riff   organ?)
2nd (3 min in   / bass tempo   mixing steel
Vowel ole at end   Give Me Blue chorus + clap hands
edit bass drums in   disemmren (chom? (guitar solo) steel. (Slow pick up
               4:35   Tamb   Strings (mellotron) Sals in intro
         3:35 I knew (chom to day) (David?) chorus.
2:30 Bring back   Hueg   clap slide. chorus
                                                 in Harps me
chorus on 8 3:9 One Day at a time. ?? Steel? PERC
4:20 Tight ass (riff) steel 2nd mellotron
                              solo?
                     3rd solo?
                   4 min left

CONTENTS

PREFACE
by Yoko Ono

John was trying to convey the message that we all play mind games, but if we can play mind games, why not make a *positive* future with it, to play a positive mind game?

I think 'Mind Games' is such an incredibly strong song. But at the time, I think that people didn't quite get the message because this was before its time.

Now, people would understand it.

I don't think in those days people knew they were playing mind games anyway.

Yoko Ono Lennon

C on down

MIND GAMES

C WERE PLAYING THE MIND GAME TOGETHER
PUSHING THE BARRIERS PLANTING SEEDS
PLAYING THE MIND GUERRILLA
CHANTING THE MANTRA PEACE ON EARTH
WE ALL BEEN PLAYING OUR MIND GAMES FOREVER
✗ SOME KINDA DRUID DUDES LIFTING THE VEIL
DOING THE MIND GUERRILLA
SOME CALL IT MAGIC THE SEARCH FOR THE GRAIL

DRUID REST 10 & 13
10 & 11

D

175 — C   D   G   Em
LOVE IS THE ANSWER ~~AND KNOW THAT SHE THE ISNT~~ THATS BLOWING IN THE WIND   D
LOVE IS A FLOWER WITH POWER ~~FOR ALL   ENOUGH THAT OFF WHICH~~ GROES WITHIN
C   D   G   Em   ~~KNOWEHX~~ (THATS ~~GROWING THAT GROWS WITHIN YOUR MIND~~) D
you gotta let it grow

C
SO KEEP ON PLAYING THOSE MIND GAMES TOGETHER
FAITH IN THE FUTURE OUTTA THE NOW ◄   gotta
YOU JUST CANT BEAT ON THE MIND GUERRILLAS
✗ ABSOLUTE ELSEWHERE IN THE STONES OF YOUR MIND
YEAH WE BEEN PLAYING THOSE MIND GAMES FOREVER   2nd verse   10 & 11
PROJECTING OUR IMAGES IN SPACE AND TIME

10 & 15

327 YES IS ~~THE~~ ANSWER ~~NO ISXXHSIXAXWHKHXANOTHERXWORR~~ THATS MIRRORED IN YOUR SOUL
YES IS SURRENDER ~~REKENDERXWHXXTHEXEAXXTHE~~ MESSAGE IS OF OLD
you gotta let it go
10 & 11

V2
2
SO KEEP ON PLAYING THOSE MIND GAMES TOGETHER
DOING THE RITUAL DANCE IN THE SUN ──
MILLIONS OF MIND GUERRILLAS
PUTTING THEIR SOUL POWER TO THE KARMIC WHEEL   10 & 11
YES KEEP ON PLAYING THOSE MIND GAMES FOREVER
RAISING THE SPIRIT OF PEACE AND LOVE

SOO ─────

4 x's
|| C / Em/B / | Am⁷ / C/G | FMa⁷ / Am/E - | D⁷ / D⁷/C / ||

2 x's
||: C / D / | G / G⁷/F / | Em / G/D / | D⁷ / D⁷/C :||

MIND GAMES

We're playing those mind games together
Pushing the barrier planting seeds
Playing the mind guerrilla
Chanting the mantra 'Peace on Earth'

We all been playing those mind games forever
Some kinda druid dude lifting the veil
Doing the mind guerrilla
Some call it magic the search for the grail

Love is the answer
And you know that for sure
Love is a flower
You got to let it
You got to let it grow

So keep on playing those mind games together
Faith in the future outta the now
You just can't beat on those mind guerrillas
Absolute elsewhere in the stones of your mind
Yeah we're playing those mind games forever
Projecting our images in space and in time

Yes is the answer and you know that for sure
Yes is surrender you got to let it, you got to let it go

So keep on playing those mind games together
Doing the ritual dance in the sun
Millions of mind guerrillas
Putting their soul power to the karmic wheel
Keep on playing those mind games forever
Raising the spirit of peace and love

Love

I want you to make love not war
I know you've heard it before

MIND GAMES

John: 'Mind Games' – that was a fun track, because the voice is in stereo and the seeming orchestra on it is just me playing three notes with slide guitar. And the middle eight is reggae. Trying to explain to American musicians what reggae was in 1973 was pretty hard, but it's basically a reggae middle eight if you listen to it. They didn't know what reggae was then. I'm glad I played; it ain't bad.

I was thinking of it in terms of guerrilla warfare. A mind guerrilla. A conceptual guerrilla. We all were playing them, whether we knew it or not.

'Love is the answer and you know that for sure' – with this one, I've really been into it. In Denmark (in 1969–70), I was just playing it for hours and hours until the rhythm was just really owned. And I was really high on it. I was really getting into it, like you never do on tape, that's the thing. [laughs] So, I know that in there somewhere I've got it, I just gotta coast myself up to it, you know. It took me a long time to be able to do it – and you'd think it was easy, you know. It's like singing a different rhythm on the top; it'd be easier to sing if somebody else was doing it.

Mind Games was actually a book that somebody sent me, which I wrote an intro to: 'I have read three important and revolutionary books in the last three years: Yoko Ono's *Grapefruit*, Arthur Janov's *Primal Scream*, and now *Mind Games*. I suggest you read and experience them.' It was an interesting book, I enjoyed it. And it just came out as a song. The lyrics have nothing to do with the book except for it's a mind game itself, the lyrics. The games are going on – so we can choose what kind of games we want to play or which side we want to play on.

People have told me that the album's title indicates I like to struggle with things in my life. But I've never seen my life that way. The record's full of songs and words. That's all. At least, that's all I was trying to do. I don't any feel different now than I ever have. I'm still a bit of an adolescent; I keep changing all the time. But I don't want to stop doing that. All my old friends from Liverpool got jobs after they left school. And I'd see them six months later and their hair would be going thin and they'd be getting fatter. They were becoming old men, while I was with the Beatles. I just keep going.

What I'm back to is believing in everything until it's disproved. But I don't think I should sit down, write a list, and sing 'I believe in everything until it's disproved, I believe in everything until it's disproved.' Whatever you call it, it is. Whatever you call what you're doing, whether you call it magic or therapy or politics, it is something you know instinctively.

There's no new myth there. It's the same thing but it's called 'Mind Games'. Whenever people say, 'What do you mean "peace"? Are you ever going to get it? Isn't it naive?' and all the rest of the shit, the answer is that we didn't fly for thousands of years but we talked about it amongst many, many other dreams. So whatever we project, we get. So I try to keep on projecting the dream of peace and love or whatever the cliché is, because I prefer that.

All I'm doing, along with millions of others in all walks of life – creatively or quote uncreatively unquote, carpenters or artists – is projecting the dream we're all going to, whether it's 'go to the moon', 'fly in the air', or 'everybody happy'. Whatever the dream is, have the dream, because I think we'll get it. And if not, well, sod it. I won't be around anyway!

I was brought up mostly on American stuff, as were a lot of the English and most of the world. It's Doris Day and Dick Tracy and Flash Gordon and all the Hollywood movies. All American music. Even the music my parents liked, or that generation, was American music. We were the fifty-first state and we spoke English too. It wasn't the other way around. They ask me why all the English groups sang in American voices and it was because that's all we heard and that's all we wanted to hear. You didn't listen to the BBC unless you had to. Music is an uplifting, spiritual ritual which enables us to carry on. That's what its origins were and I think that's what it is.

Living in the Village in New York was a bit like shaking off the dust. I don't know how conscious an effort it was. I like to think I know what I'm doing but I don't usually, until I've done it. I felt as though whatever it was, I was shaking it off. But I used to do that in the Beatles too, crash out or whatever the expression is, to try to survive as 'me' so as not to get sucked in and vanish.

There was a period when…I think if you get down to basics, whatever the problem is, it's usually to do with love. People's neurotic need for love. So I think 'All You Need Is Love' is a true statement. I'm not saying 'All we have to do is to….' Because 'All You Need' came out in the Flower Power Generation time, it doesn't mean that all you have to do is put on a phoney smile or wear a flower dress and it's gonna be alright.

Love is not just something that you stick on posters, or stick on the back of your car, or on the back of your jacket, or on a badge. I'm talking about real love. So I still believe that. Love is appreciation of other people and allowing them to be. Love is allowing somebody to be themselves and that's what we do need.

Artwork used by EMI Records to promote the 'Mind Games'
Apple single R994 in the UK and elsewhere in Europe during 1973.

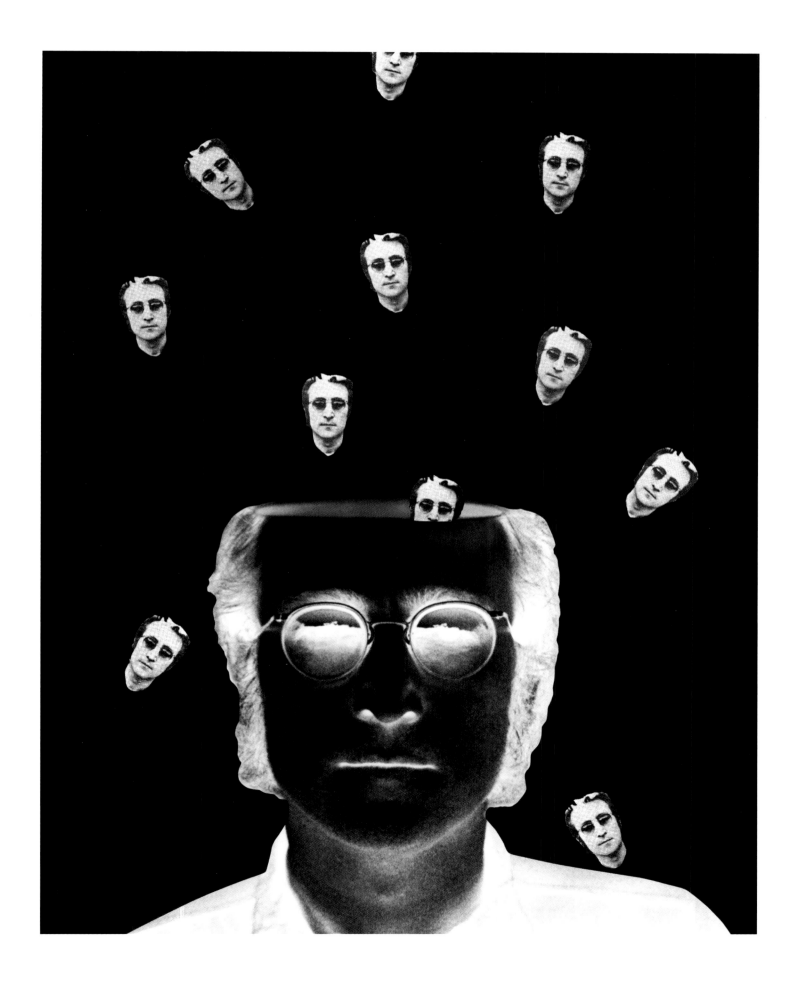

Early draft of the lyrics for 'Mind Games' on Apple memorandum
stationery, 1973.

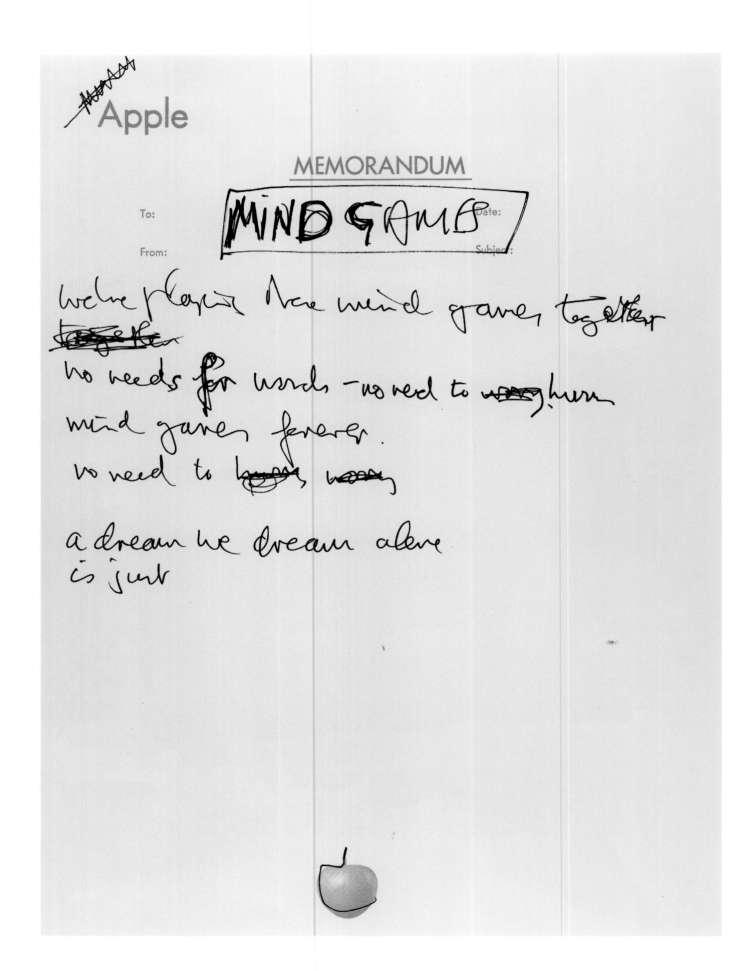

Yoko: We're all worried about this love generation because it's dying down, or something like that. The reason for that is, like John said, they were really taking the message on a superficial level – like, 'Alright, let's just stick a little label on their car,' kind of thing. But this is the age when people finally drew the conclusion that we failed in a form of communication between two people. Just see the divorce rate – you'll see what it's like. And young people not believing in marriage, which is understandable, and the reason for that is because they had a lot of bad experience in that area. But when you think about the group situation, the communication has to start with one to one.

A relationship of two people is really a very basic need and a basic starting point. The society. If two people can't get along with each other, then how could a society operate smoothly? So the thing is, we have to start to pick up on that again, not lose any faith in it, and start to understand each other, start to establish communication between two people. And listen between us; if we can't get along, nobody can. And we really, really love each other. At the same time we really work on it, because love doesn't just come like a drop of rain – you have to really work at it and water it.

John: It's like a flower you have to water every day.

Yoko: And really try to grow it. Between us, we really try to expose ourselves to each other, try to understand each other. All that effort and energy we put into understanding each other – if everybody tries that in a relationship, it's gonna work.

John: Well, you see, I / we / they always said, 'We were all part of [the cultural revolution of the sixties], it happened to all of us.' I feel just the same as everybody who was affected by it. Except somehow I was supposed to be separate. And I wasn't. I was just part of it. It does tend to put your image separate, though. Or it makes people's idea of what you are separate. But I just went through it, along with all the other millions, and here we are now, right?

Things change all the time. By the time the observers write it down, it's all changed. That's why it's a joke to listen to the news, 'cause you know it happened yesterday.

Make love, not war.

Opposite: Home video of John writing and practising 'Make Love Not War' on his favourite upright 'composing' piano and Spanish acoustic guitar in the upstairs bedroom at Tittenhurst, Ascot, 8 February 1970.

Typewritten lyrics for 'Make Love Not War' by John Lennon, 1970.

```
             MAKE  LOVE  NOT  WAR


MAKE  LOVE  NOT  WAR

I  KNOW  THAT  YOU'VE  HEARD  IT  BEFORE

THAT'S  WHY  I  WANT  YOU  TO-

          FAIT  LAMOUR,  PAS  LA  GUERRE

          I  KNOW  THAT  YOUVE  HEARD  IT  BEFORE

          LOVE  IS  THE  ANSWER

          AND  YOU  KNOW  THAT  IS  TRUE



MACH  LIEBER,  NICHT  KRIEG

I  KNOW  THAT  YOU'VE  HEARD  IT  BEFORE

THAT'S  WHY  I  WANT  YOU  TO-

          TATAKAU  YORIMO

          AISHI  AOYO

          LOVE  IS  THE  ANSWER

          AND  YOU  KNOW  THAT  IS  TRUE
```

Opposite: *Make Love Not War* offset lithograph poster, 35.6 x 24.1 cm by Wilfred Weisser, Tarot Press, Los Angeles, 1967.

Top: John's handwriting on Bag Productions notepaper containing themes from his songs 'The Word', 'All You Need Is Love', 'Instant Karma! (We All Shine On)' and 'Mind Games', 1970.

Centre: 'Approx infinite universe' and 'absolute elsewhere' in John's handwriting, 1973.

Bottom: Illustration showing the relationship between the Present (Here-Now) and the Absolute Elsewhere as proposed in A. S. Eddington's book, *The Nature of the Physical World*, 1929.

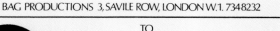

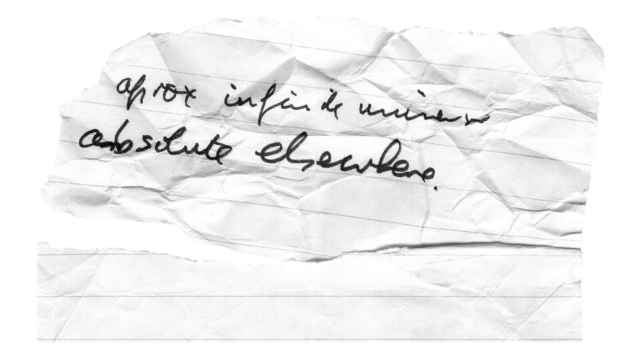

Make Love Not War badge by Penelope and Franklin Rosemont from Solidarity Bookshop, Chicago, Illinois, March 1965.

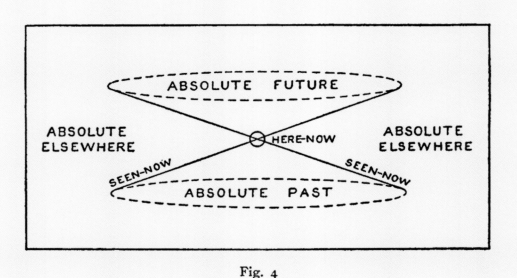

Fig. 4

THE MAGICIAN.

THE HIGH PRIESTESS

THE EMPRESS.

THE EMPEROR.

THE HIEROPHANT

THE LOVERS.

THE HANGED MAN.

DEATH.

TEMPERANCE.

THE DEVIL.

THE TOWER.

THE CHARIOT.

STRENGTH.

THE HERMIT.

WHEEL of FORTUNE.

JUSTICE .

THE STAR .

THE MOON .

THE SUN .

JUDGEMENT.

THE WORLD.

THE FOOL .

JOHN'S PORTFOLIO OF DIARIES

SHAKYAMUNI BUDDHA SURROUNDED BY SCENES OF HIS LIFE
Postcard of the hanging scroll, painting on canvas, Tibet, 18th century.

666 (THE APOCALYPSE OF JOHN 13:18)
Cut from the LP front cover of the album *666* by Aphrodite's Child (Vertigo Records, 1972).

EYE OF HORUS
Symbol of the Egyptian deity within a pyramid, representing protection and good health. Crowley believed he was instructed by Horus and that the symbol represented a new age of divine insight and awakening for the individual.

PHARMACEUTICAL LABEL
Quality control label sourced from a pharmaceutical pill container manufactured by the Upjohn Company in Michigan, USA.

ELEMENTALS
Aleister Crowley's *May Morn* (1919), featured in the periodical, *The Equinox* (Volume III, No. 1), published spring 1919. It was originally accompanied by the text: 'The picture is symbolical of the New Æon. From the blasted stump of dogma, the poison oak of "original sin", is hanged the hag with dyed and bloody hair, Christianity.'

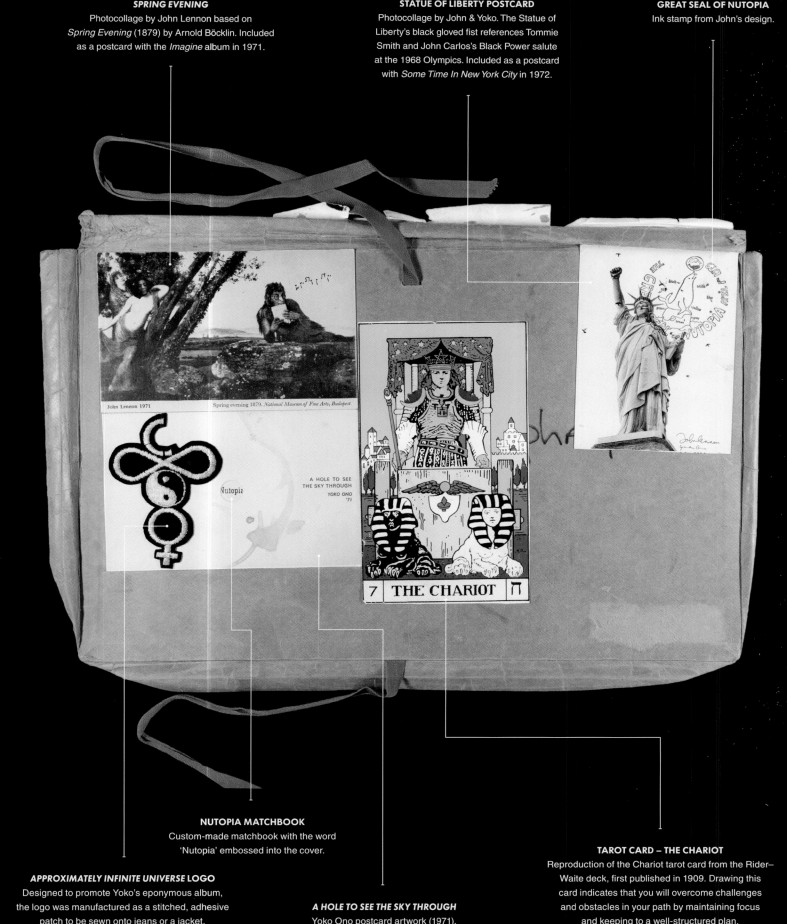

SPRING EVENING
Photocollage by John Lennon based on
Spring Evening (1879) by Arnold Böcklin. Included
as a postcard with the *Imagine* album in 1971.

STATUE OF LIBERTY POSTCARD
Photocollage by John & Yoko. The Statue of
Liberty's black gloved fist references Tommie
Smith and John Carlos's Black Power salute
at the 1968 Olympics. Included as a postcard
with *Some Time In New York City* in 1972.

GREAT SEAL OF NUTOPIA
Ink stamp from John's design.

NUTOPIA MATCHBOOK
Custom-made matchbook with the word
'Nutopia' embossed into the cover.

TAROT CARD – THE CHARIOT
Reproduction of the Chariot tarot card from the Rider–
Waite deck, first published in 1909. Drawing this
card indicates that you will overcome challenges
and obstacles in your path by maintaining focus
and keeping to a well-structured plan.

APPROXIMATELY INFINITE UNIVERSE LOGO
Designed to promote Yoko's eponymous album,
the logo was manufactured as a stitched, adhesive
patch to be sewn onto jeans or a jacket.

A HOLE TO SEE THE SKY THROUGH
Yoko Ono postcard artwork (1971).

THE GOOD SAMARITAN
Postcard of the stained-glass window by
Marc Chagall, 1967, 4.47 × 2.78 m. Union Church
of Pocantico Hills, Tarrytown, New York.

**ILLUSTRATION OF SQUARE
WITH TRIANGLE INSIDE**
Cut from the front pages of the book *The Art
and Practice of the Occult* by Ophiel, 1972.
John has drawn his signature doodle
of his and Yoko's smiling faces inside.

JOHN HOLDING A PIG
Postcard included with initial pressings of
the *Imagine* album in 1971 – John's cheeky
parody of the front cover of Paul and Linda
McCartney's *Ram* album, also released in 1971.

THE ART AND PRACTICE OF THE OCCULT
Cover art from the book on exercises in
Hermetic Qabalah by Ophiel, Peach
Publishing Co., fourth edition, 1972.

John: Many, if not all, great men and women were 'mystics' in a sense: Einstein, who at the end of his life remarked that if he had to do it over, he would have spent more time on the spiritual; Pythagoras and Newton were mystics. In order to receive the 'wholly spirit', i.e. creative inspiration (whether you are labelled an artist, scientist, mystic, psychic, etc.), the main problem was emptying the mind.

...hn playing guitar, singing songs and chanting/meditating with the Maharishi Mahesh Yogi in Rishikesh, India, February 1968. ohn: 'Eye-ing', 'eye-ing', 'eye-ing'. He picked the right mantra for e. It was quite a trip. I was in a room for five days meditating. I wrote undreds of songs. I couldn't sleep and I was hallucinating like crazy, aving dreams where you could smell. I'd do a few hours and then you'd trip off, three- or four-hour stretches. It was just a way of getting there and you could go on amazing trips. The funny thing about the camp was that although it was very beautiful and I was meditating about eight hours a day, I was writing the most miserable songs on Earth. In 'Yer Blues' when I wrote, 'I feel so lonely I could die', I'm not kidding. That's how I felt. Up there trying to reach God and feeling suicidal.

Chanting the Mantra ॐ
by Maharishi Mahesh Yogi

Mantra is a vehicle for the inward movement of the mind, and that is a word that is used for its sound value only.

The teaching has been set up in a very standard form. Actual practice involves thinking of a word (mantra) devoid of meaning. We don't know the meaning, we don't try to know the meaning. And the principle is that if we know the meaning, that meaning is a static thing. If we say, 'pencil, pencil', someone who doesn't know what 'pencil' means in English, he just hears the sound 'pencil'. And someone who knows the pencil… you see, the meaning is static.

The sound changes in its pitch. It could be a loud sound, it could be a low sound. The meaning is the same at every pitch, high or low. So if the mind is on the meaning, then there is no chance of refining the meaning.

If the mind is not on the meaning, then there's a chance of refining the sound. Then there's a chance of experiencing the sound in its finer values, till the finest could be transcended and the awareness would reach that inner wakefulness, devoid of any perception. This will be Transcendental Consciousness.

So we take a thought and experience it. And in experiencing the thought, the simple formula is that the thought functions as a motivation for impulse. Then the mind is pulsating. If we don't try to manipulate the thought in any sense – concentrate or hold it on or anything – then the thought will start to really refine, refine, refine. And it'll sink out. And if the activity starts to die out, die out, die out, die out….

So this is what we say: naturally, greater activity of the mind reaches its least value in a very natural way. Any activity has a tendency to settle down and be quiet. This natural tendency of the mind to be quiet is all that we use in meditation, and nothing else. So, in a very innocent manner, we think of the thought, and every time we think it becomes finer and finer and finer.

We experience its finest state and then it dies out. The mind is left wide awake, by itself, without any sound to experience.

That inner wakefulness is that unbounded awareness. No boundaries. It's like the wave settling down. And it settles down and [there's a] flat surface of the water throughout the whole range of the lake.

This unbounded awareness where the perception is no longer within boundaries. It is unbounded. This is a silent state of the mind and it is so fulfilling that the physiology, having tasted this kind of quietness of activity, it cherishes that.

And because it's cherishing to the whole physiology, to the whole experience, the physiology tends to maintain that state naturally, even when there are activities, like that, like that, like that….

So, by nature, that state of experience, by nature, through practice, becomes stabilized in the field of activity.

And once that is stabilized in the field of activity, we have life on all levels, all possibilities. The level of all possibilities, perfect orderliness.

And all that we know from quantum mechanics to be the characteristics of waking state becomes one's own personal experience throughout life. That kind of life we want to generate.

By reading, it's very difficult. Because to have that effortless thinking, one needs a little verification from the teacher, a few times – two, three, four times – and then one knows what it means to have a thought without effort. There's that experience.

And then in the process of teaching, the procedure of teaching, we have laid out three days of 'checking' that one experiences, and then the next day the teacher tells [the pupil] certain things, which by experience of years of teaching we have established… are the points which the beginner must know the first day.

Now: second day experiences. These are the points which the beginner must know as an explanation of his two days' experience. Experiences are very subtle. In this case, the experiences are fading of the experiences.

With some experiences, we think the thought, it's a direct experience of the thought. And then it begins to fade and fade and fade and fade.

So, the disappearing of the experiences – first day, second day, third day – every day it becomes a little bit clearer what this means.

In three days, the experiences become fairly clear [and one is able] to understand the entire process, and on that basis all the future possibilities.

So three days of checking is a vital aspect of the beginning of the process.

The whole thing is very simple. There is nothing of any complication or anything. Absolute natural process.

That is the reason why everyone succeeds in it. Only those three days of checking and one has understood those points, no problems.

It's purely on an instructional basis. Otherwise…the whole complication is not very scientific. [laughs]

Some Call It Magic

Yoko: John was the one who was first into astrology and mediums and all that. Because of his mother's death, he [wanted to talk to her]. He went to all sorts of mediums, but none of them were good enough. When I met him and I started to go to Apple in London, John had a hired astrologer who was paid by the week.

Richard DiLello: At Apple there was an astrologer named Caleb [Rupert Ashburton-Dunning] who subbed as a fortune teller for John Lennon, Paul McCartney and the Apple staff. His job was to read the stars daily and make a prediction: to move or not to move. Splitting his hours between his astral charts and the *I Ching*, he would make the daily rounds of the staff, throwing three pennies and interpreting everyone's lines. After a while, having been asked for a chart prediction in *Billboard* one too many times, he decided it was time to go home forever.

Derek Taylor: He used to manage the [Apple] boutique, but when the Beatles learned about his interest in the *I Ching* they took him on to study it in relation to the organization. All the Beatles threw for the *I Ching* and they took it seriously. Caleb gave them reports and they studied them at business meetings. But I don't know what was in them. They were confidential. Caleb had to be let go after a few weeks of trying at £50 a week. Despite this, he put up a fine show of skill and instinct in trying to sort us all out for the benefit of the Fab Two, John and Paul, still in search of a leader for the company. Ask not for whom The Caleb throws, he throws for you.

Yoko: I was one of those orientals who were westernized so I was not into those things at all. The Indian philosophy and all that – all of that came from John, not from me. I was into Jean-Paul Sartre and existentialism and all that kind of thing. I was the one who was cynical about Maharishi and when John came back he said, 'You were right!'

John: A guy in England, an astrologer [Patric Walker] once told me that I was going to not live in England. And I didn't remember that until I was in the middle of my immigration fight to stay in this country [when I was thinking], 'What the hell am I doing here? Why the hell am I going through this?' I didn't plan to live here, it just happened. There was no packing the bags. We left everything at our house in England. We were just coming for a short visit but we never went back.

I was in court, and people were saying I wasn't good enough to be here, or that I was a communist, or whatever the hell it was. So I thought, 'What am I doing this for?' And then I remembered that astrologer in London telling me, 'One day you'll live abroad.' Not because of taxes. The story was that I left for tax reasons, but I didn't, I got no benefit, nothing. I screwed up completely, I lost money when I left. So I had no reason to leave England.

And then it clicked on me, 'Jesus, that guy predicted I was going to leave England!' Though at the time [when] he said that to me, I was thinking, 'Are you kidding?'

Sometimes you wonder, I mean really wonder. I know we make our own reality and we always have a choice, but how much is preordained?

Is there always a fork in the road and are there two preordained paths that are equally preordained? There could be hundreds of paths where one could go this way or that way – there's a choice, and it's very strange sometimes.

Yoko: In 1974 I pursued everything, because basically I'm sitting here, right? Somebody said Nam Myōhō Renge Kyō, I went into Nam Myōhō Renge Kyō. Somebody said EST [Erhard Seminars Training] is very good, I went to EST. Somebody said there's a good psychic, I'll see them. For me it became a time of pursuing alternate reality, exploring everything, including the food scene, *East West* journal, about health and mind orientation. I read all the books about magic, colour – what colour does to your life and what each colour means.

John and I decided at one point that we would check a lot of things through astrology and psychics. The reason for getting psychic advisors instead of a financial advisors was because we were suddenly finding ourselves in a reality that had no signposts. It was not on the map. John and my life was a totally different kind of life. So a usually conservative financial advice would not be applicable. We wanted an opinion that was transcending all that.

We never wanted to be dependent on one psychic, so we'd always have three or four of them and double-check and whatever, you know? [laughs]

One of the psychics was upset and said, 'You never listen to me, you never do what I tell you to do.' But I mean, the point is, that is because we were double-checking as well. You get advice and [you do not] follow the advice necessarily but that gives you a perspective and then you decide what you want to do.

It's like someone who's going to do stocks. You read the stock market, you consult the lawyers, you consult the business end, and you also take this as another perspective. We thought it was probably better than getting advice from a relative, because relatives would have ulterior motives – but of course, we never thought astrologers and psychics would have ulterior motives! [laughs]

There's a time in your life when you trust the policemen, the politicians and the professors. And then…you don't really trust them necessarily – *because* they're policemen or because they're politicians or professors.

Now you trust the new aristocrats, [who are] maybe the pop stars, maybe the next is photographers…. The psychic was definitely the kind of new pop stars of the alternative reality. But they're human too.

I learnt a lot from that and don't regret the fact that I went into that and had that experience. In the end, you have to trust yourself because what happens is something that you're going to have to pay for.

Patric Walker: I saw [John] at Christmas [in 1978] and he was fantastic, very relaxed and joking that he was the highest paid house-husband in the world.

One curious coincidence, which John has read significance into, is the fact that he and Sean both share the same birthday: 9 October.

But that apart, the ego trip is over. He's been to hell and back and he's been searching for something, and he thought he would find it in meditation, or by going to India and by gurus and astrology and drugs, or whatever it was. And I think he became even more confused in the search and lost that marvellous Northern insight, that straight-on answer he used to give.

And here he is, back. For me, he's exactly the same as he started and has found himself again. And he doesn't need concerts and he doesn't need adulation and he doesn't need applause. I think he's the one Beatle that is really happy the way he is.

John: You breathe in and you breathe out. We breathed in after breathing out for a long time. The *I Ching* calls it sitting still. A lot more can happen when you're not doing anything than when you appear to be doing something. So now we are breathing out. One must do both. One withdraws, one expands; tide in, tide out. It's better to breathe in and breathe out rather than just always trying to breathe out. You run out of breath. [laughs]

NUMEROLOGY

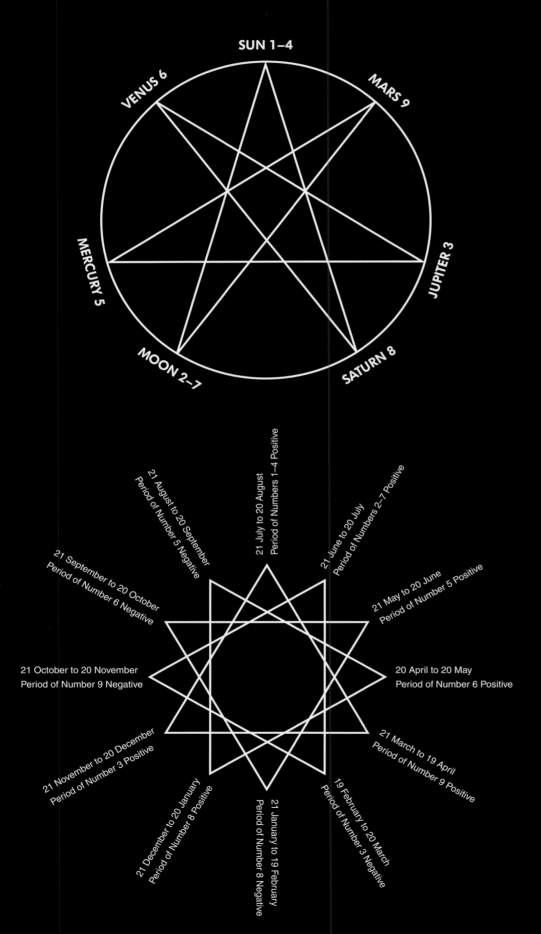

SUN 1–4

VENUS 6

MARS 9

MERCURY 5

JUPITER 3

MOON 2–7

SATURN 8

21 July to 20 August
Period of Numbers 1–4 Positive

21 August to 20 September
Period of Number 5 Negative

21 June to 20 July
Period of Numbers 2–7 Positive

21 September to 20 October
Period of Number 6 Negative

21 May to 20 June
Period of Number 5 Positive

21 October to 20 November
Period of Number 9 Negative

20 April to 20 May
Period of Number 6 Positive

21 November to 20 December
Period of Number 3 Positive

21 March to 19 April
Period of Number 9 Positive

21 December to 20 January
Period of Number 8 Positive

19 February to 20 March
Period of Number 3 Negative

21 January to 19 February
Period of Number 8 Negative

THE SEVEN-POINTED SEAL OF SOLOMON
The seven-pointed star contains the nine numbers that constitute the base of all calculations, and is the root of the system of numbers as applied to human life.

THE SUN
The Sun, with the numbers 1–4, represents the combination of the Sun and the planet Uranus (the male quality of creation being the Sun, with the feminine Uranus of the mental or spiritual plane).

THE MOON
The Moon, with the numbers 2–7, represents the Moon and Neptune, the Moon being feminine on the material or Earth plane with Neptune (masculine) on the mental or spiritual plane.

THE MEANING
The meaning of the lines of the Star being that life starts from the Sun, proceeds to the Moon, from that to Mars, from Mars to Mercury, Mercury to Jupiter, Jupiter to Venus, Venus to Saturn, and from Saturn (symbol of death) it returns to the Sun – or God from whence it came – to begin all over again in another cycle, and so on through eternity.

THE FOUR DIVISIONS OF THE ZODIAC – FIRE, WATER, AIR, EARTH

THE FIRE TRIANGLE
1st 'House' 21 March to 19 April
2nd 'House' 21 July to 20 August
3rd 'House' 21 November to 20 December

THE WATER TRIANGLE
1st 'House' 21 June to 20 July
2nd 'House' 21 October to 20 November
3rd 'House' 19 February to 20 March

THE AIR TRIANGLE
1st 'House' 21 May to 20 June
2nd 'House' 21 September to 20 October
3rd 'House' 21 January to 19 February

THE EARTH TRIANGLE
1st 'House' 20 April to 20 May
2nd 'House' 21 August to 20 September
3rd 'House' 21 December to 20 January

Chaldean Numbers: A = 1, B = 2, C = 3, D = 4, E = 5, F = 8, G = 3, H = 5, I = 1, J = 1, K = 2, L = 3, M = 4, N = 5, O = 7, P = 8, Q = 1, R = 2, S = 3, T = 4, U = 6, V = 6, W = 6, X = 5, Y = 1, Z = 7

Pages from John's paperback copy of *Cheiro's Book of Numbers*, with notations in John's handwriting. Cheiro was the sobriquet of William John Warner (1866–1936), an Irish astrologer and colourful occult figure. The name 'Cheiro' derives from the word 'cheiromancy', meaning palmistry. He was a self-described clairvoyant who claimed to have learned palmistry, astrology and Chaldean numerology in India. He was celebrated for using these forms of divination to make personal predictions for famous clients and to foresee world events.

(Handwritten notes, facing page)

JOHN = 18 = 9 }
LENNON = 30 = 3 } = 12 = 3
WINSTON: 4.   victim sacrifice.
ONO: 1. (19)
9 = 9 }
10 = 1 } : 1(0) } 15. = 6
1940 = 14 = 5 }
= 23 = 5

9 = Mars
3 = Jupiter   = perpentualmotion
6 = Venus   relationship (of the moon). trinity.

1940 = 14 = 5   1940
1 4   15.
1954   1955

Mercury = 5
LIVERPOOL = 6   J.W.L. = 16 = 7
NEW YORK = 1   J.W.OL. = 17 = 8
LONDON = 4.   J.OL = 4
TOKYO = 3
Edinburgh = 6
Paris = 6
FRISCO = 6
Berlin } = 9
Rome }
Dublin = 3
TORONTO = 9.

All occult studies point to the fact that the ancient students had a foundation for ascribing to every human being *his number in the universe*, and if we admit, as we do, that there is a moment for birth and a moment for death, so also in the links of years, days and hours, that make up the chain of life, it is not illogical to assume that *every link of life has also both its number and place*. I claim that by such a study man may become more perfect by his fitting in with the laws, system, and order of things to which he owes his being.

In this study there is nothing antagonistic to Religion or to our present-day acceptance of the idea of God. On the contrary, man will but honour God the more by his more perfect obedience to Nature's laws. In no text or passage in Holy Writ are we told that God desires human beings to suffer except as the consequence of their own acts; on the contrary, we are everywhere shown that man brings suffering and punishment on himself by his disobedience of Nature's commands. As a logical sequence, it must follow then *that if we move with the laws of life* and *are in harmony with them we must become more happy, healthy, and successful*, and consequently nearer that state of perfection that is the ultimate object of Divine design.

What would you think of a workman in a factory who, instead of moving with the wheels of, say, a weaving machine, attempted to force them in a contrary direction? Would not such a man be crushed, injured, or perhaps lose his life? You would call him a fool, and he would not even gain your sympathy, and if such a man brought such a fatality on himself *by ignorance*, your sentence on him would be perhaps even more severe. Yet you call Nature unjust, cruel, or any other name that may fit into the circumstances —you! *who do not even take the trouble of seeing which way her irresistible forces are moving*. You pray, "Thy will be done on earth as it is in heaven," but you have no more intention of even trying to find out what is the "will" which is obeyed in heaven, and broken by you every second, than if the sacred prayer had never been made.

---

in the ancient Hebrew of the Book of Solomon we can yet read his inspiring words:

I thank Thee, O Great Creator of the Universe, that Thou hast taught me the secrets of the Planets, that I mayst know the Times and Seasons of Things, the secrets of men's hearts, their thoughts, and the nature of their being. Thou gavest unto me this knowledge which is the foundation of all my Wisdom.

It is these self-same "Secrets of the Planets" that I have endeavoured to teach in these pages.

I now ask my readers to give their attention and concentration to the following system which I will put as briefly and in as clear language as possible.

To find the exact day in any month of the year whose vibration will be favourable, or in other words "lucky" to any individual, the simplest rule is to work out by the following table the occult number produced by the letters of their name.

This ancient Chaldean and Hebrew alphabet sets out the number or value of each letter. It is the best system I know for this purpose; its origin is lost in antiquity, but it is believed that it was originated by the Chaldeans, who were masters in all magical arts, and by them passed to the Hebrews.

A	= 1	N	= 5
B	= 2	O	= 7
C	= 3	P	= 8
D	= 4	Q	= 1
E	= 5	R	= 2
F	= 8	S	= 3
G	= 3	T	= 4
H	= 5	U	= 6
I or J	= 1	V	= 6
K	= 2	W	= 6
L	= 3	X	= 5
M	= 4	Y	= 1
		Z	= 7

It will be seen that there is no number 9 given in the above alphabet, for the simple reason that those ancient

(Handwritten at bottom)
JOHN   LENNON   WINSTON
1755   355575   6153475 -31-4
18 (9)   (3)30   12 = 3   ONO-1.

---

masters of Occultism knew that in the "Highest Sphere" the number 9 represents the 9-lettered name of God, and for this reason no single letter was ascribed to it.

If, however, the letters in a name should total up and produce the number 9, the meaning of it is that given as I set out in the previous chapter dealing with the number 9, and for the compound numbers of the 9 such as the 18, 27, etc.

The next important question to answer is the following: Are all the Christian and Surnames to be added together to find the last digit or number?

The answer to that is, that it is *the most used* Christian and Surname that must be added together to give the Key number; when the Surname is more used or more in evidence than the Christian name, then it is taken to give the Key number.

I have only space in a book of this description to give illustrations of a few well-known names. One I will take was always spoken of as Lloyd George—the other, Ex-Prime Minister, was called simply Baldwin.

The names Lloyd George and the Ex-Prime Minister of England, if transcribed into numbers are as follows:

L	= 3	G	= 3
L	= 3	E	= 5
O	= 7	O	= 7
Y	= 1	R	= 2
D	= 4	G	= 3
18	= 9	E	= 5
		25	= 7

B	= 2
A	= 1
L	= 3
D	= 4
W	= 6
I	= 1
N	= 5
22	= 4

(Handwritten at bottom)
7347252
OCTOBER = 11 = (0)

Suppose your name to be John Smith born 8th January, work the name out as follows:

J	= 1	S	= 3
O	= 7	M	= 4
H	= 5	I	= 1
N	= 5	T	= 4
18	= 9	H	= 5
		17	= 8

(Handwritten over table)
L = 3
E = 5
N N O N
30 = 3

EXAMPLE.—You now add the 9 and the 8 together, which gives you the "compound" number of 17, whose units added together give 8. To this add the 8 produced by similar means from the 26th April, this gives you the number 16, with 7 for the single number; now add the Birth number 8th January to this 7 and you obtain 15 for the last compound number with 6 for the last single number.

Look up the meaning I have given to the compound Number 15: you will find it stated "for obtaining money, gifts, and favours from others, it is a fortunate number." Therefore the occult influences playing on John Smith, born 8th January, would be favourable on the 26th April for his using that date to ask favours or carry out his plans. If it had not given favourable indications "John Smith" should then work out the 27th April, or the next day or the next, until he found a date indicated as fortunate.

The same rule applies for every name and every date of birth.

(Handwritten at bottom)
12 is compound (#3) } 3+6 = 9.
9/10/1940 = [15] = 6
October
734 72 5 2
9 1

CHAPTER XIV

MORE INFORMATION OF HOW TO USE "SINGLE" AND "COMPOUND" NUMBERS

FOLLOWING the publication of some articles I published in a leading London paper, I received some thousands of letters asking for further information as to how to make the Birth number and the Name number accord. I have, therefore, worked out the following example.

If possible, make the Birth number and the number given by the Name agree; the vibrations will then all be in harmony, and will give a greater promise of success if the number is a favourable one.

As an illustration, take again the example I gave in the previous chapter, of John Smith:

J	= 1	S	= 3
O	= 7	M	= 4
H	= 5	I	= 1
N	= 5	T	= 4
		H	= 5
18 = 1 plus 8 = 9		17 = 1 plus 7 = 8	

The single number of John totals a 9, and the single number of Smith equals an 8; the 8 and 9 added together make 17, and 1 plus 7 makes 8. The number of the entire Name is therefore an 8. If John Smith were born on any day making an 8, such as the 8th, 17th, or 26th of a month, the number of the Name and the number of the Birth *would then be in harmony*, and although the 8 is not such a lucky number to have in an ordinary way, yet in such a case there would be *no clash in the numbers*; and if John Smith, knowing this, used the dates making an 8, such as the 8th, 17th, or 26th, for his important transactions, he would find himself more fortunate.

On Numbers, by Yoko Ono

ONE is before it becomes two – before the cell splits into two. Before one proceeds. One is an immobile number. One step is only half a move. Since we have two legs, we have to take two steps or jump in order to move from one position to the next. One is a number found in our bodies often as fixed parts. We count ourselves as one but it might be better to count as half a pair or a half when you think of the fact that our reproductive organs can only function by meeting the other half. One as a force is a point – which does not extend like a line but stays like eternity. One constantly seeks for state of zero and two. One is mobile only in the process of becoming two. To become mobile one tries to be two (i.e. to meet or to become schizophrenic). When one meets it becomes two.

TWO is a state that is mobile by nature – like the footstep that goes one, two. It moves from one position to the next. Two as a force is a line. It extends and unlike one, does not have to move to another number to become mobile. Two is a state after splitting of the cell. While splitting is the characteristic of one, two does not split – it comes together. When it splits, it is only as two separate numbers independent from each other. So then they are to be regarded as two ones. Two as a pair (not as separate numbers but as a joint number) constantly seek for the state of one and three.

But two is a compound number of two immobile numbers and therefore there is no conflict, so it is active towards outside rather than towards the inside. When two is active towards inside, again, it is working as two separate numbers – as two separate ones – working towards each other or towards the state of two. Two can be found in our bodies quite often as a pair. When two meets it becomes one. Two is our heartbeat. After one and two,

all numbers are combinations of one and two. Therefore, there are actually only three basic states of numbers in the world: one, two and three, which is the combination of one and two.

THREE is a number we cannot find in our bodies, but we find it in nature around us (birds with three fingers, etc.). I call it a time number, because we use it to divide time and the days. When the heart beats in three, it is when the heart is moving faster than what is natural. It goes one, two, one, two. And one number out of these repetitions of two gets abbreviated because of the speed. That is three. So that means we set the time to the number which is one beat faster than our natural heartbeat. No wonder the culture is suffering from accelerated speed. The world will slow down when you dispense with clocks and watches and just follow your heartbeat.

Three is very fast, very mobile. In music, it is [a] waltz – very rhythmic. It is a running rhythm as opposed to walking rhythm of two and four. Three as a force is a three-dimensional point. Three functioning as a joint number will always seek for a state of two and a state of four. Just as two can often function as two separate ones, three can function as a pair and one, or as three separate ones, in addition to functioning as a joint number three. When it functions as three separate ones, it will move by splitting of the cells to six.

Compared to two, which has no inside conflict, three is a number of basic paradox. Two, which is a mobile number, and one, which is an immobile number, exist together and equally in three. Paradox makes three extremely active towards inside, but not very active towards outside. When two is a travelling number, three is a whirling number (it moves spirally forward). When three acts as one, it becomes immobile as one.

When it acts as two, it becomes mobile and active towards outside as two does. Three has no meeting point as two or one and it is a number of instability. Three is an abbreviated four. After three, all numbers are combinations of states of one, two and three.

FOUR is two sets of twos. Two mobile pairs, however, put together become two sets of meetings, and there's no forward movement, and they become immobile. It corresponds to two and eight. It has mobility only when it works as three and one or two and one and one. There is no trace of this number in our bodies except as two pairs. Spacially it is a square, and the force has a quality of coming back to oneself rather than going forward in a straight line, as two does, or whirling around and making spiral forward movements, as three does.

FIVE is a celestial number that exists mostly in the sky as points of stars (but, of course, we all know that there are no such things as points of stars, actually) and very rarely on Earth. And unlike two (which has four and eight), and three (which has six and nine), and one (which has zero and two), has no corresponding numbers in the series. In this sense, it is very similar to seven.

In our body, it exists only on our hands and feet – as if that were the sign of sky in us. Also, an apple has five seeds. The parts of our body where five exist are the only parts that have something to do with physical connection to things outside our bodies. It becomes the connection number. Our hands reach to other things and our feet take us to other places. But just as the fingers will not work unless the thumb moves in an opposite direction from the rest of the fingers, five will be immobile unless it has opposing elements of one, two and three in it. And it also has characteristics of five ones, one

Yoko: My first meeting with John was when I was having my first show in London at the Indica Gallery. John had just come to the gallery directly from Abbey Road Studios at 3 Abbey Road and the number three in numerology stands for music. I was at Indica Gallery at 6 Mason's Yard and the number six stands for love. So on that very day, music came to love.

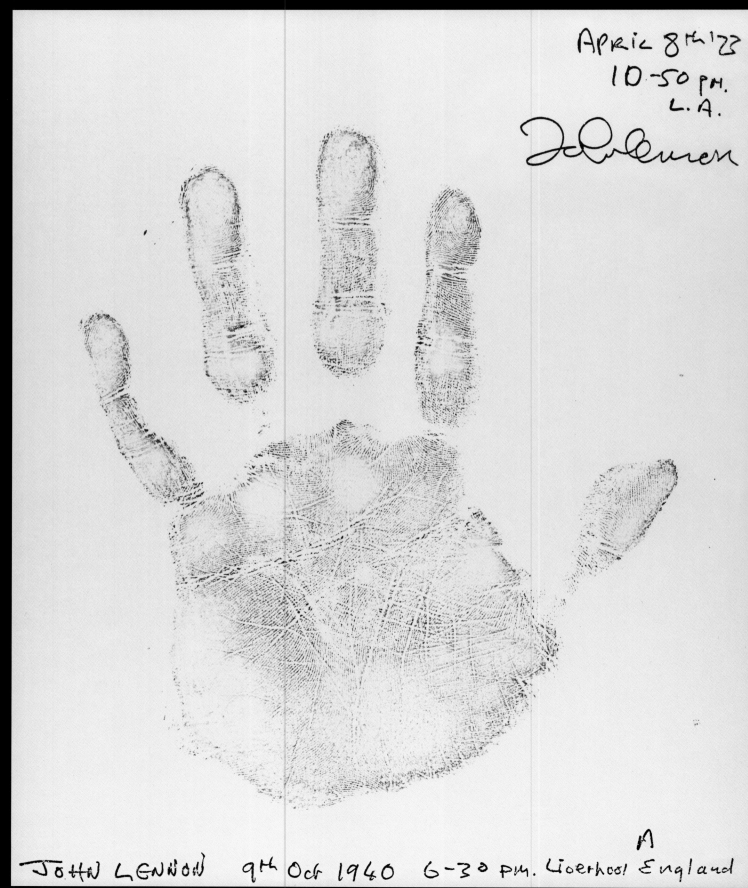

APRIL 8th '73
10-50 PM.
L.A.

JOHN LENNON   9th Oct 1940   6-30 pm. Lioerhool England

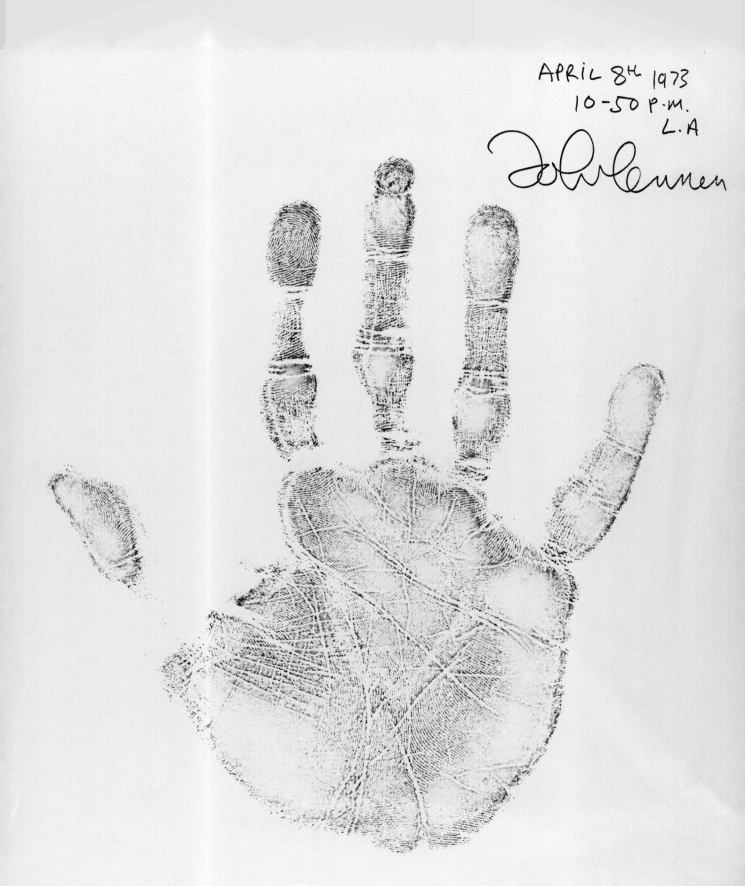

APRIL 8th 1973
10-50 P.M.
L.A

John Lennon

JOHN LENNON 9th Oct 1940 6-30 PM   Liverpool England

I CHING

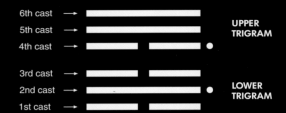

John's personal *I Ching* coins – made from copper in the 18th century during the Chinese Qing dynasty: a Qianlong Tongbao and two Daoguang Tongbaos that he kept in a grey leather pouch.

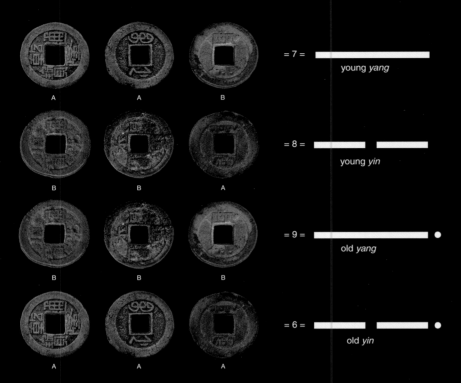

= 7 =
young *yang*

= 8 =
young *yin*

= 9 =
old *yang*

= 6 =
old *yin*

EXAMPLE HEXAGRAM

6th cast →
5th cast →   **UPPER TRIGRAM**
4th cast →

3rd cast →
2nd cast →   **LOWER TRIGRAM**
1st cast →

Each hexagram is built from the bottom up with a separate toss of the three coins. Two of the values – 6 and 9 – result in 'old' lines, meaning 'moving' or 'changing'. Two values – 7 and 8 – result in 'young' lines, meaning 'static' or 'unchanging'.

FIRST HEXAGRAM   SECOND HEXAGRAM

6th cast
5th cast
4th cast   →

3rd cast
2nd cast   →
1st cast

After the commentaries relating to the hexagram have been studied, a second hexagram is formed by changing any old *yin* lines to young *yang* lines and any old *yang* lines into young *yin* lines. The second hexagram is then also studied.

Three coins are used to build a hexagram, which then provides guidance according to the description attributed to it in *I Ching*. Three coins are tossed simultaneously. A coin that lands heads up has a value of 2 and a coin that lands tails up has a value of 3. By adding the three values together you arrive at the number 6, 7, 8, or 9. The numbers 7 and 9 create *yang* lines and 6 and 8 create *yin* lines.

1	2	3	4	5	6	7	8	9	10	11
Qián	Kun	Zhun	Meng	Xu	Song	Shi	Bi	Xiao Chu	Lu	Tai

12	13	14	15	16	17	18	19	20	21	22
Pi	Tong Ren	Da You	Qian	Yu	Sui	Ku gu	Lin	Guan	Shi Ke	Bi

23	24	25	26	27	28	29	30	31	32	33
Bo	Fu	Wu Wang	Da Chu	Yi	Da Guo	Kan	Li	Xian	Heng	Dun

34	35	36	37	38	39	40	41	42	43	44
Da Zhuang	Jin	Ming Yi	Jia Ren	Kui	Jian	Xie	Sun	Yi	Guai	Gou

45	46	47	48	49	50	51	52	53	54	55
Cui	Sheng	Kun	Jing	Ge	Ding	Zhen	Gen	Jian	Gui Mei	Feng

56	57	58	59	60	61	62	63	64
Lu	Xun	Dui	Huan	Jie	Zhong Fu	Xiao Guo	Ji Ji	Wei Ji

There are 64 hexagrams in the *I Ching*, each composed of six horizontal lines of two kinds – a solid *yang* line and a broken *yin* line. Each hexagram is created by casting three coins six times, thus forming two trigrams – an upper and a lower. A cryptic description accompanies each hexagram; for example, hexagram no. 1 is attributed the word 'Qián' or 'Force'.

UPPER TRIGRAM / LOWER TRIGRAM	HEAVEN	THUNDER	WATER	MOUNTAIN	EARTH	WIND	FIRE	LAKE
HEAVEN	1	34	5	26	11	9	14	43
THUNDER	25	51	3	27	24	42	21	17
WATER	6	40	29	4	7	59	64	47
MOUNTAIN	33	62	39	52	15	53	56	31
EARTH	12	16	8	23	2	20	35	45
WIND	44	32	48	18	46	57	50	28
FIRE	13	55	63	22	36	37	30	49
LAKE	10	54	60	41	19	61	38	58

Each hexagram is composed of two trigrams, each of eight possible configurations of *yin* and *yang* lines. Each trigram has an affinity in nature, and this element can form part of the overall reading; for example, hexagram no. 4 is mountain above water.

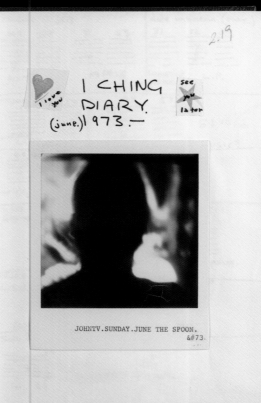

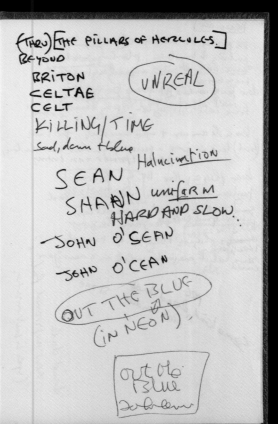

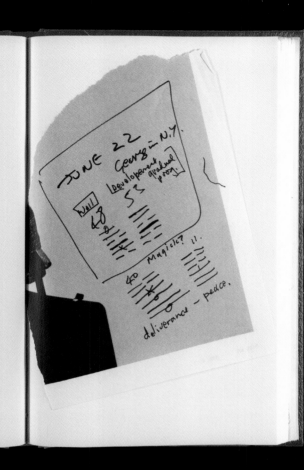

I know

mindee 8. (at in thing)
3,000 over the ocean
I will light you onta the san.

weakness.

When i wake will
your + (mmm)
body
etc

A.A.
god grant me the (right) to change the thing i can
accept the things i cant
and the wisdom to know the difference.

life
Real Slow Knife
↑ AUSLINASON.

Pepsi

GA-DEN TANKA PROTECTION

While on holiday in Greece in July 1967, John purchased five Ga-den Tanka coins on a red coral necklace, which he was told would provide prosperity and protection. He wore them for a brief period in 1967 and then, more regularly, in 1972–74, particularly during the writing and recording of the *Mind Games* album and especially when out in public.

TYPE	OUTER REV.	WATER-LINE	OUTER OBV.	OBV. CTR.
A	⠌	None	⌣⌣⌣	Pellet
B	⠌	2 lines	⌣⌣⌣	3 Crescents
C	⠌	1 line	⌣⌣⌣	2 Crescents
D	⠌	1 line	⠌	2 Crescents
E	⌣⌣⌣	1 line	⠌	2 Crescents
F	•	1 line	⠌	2 Crescents
G	None	1 line	None	2 Crescents
H	•	1 line	•	3 Crescents

The obverse side of a Ga-den Tanka coin displays an elaborate lotus surrounded by the Astamangala, the Eight Auspicious Symbols valued by a number of Dharmic belief systems. In the Buddhist tradition, these symbols represent the gifts the gods offered to Shakyamuni Buddha when he attained enlightenment.

Opposite, bottom: The reverse side has an eight-petalled lotus at its heart, surrounded by, in Tibetan: དགའ་ལྡན་ཕོ་བྲང་ ཕྱོ་ ལས་རྣམ་ རྒྱལ་རྒྱལ།, meaning 'the Ganden Podrang is victorious in all directions'.

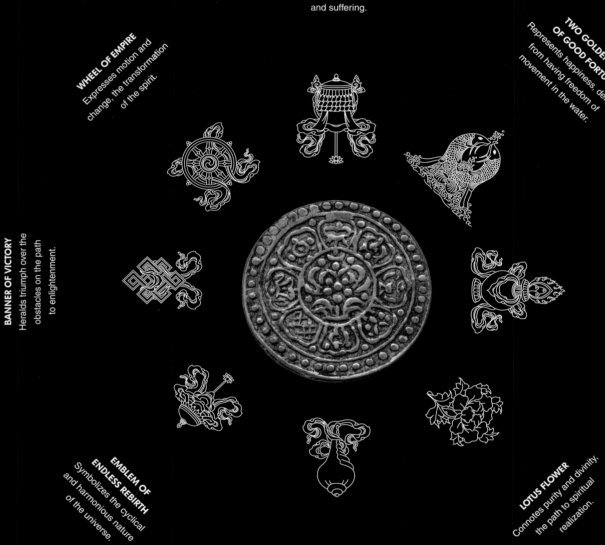

UMBRELLA OF SOVEREIGNTY
Symbol of status or royalty, protects from harm and suffering.

WHEEL OF EMPIRE
Expresses motion and change, the transformation of the spirit.

TWO GOLDEN FISH OF GOOD FORTUNE
Represents happiness, derived from having freedom of movement in the water.

BANNER OF VICTORY
Heralds triumph over the obstacles on the path to enlightenment.

AMPHORA OF AMBROSIA
The treasure vase represents wealth, prosperity and wisdom.

EMBLEM OF ENDLESS REBIRTH
Symbolizes the cyclical and harmonious nature of the universe.

LOTUS FLOWER
Connotes purity and divinity, the path to spiritual realization.

CONCH SHELL
Produces a sound that proclaims the sovereignty of the dharma's teachings.

The coins on John's necklaces are type F Ga-den Tankas, most likely minted some time between the 1910s and the early 1920s.

PALMISTRY
BY MARTINI

The
TAROT FOR TODAY
Mayananda

CHINESE
FORTUNE
TELLING

易

Divining Rods Attached

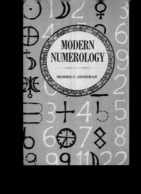

MODERN
NUMEROLOGY
MORRIS C. GOODMAN

Introduction
to
HUNA
MAX FREEDOM LONG

ETI
Space Beings
Intercept
Earthlings

The amazing true story of how ETI space beings, who have intervened at key times to direct the course of history, now return to deliver this planet into its New Age, or Heaven on Earth.

ASTROLOGY
HOW TO MAKE AND
READ YOUR OWN
HOROSCOPE

SAND AND FOAM
By
KAHLIL GIBRAN
Author of *The Prophet*

Alfred A. Knopf Publisher, N. Y.

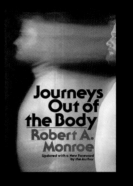

Journeys
Out of
the Body
Robert A.
Monroe
Updated with a New Foreword
by the Author

Satanism and
Witchcraft
A STUDY IN MEDIEVAL SUPERSTITION

by Jules Michele

The Ancient Mysteries
of Delphi
PYTHAGORAS
Edouard Schuré

Witchcraft
in
England
Christina Hole

Bells, Books, Candles,
Witches' Sabbaths, Fertility Rites,
Witch Hunts, and
other manifestations of
the Black Arts
that held England
spellbound for centuries

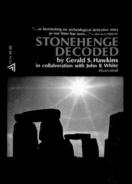

"...as fascinating an archeological detective story
as our time has seen..." —CHICAGO TRIBUNE
STONEHENGE
DECODED
by Gerald S. Hawkins
in collaboration with John B. White
Illustrated

FIVE KEYS TO
PAST LIVES
J. H. BRENNAN
PATHS TO INNER POWER

The
Master
Book
of
Candle
Burning
OR
How to
BURN CANDLES
For Every Purpose
by Henri Gamache

The CHINESE
Birthday Book
How to Use the Secrets of Ki-ology to Find
Love, Happiness, and Success
TAKASHI YOSHIKAWA
Foreword by DAMIAN SHARP

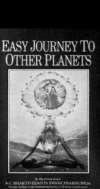

EASY JOURNEY TO
OTHER PLANETS

By His Divine Grace
A.C. BHAKTIVEDANTA SWAMI PRABHUPĀDA
Founder Ācārya of the International Society for Krishna Consciousness

LOVE, WEALTH,
AND HAPPINESS
IN THE NUMBERS
THAT GUIDE
YOUR LIFE!

The
Secret
Powers of
Numerology
by Gerie Tully

The ancient Babylonian science made simple
and easy. See what wonders it will work for you!

The Ultimate
Frontier
by Eklal Kueshana

An account of the powerful, ultra-secret
Brotherhoods and their profound, worldwide influence during the past 6,000 years.

Self
HYPNOSIS

ITS THEORY
TECHNIQUE
AND APPLICATION

MELVIN POWERS

How To Discover
Your Own Psychic Powers
in Hundreds of
Experiments You Can Do
At Home

HANDBOOK OF PSYCHIC DISCOVERIES

SHEILA OSTRANDER
and
LYNN SCHROEDER
the Authors of the
International Bestseller
PSYCHIC DISCOVERIES
BEHIND THE IRON CURTAIN

THE MUSICAL SCALE
AND THE SCHEME OF EVOLUTION

THE ROSICRUCIAN FELLOWSHIP
Oceanside, California, U.S.A.

THE LÜSCHER
Color Test
The remarkable test that reveals
your personality through color

translated and edited by IAN SCOTT
based on the original German text by DR. MAX LÜSCHER

An extraordinary and psychological
document... destined for fame —New York Times

The teachings of Don Juan:
a Yaqui way of knowledge
Carlos Castaneda

The world's most famous female medium and spiritualist

MADAME BLAVATSKY
PRIESTESS OF THE OCCULT

The incredible, bizarre life of the fascinating, eccentric and
compelling woman who founded Theosophy in America

GERTRUDE MARVIN WILLIAMS

THE LUNATION CYCLE
BY DANE RUDHYAR

Crystal Gazing
Spiritual Clairvoyance
Behind The Veil
The Trance Sleep

deLAWRENCE

REBIRTHING
The Science of Enjoying
All of Your Life

by
Jim Leonard
and
Phil Laut

TRINITY PUBLICATIONS

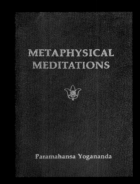

METAPHYSICAL
MEDITATIONS

Paramahansa Yogananda

ASTROLOGY
YOUR PLACE
AMONG THE STARS

EVANGELINE ADAMS

Horary Astrology

Marc Edmund Jones

est

CLARK STE...

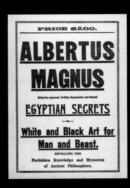

PRICE $2.00.

ALBERTUS MAGNUS

Being the Approved, Verified, Sympathetic and Natural

EGYPTIAN SECRETS

White and Black Art for
Man and Beast.

REVEALING THE
Forbidden Knowledge and Mysteries
of Ancient Philosophers.

PROPHECIES
ON WORLD EVENTS
BY NOSTRADAMUS
STEWART ROBB

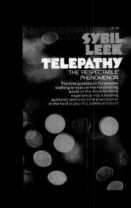

SYBIL LEEK

TELEPATHY
THE RESPECTABLE PHENOMENON

The first guidebook for anyone
wishing to explore the fascinating
world of the mind-to-mind
experience—by a leading
authority and long-time practitioner
in the field of psychic communication.

Actual case histories that
reveal there is life after death

LIFE AFTER LIFE
RAYMOND A. MOODY, JR., M.D.
WITH A FOREWORD BY
ELISABETH KÜBLER-ROSS, M.D.

The astounding bestseller
that offers true experiences of those
people declared clinically
"dead"...descriptions so similar,
so vivid, so overwhelmingly
positive that they may change
mankind's view of life, death and
spiritual survival forever.

THE ART OF
TRUE HEALING

BY
ISRAEL REGARDIE

A HELIOS BOOK

Alfred Douglas

THE TAROT
The Origins, Meaning and Uses of the Cards

Illustrated by David Sheridan

THE FOOL   THE PAPESS

"The most objective, direct, and clearly
written book to date on the complex
subject of the tarot."
—Library Journal

A PRACTICAL GUIDE TO
QABALISTIC SYMBOLISM
VOLUME ONE

by Gareth Knight

A PRACTICAL GUIDE TO
QABALISTIC SYMBOLISM
VOLUME TWO

by Gareth Knight

HOW TO READ
THE AURA

W.E. BUTLER

LOST
SECRETS OF
ASTROLOGY

ROBERT W. PELTON

A FASCINATING AND USEFUL COLLECTION OF THE
SECRET WRITINGS AND WISDOM OF THE AGES

INSTANTANEOUS
PERSONAL MAGNETISM

the wisdom of the
KABBALAH

foreword by
Dagobert D. Runes

CHEIRO'S
BOOK OF
NUMBERS

by Cheiro, the world's most famous seer
THE COMPLETE SCIENCE OF NUMEROLOGY
HOW NUMBERS AFFECT YOUR HEALTH,
FORTUNE, LIFE, MARRIAGE

ARCO

THROUGH AN
EASTERN
WINDOW

JACK HUBER

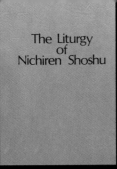
The Liturgy
of
Nichiren Shoshu

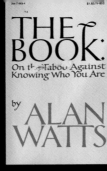
THE
BOOK:
On the Taboo Against
Knowing Who You Are

by
ALAN
WATTS

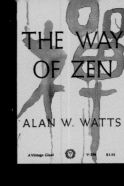
THE WAY
OF ZEN

by ALAN W. WATTS

ALAN WATTS
THE SUPREME IDENTITY
AN ESSAY ON ORIENTAL METAPHYSIC
AND THE CHRISTIAN RELIGION

Zen Buddhism
and Psychoanalysis
by D.T. Suzuki,
Erich Fromm, and
Richard De Martino

HESSE

The Journey to the East

Manual
of
Zen
Buddhism
by
D. T. Suzuki

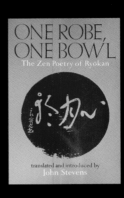
ONE ROBE,
ONE BOWL
The Zen Poetry of Ryōkan

translated and introduced by
John Stevens

Over 25 Weeks On The Bestseller List!
TM
DISCOVERING
INNER ENERGY
AND
OVERCOMING
STRESS

by
Harold H. Bloomfield, M.D.
Michael Peter Cain
Dennis T. Jaffe
and Robert B. Kory

Transcendental Meditation

The
Sound
of the
One
Hand

281 ZEN KOANS
WITH ANSWERS

The
Life of MILAREPA
A New Translation from the Tibetan by
LOBSANG P. LHALUNGPA

A MENTOR BOOK

The teachings of the
Compassionate
Buddha Early discourses,
the Dhammapada,
and later basic writings. Edited, with
commentary, by E. A. Burtt

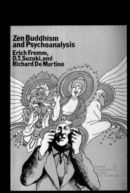
Zen Buddhism
and Psychoanalysis
Erich Fromm,
D.T. Suzuki, and
Richard De Martino

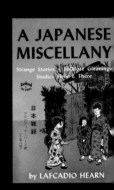
A JAPANESE
MISCELLANY
Strange Stories · Folklore Gleanings
Studies Here & There

日本雑録

by LAFCADIO HEARN

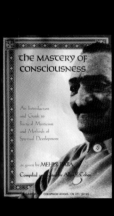
the MASTERY OF
CONSCIOUSNESS

An Introduction
and Guide to
Practical Mysticism
and Methods of
Spiritual Development

as given by MEHER BABA

THE PANJIKA

The Hindu Astrological Almanac

THE
HINDU ART
OF LOVE

The Classic Companion
to the Kama Sūtra

SIR RICHARD BURTON'S
Translation of the Ananga Ranga

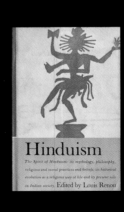
Hinduism

The Spirit of Hinduism: its mythology, philosophy,
religious and moral practices and beliefs; its historical
evolution as a religious way of life and its present role
in Indian society. Edited by Louis Renou

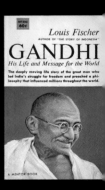
Louis Fischer
AUTHOR OF "THE STORY OF INDONESIA"
GANDHI
His Life and Message for the World
The deeply moving life story of the great man who
led India's struggle for freedom and preached a phi-
losophy that influenced millions throughout the world.

A MENTOR BOOK

GLIMPSES
OF ANCIENT INDIA

BY SUSHILARANI BABURAO PATEL

THE
SUFI MESSAGE
OF HAZRAT INAYAT KHAN

Volume II
The Mysticism of Sound
Music
The Power of the Word
Cosmic Language

The
Power
of the
Spoken
Word
Florence Scovel Shinn
FOREWORD by Emmet Fox

The Myth
of God
Incarnate

Edited by
JOHN HICK

THE ESSENE GOSPEL
OF PEACE

Translated from the Third Century Aramaic Manuscript
by
EDMOND BORDEAUX SZEKELY

The Way of Life
道
According to
LAO
TZU
Translated by WITTER BYNNER

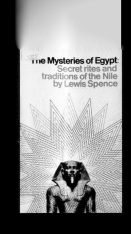

The Mysteries of Egypt:
Secret rites and
traditions of the Nile
by Lewis Spence

The Scrolls from the
Dead Sea
EDMUND WILSON

LOST GODDESSES
OF EARLY GREECE
A Collection of
Pre-Hellenic Mythology
Charlene Spretnak

THE
SOUND OF
MUSIC AND
PLANTS
by DOROTHY RETALLACK

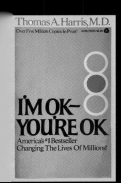

Thomas A. Harris, M.D.
Over Five Million Copies In Print!
I'M OK—
YOU'RE OK
America's #1 Bestseller
Changing The Lives Of Millions!

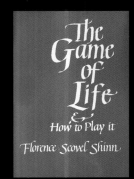

The
Game
of
Life
&
How to Play it
Florence Scovel Shinn

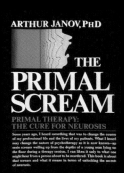

ARTHUR JANOV, PhD
THE
PRIMAL
SCREAM
PRIMAL THERAPY:
THE CURE FOR NEUROSIS

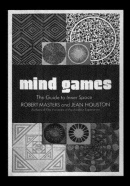

mind games
The Guide to Inner Space
ROBERT MASTERS and JEAN HOUSTON

THE
LSD
STORY
Here is a complete, comprehensive report
on LSD and all the amazing hallucinatory
pills, plants and chemicals that are cre-
ating headlines and causing a revolution
in the thinking of an entire generation
The Drug That Expands the Mind
BY PRIZE-WINNING REPORTER
JOHN CASHMAN

A RODALE BOOK 95¢
BIG TYPE
LOWER YOUR
PULSE
AND
LIVE
LONGER
by J. I. RODALE

18 PRINTINGS IN HARDCOVER!
THE BATES METHOD FOR
BETTER
EYESIGHT
WITHOUT
GLASSES
W. H. Bates, M.D.
A tested method for improving vision,
by the doctor
who originated and perfected it.
Revised Edition
INCLUDES DETACHABLE TEST CARD FOR IMPROVING YOUR VISION AT HOME

Revised Enlarged Edition
RAW Vegetable
JUICES
WHAT'S MISSING
IN YOUR BODY?
N. W. WALKER, Doctor of Science

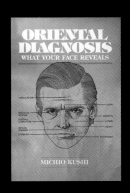

ORIENTAL
DIAGNOSIS
WHAT YOUR FACE REVEALS
MICHIO KUSHI

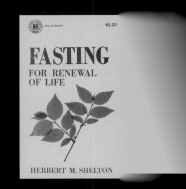

$2.25
FASTING
FOR RENEWAL
OF LIFE
HERBERT M. SHELTON

Now! Available for the first time
at a popular price!
A complete
guide to
herbal medicine
and natural
living.
The standard
reference book
since 1939.
JETHRO KLOSS
Back to eden

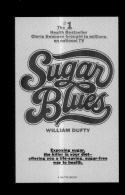

#1
Health Bestseller
Gloria Swanson brought to millions.
on national TV
Sugar
Blues
WILLIAM DUFTY
Exposing sugar,
the killer in your diet—
offering you a life-saving, sugar-free
way to health.
A NUTRI BOOK

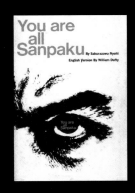

You are
all Sanpaku
By Sakurazawa Nyoiti
English Version By William Dufty

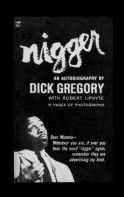

nigger
AN AUTOBIOGRAPHY BY
DICK GREGORY
WITH ROBERT LIPSYTE
16 PAGES OF PHOTOGRAPHS
Dear Momma—
Wherever you are, if ever you
hear the word "nigger" again,
remember they are
advertising my book.

A MENTOR BOOK • MQ961 • 95¢
Chronicles of
Black
Protest
The original texts and
historical meaning
of the documents that
are the major milestones
in the road from
Black slavery to Black Power
Compiled and edited with a commentary by
Bradford Chambers
with an Introduction by
Dr. C. Eric Lincoln

The
Greening
of
America
There is a revolution coming. It will not
be like revolutions of the past. It will
originate with the individual and with
culture, and it will change the political
structure only as its final act. It will not
require violence to succeed, and it cannot
be successfully resisted by violence. This
is the revolution of the new generation.
Charles A. Reich

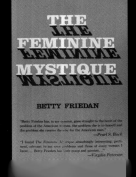

THE
FEMININE
MYSTIQUE
BETTY FRIEDAN

"Exhilarating, controversial plus!"
—PUBLISHERS WEEKLY
The
FIRST
SEX
The book that proves that woman's contribution
to civilization has been greater than man's
Elizabeth Gould Davis

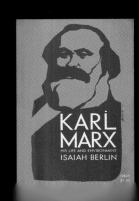

KARL
MARX
HIS LIFE AND ENVIRONMENT
ISAIAH BERLIN

WOODSTOCK
NATION
Abbie
Hoffman

Some Time in New York City
by Yoko Ono, March 1972

We live in a small apartment in the Village. The largest thing in our apartment (after John, that is) is the bed. In the morning, we wake up with thousands of birds singing outside our bedroom window. The yard belongs to the neighbour, but the birds sing for us just the same.

I call Peter (Bendrey, our assistant) in the next room for a morning tea, and the large black dog who has become our friend – though he also belongs to our neighbour – runs to our window and starts to whine. 'Here's our friend,' John says. The dog somehow fell in love with John. He keeps whining until John goes to the window and says 'good morning'. 'You see, we can talk to each other, you know, dogs and cats,' John says, 'but they never really understand until we touch them.'

'Wait, that's a good one, it proves my point about communication…' and I start to look for some paper to scribble some notes on. We can never hold on to our notebooks. So John and I scribble our ideas on anything. Backs of envelopes, fan mail, bills, etc. And if we are lucky, someone collects them and puts them in a file for us. My drawer is full of notes like that which I intend to make into a book some day when I have time.

When we wake up very early in the morning, we chat awhile and go back to sleep again. Sometimes we watch the morning TV. John changes the channel for me quickly when a child of Kyoko's age is on the screen. All Kyoko's clothes are packed away somewhere so I won't come across them. Sometimes I wake up crying because of a scary dream I've had. When this happens, no matter how sound asleep John is, he puts his hand on me and pats me, still with his eyes closed. If he is in a condition to talk at all, he would ask what the dream was about. 'Now, you'd better tell me so you'll feel better,' he says,

still with his nose buried in his pillows. 'Kyoko was in this island and she was calling us…' I say. 'Oh, that's because I told you yesterday she might be in New Zealand. Don't worry and go to sleep.'

Sometimes in a dream Kyoko is still in the back room of that coffee house, where I used to be afraid to leave her alone because of the mice. I haven't seen my daughter for two years now, so in a dream she comes out usually as a three-year-old, which was when she lived with me in that back room of the coffee house. She was at the age where she was getting to be too heavy for me to carry but couldn't walk long distances by herself. I still remember her weight in my arms.

John used to make fun of my love for New York. His experience of New York before we met was extraordinary to say the least. But now we are both in love with the city. Yes, it is a dangerous city, we know that. People say we must be crazy to want to stay in a city like this. But when people start to say that, I say, 'But did you know that this is one town where there's more Jews than in Israel, more Greeks than in Greece, more….' And John who has heard this so many times from me, finished my line by saying something like 'And more Italians than in Sicily, right? And they are all living together pretty well. It's a real cosmopolitan city, Yoko!'

It's a city with guts, I think. And you can't deny the beauty of the Manhattan island. What an electric scene for a small island! In fact, for John, New York is more like a 'super Liverpool' than London. He feels alive here. Liverpool is a tough port city as well, and John feels at home here more than in any city he's lived in. There is a particular mentality of people who finally come to this city to make their life here. John, though he is a latecomer, is one of them, I suppose.

When somebody asks me why we want to stay in New York and why we like this city, I don't know what to say. London is a beautiful city and we miss the good food in Paris, and Tokyo is where I was born and educated until I was nineteen. John likes Tokyo too and he loves London. But when we went back to London, we both realized how we miss New York. New York is a city that haunts you when you are away from it. Also we discovered that both of us get more ideas and write songs more than in any other city. It's a very stimulating city creatively.

We don't go to parties and gatherings too much, though we communicate a lot with friends over the phone and sometimes they visit us. We just like to relax at home reading, watching TV and chatting between us.

The only exercise we get is going for a ride on a bicycle. When it's warm, we go for a long ride. Mostly around the outskirts of the Village and around the piers. Riding around the Wall Street district during the weekends is our favourite route. We call it our little adventure. John shouts, 'Hey, why don't you like us? Say something will you?' He is shouting to the city. 'The Statue of Liberty said it's okay for us to stay here.' And he makes a large circle with his bike without using his hands. 'They probably don't like mixed couples,' I shout back on my bike. 'Mixed-up couple is more like it,' says John.

We also go to theatres, movies and shopping a lot. John especially likes doing these things in this city because we don't get hounded by fans too much and also he can watch the TV even when we come home at two in the morning. You can't do that in London.

Two years ago, John was arrested in London for possession of marijuana. Actually, though, two weeks before the arrest, a friend of ours in the press told us that there would be an arrest.

Pages 50–51: John & Yoko photographed by Bob Gruen strolling in Central Park, New York, 2 April 1973, after the Declaration of Nutopia press conference and before viewing their Dakota apartment for the first time.

Pages 52, 54–55: John & Yoko photographed by Brian Hamill reviewing photographs from the *One to One* concert, on the phone and on the bed in their West Village apartment at 105 Bank Street, New York, 13 October 1972.

We were on a macrobiotic diet then. And in order to maintain purity of body, we didn't even smoke cigarettes. We cleaned up the whole house just to make sure. The marijuana was brought in by the officers. The officer in charge, Sgt Pilcher, who arrested Keith Richards, Mick Jagger, Donovan and George Harrison, has since been questioned in London for his method of arrest and suspended from his job.

Our lawyer advised John to plead guilty, and pay the fine of £200 rather than prolong the case. At the time I was three months pregnant, with a record of two miscarriages before that. Therefore, John finally agreed with the lawyer. It would be detrimental to my health if the case was prolonged. The shock of the case resulted in my miscarrying anyway.

Since then US Immigration has been following our case very closely, and actually advised us at the time of application for the visa to the States that we should consider their permission given, if given at all, as a special favour to us.

We are not asking to be treated in any special way, but we feel that we have been extremely careful with the Immigration people, and that we have been treated rather unfairly.

If the regulation is such that everybody who has a past criminal record is not allowed to be permanent residents of this country, then we understand that we have to obey that law. But the strange thing about all this is that many people who have become citizens of this country have past records of a worse nature than that of John's. Some of them are murderers, and still they were able to become citizens here.

It is especially hard to understand their rejection of my residency application on the grounds that they would not like to split up a family, while they do not consider the fact that by rejecting my application they are splitting up a mother and child, When I mentioned this at the Immigration office, the man said, 'Oh, naturally, you would be allowed in to the States anytime to visit your child.' This, he said to me, not to John. But the man doesn't understand the case at all if he thinks that that is going to make me feel better.

I have received temporary custody of my daughter, Kyoko (eight years old), in Texas court on the grounds that she, an American citizen, would be brought up 'within the United States region', though we still have been unable to locate her.

A testimony was given by a Texas school teacher to the effect that, though Kyoko was unusually intelligent for her age, she was three years behind in her schooling due to her family life, of simply moving from one town to another all over the world. A mutual friend has told me that my ex-husband mentioned that since he is a US citizen, all he has to do is stay in hiding until my visa expires here. He also exercises violence to anybody around him. John and I are genuinely worried about Kyoko.

As people, we love this country and its people. As artists, we enjoy working in the stimulating atmosphere of New York City. As parents, we would like to live in a place where we could best have access to our daughter, Kyoko.

Judging from the attitude Immigration has shown our lawyer (one of the immigration officers called our lawyer and said, 'Maybe you may think I'm square, but what exactly do John & Yoko do?') I don't think that there is any serious antagonism against us.

Also, I think that since our work appeals to the younger generation, they suspect that we represent the youth culture and their problems. For instance, there are people who suspect that we promote drugs and violence. We don't. We think violence is terrible. We think it's terrible that young people are hooked on hard drugs and waste their beautiful lives.

We think the young should register to vote as well. Because we must share responsibility in what happens to society. In fact, if anything, we pride ourselves in having influenced some of the young radicals since our stay here, to realize the futility of violence and to promote peace and love.

We do believe in the change of society, but we do not believe in violent revolution. Our slogan from the start of our relationship has been 'Peace and Love'. We don't even represent the free-love, free-ride lifestyle of the youth, since we have sufficient means to support ourselves and we are very happily married and indulge and share between us one hobby – our work.

While the nature of John's record – possession of grass – even if for a moment we suppose that it wasn't planted, is something that is considered in most states now as a misdemeanour not a felony. The immigration law has not changed as yet, but it is obvious to anybody that it is [only] a matter of time [before] the immigration laws would follow the state law, and regard possession of pot as a misdemeanour.

On our third anniversary morning, sometime last week, John suddenly woke up and said, 'Why don't we go to Canada and stay there, where we can stick one foot in America and stick it in once every day?'

Then I remembered my piece about erasing lines. It seemed as though John was getting more crazy about New York than me. I wish we could erase all the border lines. John was too sleepy to acknowledge me. I went back to sleep also and in my dream John and I were erasing a border line with a huge piece of rubber.

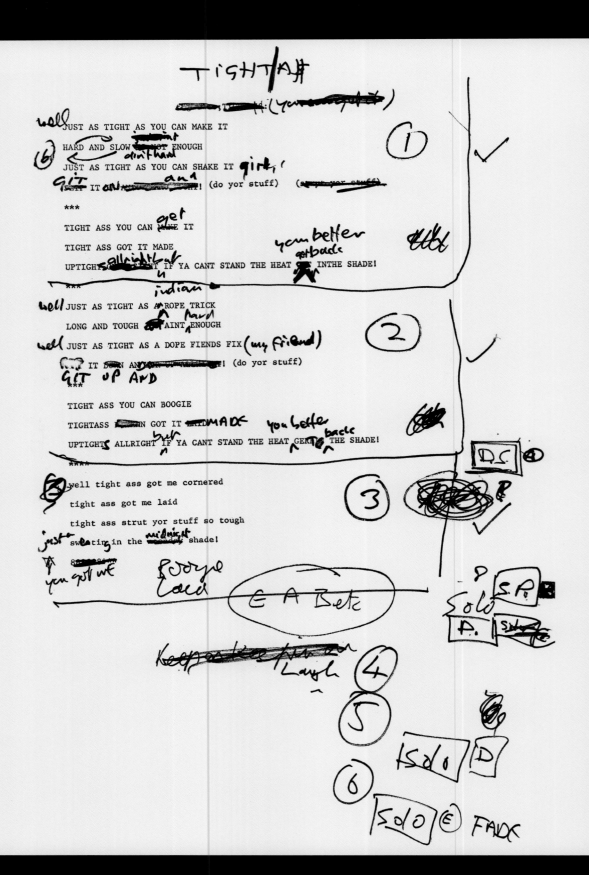

TIGHT A$

Well, just as tight a$ you can make it
Hard and slow ain't hard enough
Just as tight a$ you can shake it, girl,
Get it on and do your stuff

Tight a$ you can get it
Tight a$ got it made
Uptight's alright but if ya can't stand the heat
You better get back in the shade

Well, just as tight a$ an Indian rope trick
Long and tough ain't hard enough
Just as tight a$ a dope fiend's fix, my friend,
Get it up and do your stuff

Tight a$ you can boogie
Tight a$ got it laid
Uptight's alright but if ya can't stand the heat
You better get back in the shade

Well…. Alright…. Alright….

Well, tight a$ you can make it
Hard and slow ain't hard enough
Just as tight a$ you can shake it, girl,
Get it on and do your stuff

Tight a$ you can get it
Tight a$ got it made
Uptight's alright but if ya can't stand the heat
You better get back in the shade

Well, tight a$ an Indian rope trick
Hard and long ain't hard enough
Just as tight a$ a dope fiend's fix, my friend,
Get it up and do your stuff

Tight a$ you can boogie
Tight a$ got it laid
Uptight's alright but if ya can't stand the heat
You better get back in the shade

Well….

Well, tight a$ got me cornered
Tight a$ got me laid
Tight a$ strut your stuff so tough
Just a-sitting in the midnight shade

Tight a$ she can boogie
Tight a$ she got laid
Uptight's alright but if ya can't stand the heat
You better get back in the shade
Well, go! Aw, get it!

John: It's just one of those things that just comes into your mind. I wasn't thinking anything. It suddenly just started running through my head: 'Just as tight as this, just as tight as that.' And everybody has to read their own message. It's supposed to be a dollar sign.

It was like that early Sun sound. That's the kind of sound I like. You know, just get it on and dig it. Yeah. I was trying to recreate the feeling of buying Elvis's records in the old days.

Being famous – it's just impossible. It's like being permanently in a white bag, and people are looking, but they don't ever see. So I'm on like a permanent trip, with everyone's voices slightly in the distance. I'm in a permanent high state. So with what I've done and what people have done to me, they've cocooned me, my life and my wife, in this sort of bag. So I'm immune to a lot of things and very un-immune. It's a bit of both.

Like, when you're in a white bag, there's a risk you'll get kicked when you're sitting on the floor, because people are so interested. But there is also the womb thing. I'm in this sort of polyethylene womb, and every now and then something gets through and I actually get touched. And I say, 'What are you doing in my kitchen, or demanding my arm?' And then I have to think about that, but mostly it's just a kind of high or low.

If it's a low, I never go anywhere without being attacked. But then I think, 'If you really wanted to, you could shave your hair bald, shave off your moustache, and go to Egypt or India, so who are you kidding?'

There isn't Beatlemania going on and I'm acting more naturally. I don't have to keep up any image. I'm an artist now, an individual. I'm not responsible for a Beatles image or anybody else's and I don't have to sign an autograph unless I feel like it. They're beginning to accept that, though one or two people still get uptight. I had to stop it, because as a Beatle I had to sign everything and be everything they wanted and always smile and react 'Hi' and all of that. Or we went the other way, which was hiding, and we wouldn't see anyone, wouldn't see the press, kept the gates locked. But now I do it on a whim, just let it roll.

Yoko coined a phrase, 'Rock Square'. And I was definitely in that box. I would never have admitted it while it was happening, but nevertheless, it was going on. What happens is that you suddenly become exactly what you didn't like about other forms of music, be it jazz or classical or whatever, and then you have to admit that it should really be like this or that. Now, when someone comes along and says 'no', it can be whatever you want it to be. That's a very big

change to go through. But after you experience it, then you loosen. You feel free to do whatever you want.

Just being – quote – a 'star' or whatever it was that happened, made it a little more unreal. So perhaps the periods lasted just a little bit longer. Look, a working guy will get lost for a weekend, get pissed, and forget who he is or dream that he's so-and-so in his car. Well, it was just the same with us. But instead of getting blotto for a weekend, we got blotto for two months, trying to forget whatever it is that everybody tries to forget all the time.

The bigger you become, the more insecure you feel. I'd like to think that people could learn from the mistakes others have made. But they don't. It's like you can't tell anybody nothing, ever. I can't learn myself from other people's mistakes. You can sing about it, because that's your own experience, but you can't expect anyone to think along the lines, 'Oh, so they did that and that happened, so we won't do that.' You can't do it. It never works.

When people say I'm self-indulgent, it's only because I'm not doing what they want me to do. Simply because they're still hung up on my past. If you've noticed, when they say such things, they don't usually refer to the music. Actually, I got it down the other day. People talk about not what you do, but how you do it, which is like discussing how you dress or if your hair is long or short. They can say what they want, but the artist knows best and when you work at such an energy level, like Yoko and me, then you're doomed to be heavily criticized.

The business began to take over, because the Beatles were a helluva big business. I mean, [we're] talking about hundreds of millions of dollars. And after our first manager died, it became apparent to us that somebody's got to run this thing. We were so busy being the Beatles and suddenly we found ourselves in charge of this vast array of complicated companies within companies within companies.

We were out to be famous rock 'n' rollers and play good music and have a bloody good time. You start out with different intentions; you don't know what fame is, you don't know what being rich is till you're rich, you don't know what any of it is. It just escalated onto a world scale and next minute we turned around and people are calling us for decisions on vast things [and] we have no clue what they're talking about! 'What do you mean, Beatles concessions on lunch boxes; what are you talking about?' We didn't even know there were lunch boxes! I thought, hells, bells, I didn't set out…I'm an artist. I always was an artist and an artist is what I'm going to be. So, just leave me enough air to breathe and let me get on with it!

John & Yoko photographed by Brian Hamill window shopping in the West Village, New York, 13 October 1972.

Two photographs by Abbie Hoffman's wife Anita. Top: Jerry Rubin, Yoko, John and Abbie in New York's East Village outside the Hoffmans' apartment at 30 St Mark's Place with 2nd Avenue in the background. Bottom: Abbie and John share a smoke and a Coke and a smile on the Hoffmans' roof terrace, June 1971.

The Price of Fun

John: Our 'revolutionary period' blossomed shortly after we landed in the States for a visit. I had no intention of leaving home, for tax or any other reasons. It just happened that way. Anyway, upon our arrival in the US, we were practically met off the plane by the 'Mork and Mindy' of the sixties – Jerry Rubin and Abbie Hoffman – and promptly taken on a tour of New York's 'underground', which consisted mainly of David Peel singing about dope in Washington Square Park.

Jerry and Abbie – two classic, fun-loving hustlers. I can do without Marx and Jesus.

It took a long time and a lot of good magic to get rid of the stench of our lost virginity, although it was fun meeting all the famous underground heroes (no heroines): Bobby Seale and his merry men; Huey Newton in his very expensive-looking military-style clothes; Rennie Davis and his 'You pay for it and I'll organize it'; John Sinclair and his faithful Ann Arbor Brigade; and dear old Allen Ginsberg, who if he wasn't lying on the floor 'ohm-ing' was embarrassing the fuck out of everyone he could corner by chanting something he called poetry very loudly in their ears (and out the other).

The price of that kind of fun was too high. It was almost five years before our battle with the Nixon government was over (presuming it is over). It was Strom 'May He Be Enlightened' Thurmond who cast the first stone; he wrote to the then Attorney General of the United States, John 'Take My Wife' Mitchell (they took her; RIP Martha), suggesting that somehow they throw us out of America before the Republican National Convention in San Diego. I understand the reasoning behind the attack, especially after one of our big-mouthed revolutionary heroes had broadcast to the world that John & Yoko were organizing a massed rally to blow away the Republicans at San Diego.

Abbie Hoffman: John & Yoko did come and look up myself and Jerry Rubin, and they wanted it known around the New York scene that they had a political side to them. They – before they even got here, they had a lot more political consciousness than just say the bed-ins or other things that they were kind of involved in that might appear a little flaky.

We must have met at least a dozen times, and we started to organize demonstrations at the Republican Convention, which at that time was still in San Diego. All of these conversations were monitored by the FBI and God knows who else, you know. And it was these conversations that, number one, forced the convention to move to Miami, and number two, got the Immigration Service on John Lennon's back. And I think it's wise to remember that for six years he was hounded, not just because of some pot possession charge. I mean, there's probably one hundred to two hundred people a week that want to come into this country with many more charges, but because that he was both political and was forming alliances with radicals.

He talked sheer poetry. I mean, you totally hung on every word, and he was extremely dramatic and ran the gambit from manic excitation to sad depressive, moody states. And he just pulled off one night and just went over to the corner and in three minutes wrote a song, came back and sang it. It was quite a thing to witness.

Yoko: They really tried to make us go to Miami, and we kept saying we're not going to do it, but Jerry, for political reasons, just announced that we were going to be there.

John: They think we're going to San Diego or Miami or whatever it is. We never said we're going, we ain't going, they'll be no big jam with us and Dylan because there's too much going on.

We never said we were going and that's it.

Yoko: By then John and I realized that it would have been very, very dangerous for us. We had a very distinct, clear, feeling that if we had gone to the Republican Convention we would have been in danger of our lives.

John: There had been a grand pow-wow at our Bank Street apartment. All the heroes were there. It seemed that without John & Yoko's drawing power, there wasn't going to be a revolution. The Left and Right were both labouring under that illusion. I think Ginsberg was the only one there besides ourselves who thought that the whole idea stunk, and was not only dangerous but stupid.

But apparently, the 'leaders' of the movement wanted another 'Chicago'. And we were to be the bait, only we said no. It didn't make much difference, because simply putting out the message through *Rolling Stone* that we were coming would convince enough people that we had agreed to it. It convinced Nixon's people.

Paul Krassner: They knew for a fact that they didn't want hundreds, thousands, millions of young people attending a counter-convention, especially where John Lennon would perform.

John: Mae 'They're Coming Through the Windows!' Brussel and Paul Krassner told us that Jerry and Abbie and the whole of the Chicago Seven were double agents for the CIA (except Krassner, of course). We never did find out.

They were following me around everywhere I went, but I suppose they must have got bored going to the studio and hanging around for hours at a time. And they were tapping my phone. I think they wanted me to know

they were doing it too, because I kept hearing heavy breathing. It scared me at first but now it's a bit of a joke. I wasn't on Nixon's list of unfriendlies but I was on somebody's list, that's for sure. There's a pattern to it all. Not necessarily a coordinated conspiracy but a series of connected happenings that numbered all the leading sixties cult figures.

G. Gordon Liddy (FBI): It was our perspective [on] Lennon that most of the time he was walking around stoned, whacked out of his mind. But he was a high-profile figure, and so his activities were being monitored. It wasn't so much that Lennon was being critical of US policy, it was that he was over here enjoying all the benefits of the success that we were giving him, the wealth and all the rest of it, and badmouthing us here. Our attitude was: you want to do that? Go back to London. Go back to Liverpool.

John: Senator Strom Thurmond sent a letter to John Mitchell when he was Attorney General. Thurmond was the head of a congressional committee, and whether we'll get our hands on it I don't know. But it said in essence, this guy's looking to stay here and we suggest no. And our lawyers always said that the instructions for Lennon's case are coming from Washington. And the New York people kept insisting it was a local case. But we knew it wasn't just a local case, and this letter from Thurmond could prove it.

Oh, yeah. They picked on me. I'm telling you, when it first started, I was followed in a car, and my phone was tapped. I can't prove it. I just know there's a lot of repairs going on in the cellar. I know the difference between the phone being normal when I pick it up and when every time I pick it up there's a lot of noises.

I'd open the door, and there would be guys standing on the other side of the street. I'd get in a car, and they'd be following me in a car, and not hiding, you see? That's why I got a bit paranoid, as well. They wanted me to see I was being followed. Suddenly I realized this was serious. They were coming for me one way or the other.

Now we lost the phone tapping case – because, how do you prove your phone was tapped? That was pre-Watergate, so you can imagine – 'John Lennon says his phone's tapped and there's men following him in car.' I went on *The Dick Cavett Show* – this is long before Watergate – and said this was happening to me and it stopped the next day. And I think they wanted me to know, to scare me. And I was scared, paranoid, you know.

And people just thought, 'Oh crazy Lennon. Whose gonna bother following him? What an egomaniac.'

But we had been associated with Jerry Rubin and John Sinclair and little rallies, and were seen around those people. It really was like a mini-Watergate.

The John Sinclair Freedom Rally included The Up, Allen Ginsberg with Gary Williamson, Teegarden & Van Winkle with Bob Seger, Phil Ochs, Commander Cody and His Lost Planet Airmen, Stevie Wonder and Wonderlove, David Peel & The Lower East Side and John & Yoko with Plastic Ono Band, with speeches by Bobby Seale, Rennie Davis, Jerry Rubin, and John Sinclair's wife Leni and mother, Crisler Arena, University of Michigan, 10 December 1971. Three days after the rally, after 29 months in jail for possession of two marijuana cigarettes, John Sinclair (still bottom right) was finally released and filmed in an emotional reunion with his wife Leni and daughters Sunny and Celia, Jackson State Prison, Michigan, 13 December 1971. Opposite: Jerry Rubin's report on the concert that kickstarted John's problems with Nixon – planning a huge political Woodstock at the Republican National Convention in August 1972.

A REPORT ON ANN ARBOR AND THE FREEING OF JOHN SINCLAIR

By Jerry Rubin

It was a new beginning for the movement. People went around hugging each other. Everyone at the huge Free John Sinclair rally in Ann Arbor Michigan felt they were part of something new and historic--- but like the first college sit-in or the first be-in or first rock festival, nobody knew its name or its meaning. (energy)

When you entered Chrisler Hall on the/night of XXXXXXX Friday, December 10, you felt an incredible rush. The good vibrations of 15,000 people linked XXXXXX together in that oval spaceship made everyone feel really warm inside. 15,000 people on the same wave length! What a trip!

We were all there, not just to get high or go crazy with music, but to free a brother from The Man's jail and to pool our energy together to focus attention on political prisoners throughout Amerika. The passing of joints from person to person united us all in a community of XXX saliva, all the more ironic and outrageous because John Sinclair was in jail for what XXXX we were XXXXX doing, XXXXXXXXXXXXX (at that moment) (and not welcome.)

Hard drugs and pills were nowhere to be found. Nobody was pushing or shoving. No tough guys were needed to protect the stage because nobody was rushing the stage. "When was the last time you felt so great?" everyone was saying to each other as we all looked around and saw 15,000 people united in a collective dream. Even though the stage still provided the focus of energy, everyone in the audience knew that their presence was important: that they, not the stage, were the news. The people felt their own power.

XXXXXXXX This was a political event, with a political goal and all money going to political purposes and not for profit, everyone felt united in something beyond themselves and beyond their own XXXXXXX pleasure: a community action. (already)

John Sinclair had been in jail XXXXX years for possession of two joints on a 10-year sentence. Three months earlier the Michigan State Supreme Court denied him appeal bond by a 5-2 vote. His friends were depressed that he might XXX not get out until he served his entire barbaric sentence. John himself, was locked in solitary, lonely, near freak-out. No one seemed to know or care about John even tho he was jailed because of his political activism in opposing XXXXXXXXXXXX imperialism and racism. He was a victim, a martyr, a symbol of the movement's inability to defend its own.

What was needed was some way to focus national attention on Sinclair's case. Anonymity helps the state keep people in jail. The state is repressive because people do not know or care. John's friends decided to organize a big event, and John Lennon and Yoko Ono among others offered to attend to show support. The day before the rally the Michigan Legislature reduced marijuana possession from a felony to a misdemeanor. The Free (offered)

2

Sinclair rally publicized his case on the front pages of every paper in Michigan. The vibrations reached the judges because in an incredible tribute to the power of the people, on Monday morning, 55 hours after the rally ended, they voted 6-1 to release John from jail on appeal bond.

As if the rally itself XXXXX wasn't amazing enough, we achieved our goal. We won! We freed John! The people freed John! 15,000 people freed John! And it is only the beginning.

Amazingly XXXX enough, the whole thing was organized in 10 days. What brought everyone together was the magic of John XXXX and Yoko who released a tape on Wednesday on Detroit radio saying they were coming by themselves, without the Plastik Ono band, to support Sinclair--and 15,000 XXXXXXXXXXXXXXXXXXXXXXXXXXXXXXXXXX tickets at $3 a person were XXXX sold out within one hour, with all money going to the Free Sinclair Fund. This was the first time in our history that people of John and Yoko's status have done a benefit action for the people. Everyone there felt an appreciation and love for John and Yoko that is unique in feelings between people and rock performers. Something new was in the air, and it is only the beginning.

The people on stage reflected the seeds of the new cultural and political renaissance about to hit Amerika--the second cultural revolution. One after another on the stage came Allen Ginsberg, Marge Tobankin, emcees Anne LaVasseur and Bob Rudnick, XXXXX Bobby Seale, Phil Ochs, Jerry Rubin, Ed Sanders, Rennie Davis, Dave Dellinger, David Sinclair, Sheila Murphy, the Up, Father James Groppi, Jonnie Lee Tillman, Stevie Wonder, Seger-Teagarden-Van Winkle, Archie Shepp, Commander Cody, Leni Sinclair, David Peel and John and Yoko.

Everyone who had been out doing their own thing by themselves for the past two years came together again, black and white, male and female, politics and music, young and old, revolutionary and reformist, reflecting our new unity, thrown together by Nixon, realizing how much love and power we have if we are together.

People cheered the political rock songs, and listened carefully and enthusiastically to the speeches, a merger of music and politics never before done, so that the Michigan Daily said, "one couldn't distinguish where the songs left off and the politics began." It was not a rock concert. It was not a teach-in. It was some beautiful new combination of rock and political event combined with the feeling of a be-in: some new form of mass celebration and affirmation--so new it as yet has no name or definition.

The media tells us that young people are back in the 1950's and the movement is dead. But here were 15,000 kids from the State of Michigan, working class kids, college kids, high school kids, GI's, youth from every XXXXXXX social class and every imaginable community, brought together by their desire to live in a world without oppression.

The action began at 7 p.m. but it was not 8½ hours later til 3:30 a.m. before John and Yoko got on the stage. XXXX By the time John and Yoko began singing the room was so high you felt like laughing hysterically XXXXXXXXXX

3

or crying with happiness or pinching yourself to see if it was really happening. It was farout: John and Yoko had given their energy as an opportunity for all of us to get together. An unspoken "thank you" went out from the crowd and an XXXX unspoken "thank you" went back from John and Yoko.

Yoko dedicated XXXXXXXXXXXXXX a song "to XXXXX my sisters in Ann Arbor," called, "Sisters O Sisters." John and Yoko sang XXXX two songs they wrote together: "Attica State" about the massacre of 43 prisoners and guards XXXXX at the prison, and "The Luck of the Irish," about the struggle of the Irish people against British occupation.

Then John XXX climaxed the night with the song he wrote XXXXXXX specifically for that night: "It Ain't Fair, John Sinclair," a catchy tune sung with a slide guitar.

What an incredible XXXXXX moment earlier when Leni, John's wife, began speaking to him on the phone. John was making his one phone call XXXXXXXXXXXXXXXXX a month, and prison officials did not know he was speaking on a phone hooked up live to 15,000 people and FM radio. John said, "They try to make us feel so alone in here," and then he started sobbing. For XXXXXXXXXX one minute that seemed like an hour John broke down and cried. 15,000 XXXXXX stunned people sat motionless with lumps in their throats.

The Old Dream of 1967 and '68 has floundered. Rock festivals turned into mass freakouts, with ugly rapes and mad pushing and shoving. The XXXXXXXXXX sweet pot high turned into a heroin disaster area. Rock music became a new capitalist product and rock stars became movie stars. Our streets turned into Desolation Row.

Finally, individually and collectively we said stop! and we decided to take a rest and rediscover who we are. Before we began again we knew we had to root out of our own family the evils of male chauvinism, bad drugs, capitalist rip-offs, movie stardom.

But even that necessary self-examination and turning inward got corrupted into an extreme as people began attacking themselves and each other so ferociously that we all became too scared to move--not out of fear of the Establishment but out of fear of unloving, XXXX unrelenting criticism from one's own sisters and brothers---and people went so inward XXXXXX and so deep into the country---literally and figuratively--- XXXXX that apathy, despair, cynicism and loneliness took over and we forgot who we were: a new human family, XXXXXXXXXXX linked together by love and solidarity, out to turn on and change the world.

For the past five months in New York City people have been feeling that the worst is over and that people are creating again and coming together again and something new is in the air. Somehow XXXX the arrival of John and Yoko in New York has had a mystical and practical effect that is bringing people together again. Bob Dylan signalled an omen of the return to activism when he appeared unannounced at the Bengla Desh concert in Madison Square Garden and sang, XXXXXXXXXXX "Blowing in the

---

4

"A "Mr.
Wind," "Hard Rain's A-Gonna Fall" and "Tambourine Man." It's great--- everyone is XXXXXX almost going back to the early '60's and starting out all over again.

As John Lennon said in the last words spoken at Ann Arbor: "Apathy won't XXXXX get us anywhere. So flower power failed, so what, let's start again."

This is the year for everyone to come back and start again, to come together again, in new ways, to build our culture without male chauvinism, bad drugs and crazy freakouts, We should try to build our culture once more, only this time with XXXXX more self-awareness and self-control. We need more public events, even a huge Political Woodstock at the Republican National Convention next August in San Diego.

1-2-3-4, many more Ann Arbors!

And it is only the beginning...

H

Yoko Ono, John Lennon and their immigration attorney, Leon Wildes (right), arrive at and leave the Immigration and Naturalization Service in New York on 16 March 1972.

Opposite: John & Yoko with Dick Cavett on *The Dick Cavett Show*, filmed at The Elysee Theater, ABC Studio TV 15, 202 W58th St, New York, 3 May 1972.

John: The thing that bothered most of our revolutionary brothers was the fact that we weren't against anything, just for things, you know, like peace and love and all that naive crap. That was not macho enough for the tough Jewish Haggendass (not the ice cream). I mean, man, they were the Chicago Seven and knew the Black Panthers. Whilst they tried to 'use' us, we tried to 'convert' them. We even got them on *The Mike Douglas Show*, but none of them knew how to talk to the people – never mind lead them!

The other thing no one liked was the fact that we always insisted on keeping physical and legal control over any film footage which included us in it. John Sinclair threatened to sue us, even after we helped get him out of prison! 'It ain't fair, John Sinclair.' All in all, we had a few laughs and a lot of drugs.

The bottom line was Nixon's government vs. John & Yoko, a few friends, a lot of fans, and a small black psychic from Chicago, introduced to us by Dick 'I'll Never Eat Another Thing' Gregory. All of whom we are profoundly grateful to.

The biggest mistake Yoko and I made in that period was allowing ourselves to become influenced by the male-macho 'serious revolutionaries', and their insane ideas about killing people to save them from capitalism and/or communism (depending on your point of view). We should have stuck to our own way of working for peace: bed-ins, billboards, etc.

And now here we were, fighting the US government with a lawyer who at first didn't believe that it was a politically motivated court case (he thought we weren't 'that important'), or that the FBI was harassing us with phone taps and the like. He believed later when his own phone was tapped. We stopped them when we announced on *The Dick Cavett Show* that they were following us and bugging us.

Leon Wildes (immigration lawyer): It became clear to me that John was a guy of major principle, and he understood that what was being done to him was wrong. It was an abuse of the law, and he was willing to stand up and try to show it, shine a big light on it. I sued the Attorney General, Mitchell, and a whole slew of other people who I claimed were involved in a conspiracy to deny John & Yoko's case and get them out of the US improperly.

We ultimately were able to examine the records in the case and, lo and behold, deep in John's immigration file, which was a high security file, were documents reaching all the way up to President Nixon showing improper interference in an immigration case and prejudgement.

John: So, it was 'Bell, Book, and Candle' against Mr Six Six Six Nixon. Yes, we used magic, prayer and children to fight the good fight.

Top left: 'Jerry Rubin/John Lennon & Yoko Ono.... All Extremists
Should Be Considered Dangerous', US government memo,
12 January 1972. Top right: FBI memo alledging the 'Allamuchy
Tribe' (Rennie Davis, Stu Alpert and Jay Craven) were hiring office
space in Manhattan, preparing for a tour and intent on disrupting the
Republican Convention, all funded by John Lennon, 28 January 1972.

Bottom left: Memo from Republican Senator Strom Thurmond
to Attorney General John N. Mitchell – 'many headaches might be
avoided if appropriate action be taken in time' – 4 February 1972.
Bottom right: Continuation of the Strom Thurmond memo: 'if
Lennon's visa is terminated it would be a strategy counter-measure',
4 February 1972.

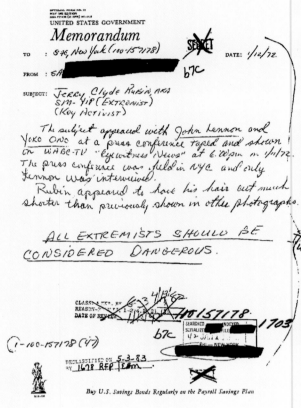

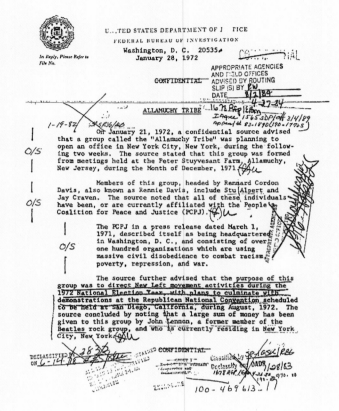

Enemy of the State: The Secret War Against John Lennon
by Tom Hayden

John Lennon cannot be memorialized without recalling his radical political attitudes at a time of roiling unrest in Britain, America and around the globe. His greatest qualities were as an artist, of course, but he would have been a different artist without the rebellious, nonconformist and subversive spirit of the sixties. Revered by all as a great musician, John also became an enemy of the state, which future generations of fans need to remember.

The forces who targeted John Lennon – some combination of London's MI5 and J. Edgar Hoover's FBI – did so clandestinely, then waged a further war to keep their embarrassing improprieties hidden and impeccable reputations intact.

Their counterintelligence campaign unfolded, as far as we know, as the Beatles evolved from an entertainment sensation to a fountain-head of a counterculture consciousness to a formidable political threat in the person of John Lennon.

Five years after the Beatles had performed a last time in San Francisco in 1966, Lennon performed a live concert in December 1971 in Ann Arbor, Michigan. His 'Give Peace A Chance' was already a peace anthem. But this cause had a harder edge, a benefit for imprisoned musician-turned-revolutionary John Sinclair. The flower children of Motown were becoming 'white panthers', consciously emulating the Black Panther Party.

According to the FBI documents obtained in a lawsuit by the historian Jon Wiener, FBI agents were in the audience of fifteen thousand that night and did not like what they heard, saw or inhaled. For years the spy agency had been frustrated by the rise of a counterculture; one 1966 strategy memo lamented that the 'nonconformism in dress and speech, neglect of personal cleanliness, use of obscenities (printed and uttered), publicized sexual promiscuity, experimenting with and the use of drugs, filthy clothes, shaggy hair, wearing of sandals, beads and unusual jewelry *tend to negate any attempt to hold these people up to ridicule*' [emphasis added; SAC, Newark, to Director, FBI, Memorandum, 27 May 1968 (Counterintelligence Program, Internal Security: Disruption of the New Left/Re. Bureau letter to Albany, 10 May 1963)].

Declassified cable traffic reveals that the key reason the Bureau attempted to deport John & Yoko Lennon in early 1972 for overstaying a visa was not a prior marijuana charge in London, but the upcoming 1972 re-election campaign of Richard Nixon. Anti-war sentiment had reached majority proportions in America and activism had acquired a militant edge with the siege of the White House and thousands of arrests in May 1971. Nixon's paranoia was seemingly boundless. That same year he illegally authorized the White House 'plumbers' to ransack the Democratic National Committee offices in Washington, steal confidential files from Daniel Ellsberg's therapist, and lay plans to suppress the planned protests at the Republican National Convention in San Diego.

John Lennon and Yoko Ono figured prominently in the plans and dreams of those hoping to upset Nixon that year. 'A confidential source who has furnished reliable information in the past' advised the FBI that Lennon gave $75,000 in early 1972 toward a plan to 'disrupt the Republican National Convention'.

On 1 March, another 'confidential source' advised that I had flown into Washington for a secret meeting with Rennie Davis to discuss an election-year plan involving demonstrations, speaking tours and a New Left-oriented 'entertainment group' composed of John & Yoko, whose 'function [was] a stimulus to encourage youths to be in the vicinity of election candidates when they are on tour' [FBI memorandum (Election Year Strategy Information Center), 8 March 1972].

On 16 March 1972, another FBI memo warned that 'subject' Lennon 'continues to plan activities directed towards RNC and will soon initiate series of "rock concerts" to develop financial support…'. The agent advised that the New York Bureau 'promptly initiate discreet efforts to locate subject' and that any information linking Lennon to drugs be 'immediately furnished to Bureau in form suitable for dissemination.'

On 21 May, the Bureau pledged to '*neutralize any disruptive activities of subject*' (emphasis added) in the chilling vocabulary of the FBI's counterintelligence (COINTEL) programme.

Somewhere between fantasy and reality, Rennie was convinced that John Lennon could transcend and unify our fragmented world with one more grand tour of protest. Abbie Hoffman and Jerry Rubin shared the same dream, and were meeting with Lennon, Rennie said. It was a time of grand and distrustful egotisms, however, despite the considerable expansion of public support for the movement's aims of peace and tolerance.

One reason is that Nixon was withdrawing ground troops from Vietnam while continuing the bombing, sending police after the Black Panthers and their friends, and indicting up to sixty separate antiwar protestors on various conspiracy charges. All this was causing activists to wonder and quarrel about whether the long war was ending or heating up. One can only speculate about the role that FBI counterintelligence programmes, and the plenitude of drugs, played in fostering this paranoia.

Top left: 'You may be assured the information you previously furnished has been appropriately noted' – response to Thurmond's memo from Nixon's assistant William Timmons – 6 March 1972.
Top right: Airtel to New York: 'In view of subject's avowed intention to engage in disruptive activities surrounding RNC, New York Office will be responsible for closely following his activities until time of actual deportation.'

Bottom left and right: Memo to E. S. Miller from R. L. Shackleford: 'New York City Police Department currently attempting to develop enough information to arrest both Lennons for narcotics use… subject's activities being closely followed…in effort to neutralize any disruptive activities of subject', 21 April 1972.

EXECUTIVE
IM/L

March 6, 1972

Dear Strom:

In connection with your previous inquiry concerning the former member of the Beatles, John Lennon, I thought you would be interested in learning that the Immigration and Naturalization Service has served notice on him that he is to leave this country no later than March 15. You may be assured the information you previously furnished has been appropriately noted.

With warm regards,

Sincerely,

William E. Timmons
Assistant to the President

Honorable Strom Thurmond
United States Senate
Washington, D.C. 20510

bcc: Mr. Harlington Wood, Department of Justice - for your information
bcc: Tom Korologos - for your information

WET:VO:jlh

Airtel to New York'
RE: John Winston Lennon
100-469910   CONFIDENTIAL

In view of subject's avowed intention to engage in disruptive activities surrounding RNC, New York Office will be responsible for closely following his activities until time of actual deportation. Afford this matter close supervision and keep Bureau fully advised by most expeditious means warranted.

NOTE:

John Lennon, former member of Beatles singing group, is allegedly in U.S. to assist in organizing disruption of RNC. Due to narcotics conviction in England, he is being deported along with wife Yoko Ono. They appeared at Immigration and Naturalization Service, New York, 3/16/72, for deportation proceedings but won delay until 4/18/72 because subject fighting narcotics conviction and wife fighting custody child case in U.S. Strong possibility looms that subject will not be deported any time soon and will probably be in U.S. at least until RNC. Information developed by Alexandria source that subject continues to plan activities directed toward RNC and will soon initiate series of "rock concerts" to develop financial support with first concert to be held Ann Arbor, Michigan, in near future. New York Office covering subject's temporary residence and being instructed to intensify discreet investigation of subject to determine activities vis a vis RNC.

- 2 -

CONFIDENTIAL

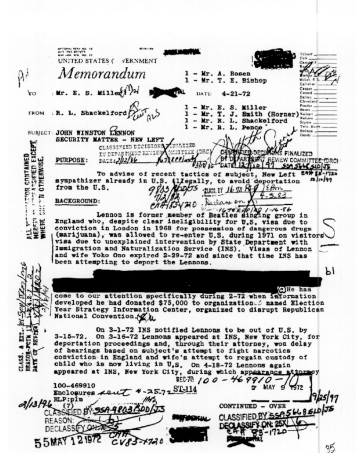

UNITED STATES GOVERNMENT

Memorandum

TO : Mr. E. S. Miller   DATE: 4-21-72

FROM : R. L. Shackleford

1 - Mr. A. Rosen
1 - Mr. T. E. Bishop
1 - Mr. E. S. Miller
1 - Mr. T. J. Smith (Horner)
1 - Mr. R. L. Shackleford
1 - Mr. R. L. Pence

SUBJECT: JOHN WINSTON LENNON
SECURITY MATTER - NEW LEFT

PURPOSE:

To advise of recent tactics of subject, New Left sympathizer already in U.S. illegally, to avoid deportation from the U.S.

BACKGROUND:

Lennon is former member of Beatles singing group in England who, despite clear ineligibility for U.S. visa due to conviction in London in 1968 for possession of dangerous drugs (marijuana), was allowed to re-enter U.S. during 1971 on visitors visa due to unexplained intervention by State Department with Immigration and Naturalization Service (INS). Visas of Lennon and wife Yoko Ono expired 2-29-72 and since that time INS has been attempting to deport the Lennons.

He has come to our attention specifically during 2-72 when information developed he had donated $75,000 to organization named Election Year Strategy Information Center, organized to disrupt Republican National Convention.

On 3-1-72 INS notified Lennons to be out of U.S. by 3-15-72. On 3-16-72 Lennons appeared at INS, New York, for deportation proceedings and, through their attorney, won delay of hearings based on subject's attempt to fight narcotics conviction in England and wife's attempt to regain custody of child who is now living in U.S. On 4-18-72 Lennons again appeared at INS, New York City, during which appearance attorney

100-469910
Enclosures
RLP:plh
(7)
CLASSIFIED BY
REASON:
DECLASSIFY ON:

55 MAY 12 1972

REC-70 100 - 469910 - 10
sent 4-25-72   ST-114   8 MAY 9 1972

Memorandum to Mr. E. S. Miller
RE: John Winston Lennon
100-469910   CONFIDENTIAL

commented that subject felt he was being deported due to his outspoken remarks regarding U.S. policy in Southeast Asia. Attorney requested delay so character witnesses could be introduced to testify on behalf of subject. Attorney also read into court record fact subject had been appointed to the President's Council for Drug Abuse, correct name National Commission on Marijuana and Drug Abuse (NCMDA), and to the faculty of New York University, New York City. As a result of these revelations, INS set new hearing date for 5-2-72, and Lennons left INS to be met by throng of supporters and news media reporters who listened to subject's press release implying he was being deported due to his political ideas and policy of the U.S. Government to deport aliens who speak out against the Administration.

OBSERVATIONS:

Irony of subject being appointed to President's Council for Drug Abuse, if true, is overwhelming since subject is currently reported heavy user of narcotics and frequently avoided by even Rennie Davis and Jerry Rubin, convicted Chicago Seven Conspiracy trial defendants, due to his excessive use of narcotics. New York City Police Department currently attempting to develop enough information to arrest both Lennons for narcotics use. WFO has contacted NCMDA under pretext and determined no information available indicating subject has been appointed to NCMDA. New York Office has confirmed that Lennon has been offered teaching position at New York University for Summer of 1972. In view of successful delaying tactics to date, there exists real possibility that subject will not be deported from U.S. in near future and possibly not prior to Republican National Convention. Subject's activities being closely followed and any information developed indicating violation of Federal laws will be immediately furnished to pertinent agencies in effort to neutralize any disruptive activities of subject. Information developed to date has been furnished as received to INS and State Department. Information has also been furnished Internal Security Division of the Department.

ACTION:

Attached for approval are letters to Honorable H. R. Haldeman at The White House and Acting Attorney General with copies to the Deputy Attorney General and Assistant Attorney General, Internal Security Division, containing information concerning Lennon.

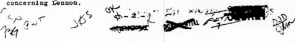

Top left: Memo to Nixon's White House Chief of Staff, H. R. Haldeman: 'Lennon continues to be a heavy user of narcotics', May 1972.

Top right: Memo to Acting Attorney General from FBI Director J. Edgar Hoover: 'Lennon has contributed $75,000 to a newly organized New Left group formed to disrupt the Republican National Convention…. Lennon felt he was being deported due to his outspoken remarks concerning United States policy in Southeast Asia', 25 April 1972.

Bottom left: Airtel to FBI Acting Director L. Patrick Gray from SAC Miami: 'subject Lennon and his wife, Yoko Ono, are planning a large rock concert in Miami during the conventions…to be held in front of the convention hall', 5 June 1972. Bottom right: Airtel to FBI Acting Director L. Patrick Gray from SAC New York: 'if Lennon were to be arrested in US for possession of narcotics he would become more likely to be immediately deportable', 27 July 1972.

CONFIDENTIAL

Honorable H. R. Haldeman

A second confidential source, who has furnished reliable information in the past, advised that Lennon continues to be a heavy user of narcotics. On April 21, 1972, a third confidential source in a position to furnish reliable information advised that there was no information available indicating that Lennon has been appointed to the National Commission on Marijuana and Drug Abuse. A fourth confidential source in a position to furnish reliable information advised that Lennon has been offered a teaching position at New York University for the Summer of 1972.

This information is also being furnished to the Acting Attorney General. Pertinent information concerning Lennon is being furnished to the Department of State and INS on a regular basis.

Sincerely yours,

NOTE:

Classified "Confidential" since information is contained from _____ first confidential source is _____ second confidential source is _____ third confidential source is pretext inquiry by WFO with _____ National Commission on Marijuana and Drug Abuse, Washington, D. C.; and fourth confidential source is _____, New York, New York.

1. See memorandum R. L. Shackelford to Mr. E. S. Miller, 4/21/72, captioned "John Winston Lennon, Security Matter – New Left," and prepared by RLP:plm.

CONFIDENTIAL

- 2 -

CONFIDENTIAL

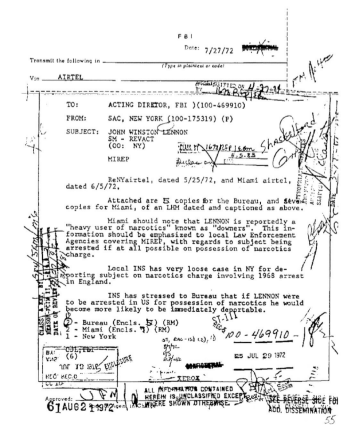

The Acting Attorney General   April 25, 1972

Director, FBI

JOHN WINSTON LENNON
SECURITY MATTER – NEW LEFT

1 – Mr. A. Rosen
1 – Mr. T. J. Bishop
1 – Mr. E. S. Miller
1 – Mr. R. L. Shackelford
1 – Mr. T. J. Smith (Horner)
1 – Mr. R. L. Pence

John Winston Lennon is a British citizen and former member of the Beatles singing group. _____ Lennon has taken an interest in "revolutionary left-wing activities in Britain" and is known to be a sympathizer of Trotskyist communists in England.

Despite his apparent ineligibility for a United States visa due to a conviction in London in 1968 for possession of dangerous drugs, Lennon obtained a visa and entered the United States in 1971. During February, 1972, a confidential source, who has furnished reliable information in the past, advised that Lennon had contributed $75,000 to a newly organized New Left group formed to disrupt the Republican National Convention. The visas of Lennon and his wife, Yoko Ono, expired on February 29, 1972, and since that time Immigration and Naturalization Service (INS) has been attempting to deport them. During the Lennons' most recent deportation hearing at INS, New York, on April 18, 1972, their attorney stated that Lennon felt he was being deported due to his outspoken remarks concerning United States policy in Southeast Asia. The attorney requested a delay in order that character witnesses could testify for Lennon, and he then read into the court record that Lennon had been appointed to the President's Council for Drug Abuse (National Commission on Marijuana and Drug Abuse) and to the faculty of New York University, New York, New York.

A second confidential source, who has furnished reliable information in the past, advised that Lennon continues to be a heavy user of narcotics. On April 21, 1972, a third confidential source in a position to furnish reliable information advised that there was no information available indicating that

100-469910
RLP:pla
(13)

CONFIDENTIAL
Group 1
Excluded from automatic
downgrading and
declassification

SEE NOTE PAGE TWO

ALL INFORMATION CONTAINED
HEREIN IS UNCLASSIFIED EXCEPT
WHERE SHOWN OTHERWISE

CLASSIFIED BY _____
DECLASSIFY ON: 25X 1.3 (4) 11/28/2031

FD-36 (Rev. 5-22-64)

FBI

Date: 6/5/72

Transmit the following in _____
(Type in plaintext or code)

Via   AIRTEL
        (Priority)

ALL INFORMATION CONTAINED
HEREIN IS UNCLASSIFIED
DATE 2/12/81 BY

TO: ACTING DIRECTOR, FBI (100-469910)
                                (100-469601)

FROM: SAC, MIAMI (100-NEW) (P)
                    (80-1353) (P)

SUBJECT: JOHN WINSTON LENNON
         SM – REVOLUTIONARY ACTIVITIES
         (OO: NEW YORK)

         MIDEM

         Re New York airtel to the Bureau dated 5/25/72, under first caption above.

         New York airtel indicated information was received from VINCENT SCHIANO, Chief Trial Attorney, INS, New York City, on 5/25/72, to the effect that he had received information that subject LENNON and his wife, YOKO ONO, are planning a large rock concert in Miami during the conventions and that the rock concert was to be held in front of the convention hall.

                    LEAD

NEW YORK

2 - Bureau (RM)
    (2 - 100-469910)
    (2 - 100-469601)
2 - New York (100-175319)
3 - Miami
    (2 - 100-NEW)
    (1 - 80-1353)
JCB:mly
(9)

REC 11

100-4699/0-17

JUN 8 1972

Approved: _____   Sent _____ M
Special Agent in Charge

57 JUN 19 1972

FBI

Date: 7/27/72

Transmit the following in _____
(Type in plaintext or code)

Via   AIRTEL

TO: ACTING DIRECTOR, FBI (100-469910)

FROM: SAC, NEW YORK (100-175319) (P)

SUBJECT: JOHN WINSTON LENNON
         SM – REVACT
         (OO: NY)
         MIREP

         ReNYairtel, dated 5/25/72, and Miami airtel, dated 6/5/72.

         Attached are 5 copies for the Bureau, and seven copies for Miami, of an LHM dated and captioned as above.

         Miami should note that LENNON is reportedly a "heavy user of narcotics" known as "downers". This information should be emphasized to local Law Enforcement Agencies covering MIREP, with regards to subject being arrested if at all possible on possession of narcotics charge.

         Local INS has very loose case in NY for deporting subject on narcotics charge involving 1968 arrest in England.

         INS has stressed to Bureau that if LENNON were to be arrested in US for possession of narcotics he would become more likely to be immediately deportable.

2 - Bureau (Encls. 5) (RM)
    Miami (Encls. 7) (RM)
1 - New York

100-469910-18

25 JUL 29 1972

ALL INFORMATION CONTAINED
HEREIN IS UNCLASSIFIED EXCEPT
WHERE SHOWN OTHERWISE

Approved: _____   Sent _____ M
Special Agent in Charge

61 AUG 2 1972

SEE REVERSE SIDE FOR
ADD. DISSEMINATION

55

Top left: FBI memo info sheet on John Lennon ('Brown to Blond' hair, 'Approximately six feet') that used an image of David Peel's face.
Top right: Memo from SAC Miami to FBI Acting Director L. Patrick Gray, 'a review of records relating to the individuals arrested…failed to reflect that the subject was one of those arrested', 24 October 1972.
Bottom left: Memo from SAC New York to FBI Acting Director L. Patrick Gray, 'It is believed that the subject did not travel to Miami for the Republican National Convention as he had previously planned…. New York Division is placing this case in a pending inactive status', 30 August 1972.
Bottom right: Airtel from SAC New York to FBI Acting Director L. Patrick Gray: 'In view of the subject's inactivity in Revolutionary Activities and his seemingly rejection by NY Radicals, captioned case is being closed in the NY Division', 8 December 1972.

John Winston Lennon

John Winston Lennon, a former member of the Beatles Rock Music Group is presently the subject of deportation hearing by the Immigration and Naturalization Service.

Lennon is described as follows:

Name: John Winston Lennon
Race: White
Date of Birth: October 9, 1940
Place of Birth: Liverpool, England
Hair: Brown to Blond
Weight: 160 pounds
Height: Approximately six feet
Build: Slender
Nationality: English
United States
Residence: 105 Bank Street
                    New York City
Arrest Record: 1968 Narcotics Arrest, in
                    England for Possession of
                    Dangerous Drugs (Cannabis)
                    Pled Guilty

UNITED STATES GOVERNMENT
Memorandum

TO : ACTING DIRECTOR, FBI (100-469910)   DATE: 10-24-72

FROM : SAC, MIAMI (100-16733) (RUC)

SUBJECT: JOHN WINSTON LENNON
         SM - RA

         (OO: New York)

Re Miami letter to Bureau, 9-28-72.

A review of records relating to the individuals arrested in Miami Beach, Florida, on 8/22 and 23/72, in connection with protest demonstrations against the Republican National Convention, failed to reflect that the subject was one of those arrested.

Inasmuch as there is no indication that the subject ever appeared in Miami Beach during either of the national political conventions in July and August, 1972, no further investigation is being conducted by Miami.

2-Bureau (RM)
2-New York (100-175319) (RM)
1-Miami
WED/al
(5)

ALL INFORMATION CONTAINED HEREIN IS UNCLASSIFIED
DATE 2/19/41 BY

REC-63   100-469910-23

3   OCT 27 1972

NOV 3 1972

Buy U.S. Savings Bonds Regularly on the Payroll Savings Plan

UNITED STATES GOVERNMENT
Memorandum

TO : ACTING DIRECTOR, FBI (100-469910) DATE: 8/30/72

FROM : SAC, NEW YORK (100-175319) (P*)

SUBJECT: JOHN WINSTON LENNON
         SM-REVACT
         (OO: NY)

Re NY airtel and LHM, 7/27/72.

Referenced communications set forth background information as requested by Miami in view of MIREP activities in that city, August 21-24, 1972.

Case Agent traveled to Miami as a member of the Weatherman Task Group (WTG). The subject was not observed by the case agent and based on informant coverage it is believed that the subject did not travel to Miami for the Republican National Convention as he had previously planned.

On August 28, 1972, Mr. VINCENT SCHIANO, Chief Trial Attorney, INS, NYC, advised that no information has come to his attention to indicate the subject traveled to Miami.

For the past several months there has been no information received to indicate that the subject is active in the New Left.

Sources; [redacted] all advised during the month of July, 1972, that the subject has fallen out of the favor of activist JERRY RUBIN, STEWART ALBERT, and RENNIE DAVIS, due to subject's lack of interest in committing himself to involvement in anti-war and New Left activities.

In view of this information the New York Division is placing this case in a pending inactive status. When information concerning subject's tentative deportation is received such information will be sent to the Bureau.

2-Bureau (RM)   REC-24 100-469910-20
1-New York

EX-104

CJL:jas
(3)

21 SEP 1 1972

Buy U.S. Savings Bonds Regularly on the Payroll Savings Plan

FBI

Date: 12/8/72

Transmit the following in _____ (Type in plaintext or code)

Via AIRTEL _____ (Priority)

TO: ACTING DIRECTOR, FBI (100-469910)

FROM: SAC, NEW YORK (100-175319) (C)

SUBJECT: JOHN WINSTON LENNON
         SM - RA
         (OO:NY)

ReLegat, London letter, 9/12/72; NYlet, 8/30/72.

Enclosed for the Bureau are ten copies of an LHM captioned "International Committee for John and Yoko," dated as above. Appropriate copies should be made available to Legat, London, as per their request.

In view of subject's inactivity in Revolutionary Activities and his seemingly rejection by NY Radicals, captioned case is being closed in the NY Division.

In event other information comes to New York's attention indicating subject is active with Revolutionary groups, the case will be re-opened at that time and the Bureau advised accordingly.

The Special Agent of the FBI who contacted INS was SA [redacted]

2 - Bureau (RM) (Encls. 10)
1 - New York

CJL:eps
(4)

ALL INFORMATION CONTAINED HEREIN IS UNCLASSIFIED EXCEPT WHERE SHOWN OTHERWISE

REC-72 100-469910-24

11 DEC 11 1972

Approved: _____ Sent _____ M _____ Per _____
           Special Agent in Charge

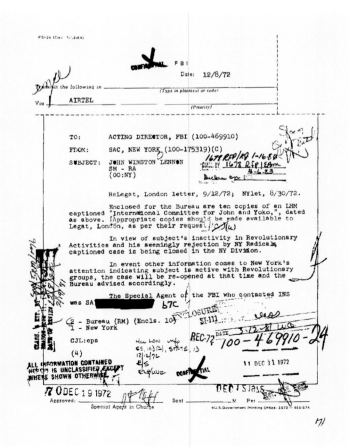

The Lennons were consumed in their government-triggered deportation hearings and could not imagine being at the storm centre of a six-month crusade of concerts and confrontations to dump Richard Nixon. They would speak out, and did, being photographed in conical hats showing solidarity with South Vietnamese political prisoners. John & Yoko endorsed a protest that resulted in cancellation of the annual Armed Forces Day in New York City. But on their deportation lawyer's advice, they dropped the convention concert plans by the end of 1971.

The whole bizarre history surrounding that convention remains to be told. Later documents would show that G. Gordon Liddy (of Watergate infamy) took part in a planning group that considered kidnapping protest leaders and dumping us in the Mexican desert. A vigilante group called the Secret Army Organization (SAO) took shots into a San Diego house filled with protest planners; one bullet pierced a wrist. An FBI undercover agent sat in the car next to the shooter.

Then suddenly the Republicans pulled out, shifting their venue to Miami, for reasons never explained to this day. The effect was to undermine and weaken the protests, spurring even greater division and paranoia. A group called the Zippies was dogging Jerry Rubin and Abbie Hoffman with charges of selling out. Rennie Davis was being shunned by feminists. I was accused of burning buses when I wasn't even in town. Even the newly formed Vietnam Veterans Against the War (VVAW) was riddled with undercover agents. Inexplicably, however, FBI memos as late as June 1972 still warned that the Lennons were planning a huge rock concert outside the Republican convention hall. In July another FBI memo urged the Miami office that the Lennons be arrested on possession of narcotics charges during the Republican

convention. They even fabricated a wanted flyer for Miami police with a photo purporting to be John Lennon saying 'The Pope Smokes Dope' and describing him as 'a former member of the Beatles Rock Music Group'.

Once the convention ended, however, the FBI folded up its mythic case, reporting in several memos that the Lennons had not been seen at all in Miami, quoting a source that the 'subject' had 'fallen out' with Davis, Rubin and Hoffman (30 August 1972). The Lennon counterintelligence case was put on 'pending inactive status' six days after the Republican convention and closed on 8 December 1972, one month after Nixon was re-elected.

No doubt British intelligence was after John Lennon in that year, not because of a token marijuana charge, but because he actively demonstrated against the British Army shootings of fourteen Irish civil rights demonstrators during 'Bloody Sunday' in January 1972. Cable traffic revealed that Lennon had 'offered entertainment' for the Deny cause, and intense efforts were devoted to monitoring links between American activists and the republican movement in Northern Ireland. One FBI document based on 'information provided by a foreign government', presumably London, was totally blacked out, apparently because the discovery of a British spy operation could provoke 'retaliation' toward the spymasters.

Having attempted to defame and neutralize this 'former member of the Beatles Rock Music Group', the FBI and government agencies fought fourteen years in court against disclosure of their covert campaign until 1992, when they were ordered to settle with plaintiff Jon Wiener and his ACLU lawyers. The following government officials and agencies were revealed to be in a single sinister loop to prevent an election-year concert tour

featuring John Lennon: the president, the vice president, the secretary of state, the director of the Central Intelligence Agency, the director of the Defense Intelligence Agency, the Department of the Army, the Department of the Air Force, the Naval Investigative Service, the US Secret Service and the attorney general [memo from J. Edgar Hoover on 'Protest Activity and Civil Disturbances', including [blacked out] 'Beatle singer John Lennon', 23 January 1972].

In the end, some of the truth was revealed, but who was left to remember? Imagine what 1972 might have been with John Lennon on tour against Richard Nixon. Instead, the full weight of one, and presumably two, state spy agencies was brought down to fabricate charges, launch deportation proceedings and discreetly set in motion a plan to 'neutralize' an artist they couldn't co-opt.

Asked in a *Rolling Stone* interview about 'the effect on history' of the Beatles, Lennon perhaps foresaw the future: 'The people who are in control and in power and the class system and the whole bourgeois scene is exactly the same, except that there's a lot of fag fuckin' middle-class kids with long hair walking around London in trendy clothes…but apart from that, nothing happened. We all dressed up. The same bastards are in control, the same people are running everything. It's exactly the same! They hyped the kids! We've grown up a little, all of us, and there has been a change and we are a bit freer and all that, but it's the same game…. The dream is over, it's just the same, only I'm thirty and a lot of people have got long hair, that's all.'

There are many ways to remember John Lennon, of course. But we should always remember the John Lennon that the FBI and MI5 will do anything to make us forget.

E7 AISUMASEN.

WHEN IM DOWN REALLY YIN
AND I DONT KNOW WHAT IM DOING
AISUMASEN AISUMASEN YOKO
ALL I HAVE TO DO IS CALL YOUR NAME
YES ALL I HAVE TO DO IS CALL YOUR NAME

AND WHEN I HURT YOU AND CUASE YOU PAIN
DARLIN I PROMISE I WONT DO IT AGAIN
AISUMASEN AISUMASEN YOKO SAN
ITS HARD ENOUGH FOR YOU JUST TO FEEL YOUR OWN PAIN
ITS HARD ENOUGH I KNOW TO FEEL YOUR OWN PAIN

ALL THAT I KNOW IS JUST WHAT YOU TELL ME
ALL THAT I KNOW IS JUST WHAT YOU SHOW ME

when I'm down real SanPAKU.
and i don't know what to do
aisumasen, aisumasen yoko
all i had to do was call yr name
yes

	E , E7,	, ,	A , A/G♯,	F♯m, , ,
B7, , D	F♯m	B7/D	A , B7,	E , G♯,	A , C♯m,
D, A ,	G , B7, || E , E7,	E7,	A , A/G♯	F♯m, , ,
B7, , D	F♯m, , B7,	, D	A , B7,	E , A♭,
A , C♯m,	D , A ,	G , , ,

||: F♯m , F♯/E , | F♯m/E , B7, :||

AISUMASEN (I'M SORRY)

When I'm down, really yin
And I don't know what I'm doing
Aisumasen, aisumasen, Yoko
All I had to do was call your name
All I had to do was call your name

And when I hurt you and cause you pain
Darlin' I promise I won't do it again
Aisumasen, aisumasen, Yoko
It's hard enough I know just to feel your own pain
It's hard enough I know to feel
Feel your own pain

All that I know is just what you tell me
All that I know is just what you show me

And when I'm down, real sanpaku
And I don't know what to do
Aisumasen, aisumasen, Yoko-san
All I had to do was call your name
Yes, all I had to do was call your name

AISUMASEN (I'M SORRY)

John: I go into these troughs every few years. It was less noticeable in the Beatles, because the Beatles image would carry you through it. I was in the middle of a trough in *Help!* but you can't see it, really. I'm singing 'Help!' for a kick-off, but it was less noticeable because you're protected by the image of the power of the Beatles. Now when it happens, I'm on my own, right, and it's easier to get sniped and so I've been in a trough. I'm coming out of it, whoopee. I'll be around for the rest of my life in this business so I don't get too serious about it, I only worry about what's happening to me.

I tried to pretend to myself that I wasn't being affected, that it was just going off my back, like water. But when I really got down to it, I realized that it was a constant thing, all the time. Just non-stop. It was like a big toothache and it didn't go away. It's still around now but I think I've come to terms with it. And it was just interfering with everything.

At one time I had this group together, Elephant's Memory and a few other people, and I was ready to go on the road, just for fun. I didn't care whether I was going to get paid, even, I just felt like going out, you know? And they started taking me to court and that, and I was getting into the court scene. I can get into any play, right? I was getting me suits on and I was talking to the judges and there's TV. It's a stage, so I got more involved in that stage.

I had to send them away. And that put me off performing for a bit. I still did my work, because I can't stop it even if I'm in a bad state of mind, but it was affecting me. It affected my whole life, actually.

Bob Gruen: The critics panned the *Some Time In New York City* album. The critics panned the *One to One* concert. One thing was going wrong after another. John didn't take it very well at all. All of John's money was being held in escrow, so he couldn't get any of [it]. He started getting legal problems and he was having additional legal problems with Allen Klein, his former manager. They were suing each other.

The Nixon administration issued a deportation order to try to throw John out of the country. And then Nixon was elected. And that night particularly was pretty ugly.

Yoko: The night McGovern lost the election [in 1972], John and I were invited to a party at Jerry Rubin's apartment in the Village. It was a gathering of New York liberal intellectuals, some artists, musicians and many journalists. John became totally drunk and pulled a woman into the next room and started to make love. Nobody could leave the party because all the coats were in that room. We were all sitting there trying to ignore what was happening. The wall was paper thin and you could hear the noise, which was incredibly loud. A considerate musician put a Dylan record on to offset the sound. But that did not drown out the sound coming from 'the room'.

In the middle of all this, a New York celeb woman chose to make conversation with me. 'I don't know how you feel about him…but we love him. He and his friend…what they did…but especially John…we all respect him tremendously. He's a great man…he is a wonderful man….' It was something like that she kept repeating to me, with an angry look as if to blame me for not rejoicing for what was happening in that room. Then there was a long silence. Some woman quietly went into the room to retrieve her coat. Others followed. When John finally came out of the room, he said, later, that he had never seen me looking so pale. 'I could never forget that face,' he used to say for a long while. I wrote a song right after that called 'Death Of Samantha', and that song says it all, in a way.

Bob Gruen: Yoko said one of the Elephants put on a record to try and muffle the sound? That was me. I put on a Bob Dylan record. I put on the wrong side, so when I put the needle down it was 'Sad Eyed Lady Of The Lowlands', which is one of his most depressing songs. Not really the song you want to play when everybody's already really depressed! So I was embarrassed about that and I went home.

The next day was a kind of sleep-it-off day and the next day we were in the studio, and we all showed up and John was still hung over. He had several days' growth of beard. He looked very sheepish, very remorseful. He knew he had screwed up. He knew, as many times as you try to apologise, it didn't erase the fact that he had embarrassed Yoko so badly in front of everybody.

After the recording session we went down to the Pink Teacup, a great soul food place in the village on Grove and Bleecker and had breakfast around 5 a.m.

In the seventies on the waterfront by Bank Street there was a huge dock that used to go three blocks out, and we walked all the way out to the end as the sun was coming up and just sort of sat there. If you look at pictures of the shadows, they're really long down the dock.

Coming back, we were taking some pictures, there's one where John's on his knees, kind of asking for forgiveness. She was still dealing with him, she knew what he did, but it wasn't okay. You know, it's just not okay to do that. And… and he knew it. And he was sorry about it.

Yoko: Something was lost that night for me.

Living with John was a very trying situation. But I thought I would endure all that for our love. I used to think that our love was a secret thing between us, so it didn't matter what people said…let them. Our love was higher than the highest sky, and deeper than the deepest water. But was it? Now it seemed that there were some clouds I hadn't noticed and the water looked murky after the splash. Jerry Rubin thought it was terrible that I couldn't 'forgive' John.

McGovern lost. All of us were totally devastated. You can imagine how John felt about it. It was a real blow to us. So he was drunk, for heaven's sake! It's not a matter of forgiving him or not forgiving him. I would not use that word. It's more like I can't 'forget' what happened. Call me a prude, but it just hit me in the wrong way. Inside, I felt like a shattered raggedy doll.

The United States government was trying to kick us out of the country because of our political stand. John and I had pretty much burned our bridge to England, with John marrying an oriental, returning the MBE to the Queen, and being arrested for possession of drugs, though the drug had been planted.

My daughter had been kidnapped by my ex-husband. I became a dragon lady in the eyes of the public and I lost my platform to express myself as an artist. The tension was compounded by nets of intrigues spun around us by sources which were sometimes not too clear.

Yet, we thought nothing was more important than how we felt about each other. We can make it. We're making it. Yes, it's alright! But that night made me think. It took almost another whole year for me to decide on what to do, and I did. Extraordinary circumstances call for extraordinary solutions.

We had moved into the Dakota because we thought it would give us more room to be alone if we wanted without bumping into each other all the time but it didn't work out quite like that. I guess we'd reached a point in our lives when we needed to be away from each other completely.

There was no fight or anything. We were having a warm conversation in the afternoon in our bed. I told John that I thought a trial separation would be a good idea. 'We're both still young and attractive, it's crazy to stay together just because we're married. I would hate that. That's not what we were about, was it? We should see what happens….' I tried to make light of it. 'What about LA? I remember you telling me how you had fun on a Beatle tour…' – that sort of thing.

'Okay, but I don't want to lose you,' John said. 'We'd probably lose each other if we stayed,' I said.

I didn't tell this to John, but I thought I would lose him. Hey, it's John Lennon. It was obvious to everybody, except to John, that I was the loser. Every man and woman of our generation was going to be happy that finally I was not around their hero.

Back in those [early] days, we wanted to do everything together – work, play, everything. Now things were different. We're a bit older and, I guess, more mature, too. Our lifestyles drifted apart as well. John was still very much the swinger. He liked to go to parties and nightclubs and play the star role, but all that kind of thing left me cold. We were two strong-minded people and neither one of us would give in to the other, so there was bound to be differences.

John: She said, 'Get the hell out' and kicked me out. I didn't go off on a 'I'm going to be a rock 'n' roll bachelor.' She had literally said, 'Get out,' you know? And I said, 'Okay, okay, I'm going!' I'm a bachelor, free – I'd been married all my life. I'd been married before Yoko, and I immediately married Yoko. So I'd never been a bachelor since I was twenty or something. So I thought, 'Whoo-hoo-ha-ha!'

Yoko: John was incredibly ecstatic for four days. He called me to thank me. 'Yoko, you're incredible. This is great! Thank you!' There was no sarcasm there. I was glad that he was happy.

After four days he called me with a totally different voice, 'I've had enough. I want to come home.' I laughed it off. It was too soon.

John: The separation was physical as well as mental. Our only communication was really on the phone. I just went there [Los Angeles] to get out of New York for a bit. Trying to do something down there. But I spent most of the time drunk on the floor with Harry Nilsson and Ringo and people like that. And ending up in the papers. That went on for about nine months. It was just one big hangover. It was hell. But that's why I was there. And why did we end up back together? [pompous voice] 'We ended up together again because it was diplomatically viable….' Come on! We got back together because we love each other. The separation didn't work out. And the reaction to the break-up was all that madness. I was like a chicken without a head.

Yoko: When we got back together, we just had a very quiet ceremony and exchanged rings in our apartment in that big white room. It had nothing to do with any particular religion and it was very nice.

ONE DAY (AT A TIME.)

| Bm , Bm/A , | Bm/G# , , , |

① YOU ARE MY WEAKNESS, YOU ARE MY STRENGTH

| C , C/B , | C , , , |

NOTHING I HAVE IN THE WORLD MAKES BETTER SENSE

| D , D/C , | D/B , C , | G, Bbaug , | F , , , |

CAUSE IM THE FISH AND YOUR THE SEA.

WHEN WERE TOGETHER , OR WHEN WERE APART

THERS NEVER A SPACE IN BETWEEN THE BEAT OF OUR HEARTS

CAUSE IM THE APPLE AND YOURE THE TREE.

| F#m , , , | B7 , , , | E , A , | B , , , |

ONE DAY AT A TIME IS ALL WE DO

| Ab , , , | Dbmin , , , | Gbm , Ab , | Dbm 2·3 |

ONE DAY AT A TIME IS GOOD FOR YOU.

| /e , , , | /B , , , | Dbgdim , D , | G , , |

② YOU ARE MY WOMAN I AM YOUR MAN

NOTHING ELSE MATTERS AT ALL NOW I UNDERSTAND

THAT IM THE DOOR AND YOURE THE KEY!

AND EVERY MORNING I WAKE IN YOUR SMILE

FEELING YOUR BREATH ON MY FACE AND THE LOVE IN YOUR EYES

CAUSE YOUR THE HONEY AND IM THE BEE!

ONE DAY AT A TIME IS ALL WE DO

ONE DAY AT A TIME IS GOOD FOR US TWO!

1973.   COPYRIGHT JOHN LENNON

ONE DAY (AT A TIME)

You are my weakness, you are my strength
Nothing I have in the world makes better sense
'Cause I'm the fish and you're the sea

When we're together or when we're apart
There's never a space in between the beat of our hearts
'Cause I'm the apple and you're the tree

One day at a time is all we do
One day at a time is good for you
(yeah)
You
(yeah)
You
(yeah)
Ooh….

You are my woman, I am your man
Nothing else matters at all, now I understand
That I'm the door and you're the key

Every morning I wake in your smile
Feeling your breath on my face and the love in your eyes
'Cause you're the honey and I'm the bee

One day at a time is all we do (be do be do)
One day at a time is good for us two
(yeah)
You too
(yeah)
You
(yeah)
Ooh….

'Cause I'm the fish and you're the sea
'Cause I'm the apple and you're the tree
'Cause I'm the door and you're the key
'Cause you're the honey and I'm the bee

ONE DAY (AT A TIME)

John: Well, that's just a concept of life, you know – how to live life. It was Yoko's idea for me to sing it all falsetto.

An artist is not usually respected in his own village, so he has to go to the next town. It's a bit of that with us really. I think it's also like Dylan Thomas and Brendan Behan – they both died of drink. Artists always die of drugs, drink and all that. Like Jimi and Janis – it's just that they're so misunderstood and tortured that they kill themselves. I refuse to do that.

I've found the way out. 'You are here'. Live for the day, minute by minute. That's the essential way. I think it's the biggest joke on Earth that everyone's talking about some imaginary thing in the sky that's going to save you and talking about life after death which nobody has ever proved or shown to be feasible. Why should we follow Jesus? I'll follow Yoko, I'll follow myself. It's the same as I did when I went looking for gurus. It's because you're looking for the answer which everybody is supposedly looking for. You're looking for some kind of super-daddy. The reason for this is because we're never given enough love and touch as children.

The whole Beatles message was, as Baba Rama Ding-Dong says, 'Be Here Now'. Some people will do anything rather than 'be here now'. That's all them gurus'll ever tell you: 'Remember this moment now.'

It's going to be alright – it's now, this moment. That's alright this moment, and hold on now, we might have a cup of tea or we might get a moment's happiness any minute now, so that's what it's all about, just moment by moment. That's how we're living, cherishing each day and dreading it, too. It might be your last day, you might get run over by a car, and I'm really beginning to cherish it.

Yoko: We all know that John was not with his mother very much when he was a child. And with me, he was with me twenty-four hours a day, so maybe I resolved his need for that kind of closeness. But that's not the whole thing.

When you compare John to other men, he was a terribly independent guy. He was financially independent. I was doing the business, but that's incidental. He could have hired lawyers and accountants. He chose to be with me. And that goes with me, too. I did not need him, but I chose to be with him. Of course he had a need to be dependent, too.

What was beautiful was that he wasn't afraid to show it. That was the difference. We all want to lean on somebody, but we are too embarrassed or too shy to show it that much. Now the fact that John became naked and took that position wasn't a private perversion but a symbolic statement to tell the female species, 'We guys have this vulnerable side, too.' And to tell the guys not to be afraid of showing it. He preferred to show that vulnerable side rather than show the sarcastic, cynical, intellectual and violent side, the typical rock 'n' roll guy image, the macho image. Which is an element he had, too. He could express himself like that because he was very confident about his masculinity.

John had the money and fame and power to dare to be himself. At the same time, yes, living with a woman might have helped. What I did, if anything at all, was to give him freedom to be himself. And he just jumped on it: 'Oh great, I can be free!' The freedom was what he enjoyed. Already there was in him the element of a rebel, and he was suffocated with having to conform. At home [in 1966] he was making little cassette tapes of crazy music and feeling like a lonely artist because he was being told by people around him, 'That is not good; it's a bit too crazy.'

When he met me he asked, 'Is this alright?' and he brought out these cassettes. I'd say, 'Are you kidding? This is beautiful.' Not because I was intentionally flattering him, but it was really hitting my soul. And he was starting to say, 'It's alright just to be myself.'

You must follow your intuition, moment to moment, with as much devotion as you can. We are not waiting for any moment; we are just living this moment as fully as we can. It's a balancing act. If you put weight on one side, you will find yourself on the other side. Try not to hold things in too much. That's a strength. Holding in is weakness. Let go. Feel better.

I'm still sharing hope for myself and for my friends and for the world because I still feel that we have the choice. We are gonna make that choice. We have to remember that we are all together, anyway. It's the boat which, if the world sinks, we all sink together. When on Earth, even when we are dreaming, our hearts are beating together in unison.

John: I believe the universe is in your head. Literally, in your head. Physically we're insignificant when you look around to the size of it but the physical bit is a load of crap. It's like you're worrying about your car and talking about it as if there's no driver. The driver's the bit, and the car is nothing. The car just happens to be the thing you are driving.

But the driver's the bit and the driver's your soul. And that's universal, omnipresent and all the rest of it. And it is. And you can realize it. If you realized it once, you remember when you've realized it before – as a child or any time in your life – and it's there.

Pages 87–89: Contact sheet and selected photographs from it of John & Yoko on the steps, on the balcony and inside their suite at Bungalow 19, Beverly Hills Hotel, California, March 1973.

Drawings by John Lennon containing themes of telephones, clouds, an elephant, eight dogs, a home and a sunrise or sunset, 1973.

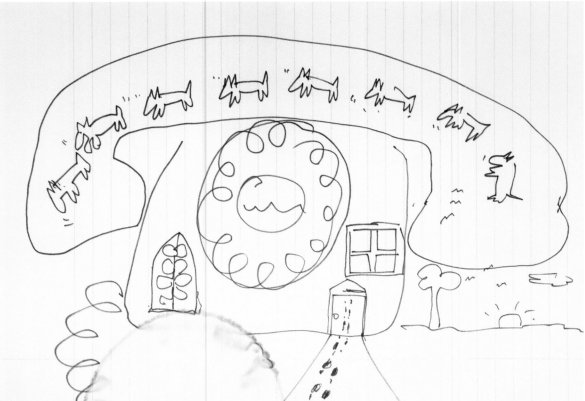

John & Yoko on the phone in their suite at Bungalow 19 at the Beverly Hills Hotel, Beverly Hills, California, March 1973. They lived there for most of February, March and April 1973 to search for Yoko's still-missing daughter, Kyoko; promote Yoko's *Approximately Infinite Universe* album; work on Ringo Starr's new album with Ringo, George Harrison, Klaus Voormann and Billy Preston; take care of some Beatles business and Capitol Records business; and generally take a break from New York to escape the harassment from the writs, lawsuits, FBI, CIA and the crazies like 'Jesus from Toronto' knocking on the front door and breaking into their Bank Street apartment. They returned to New York in mid-April, having found the Dakota apartment, and moved in there in early May 1973.

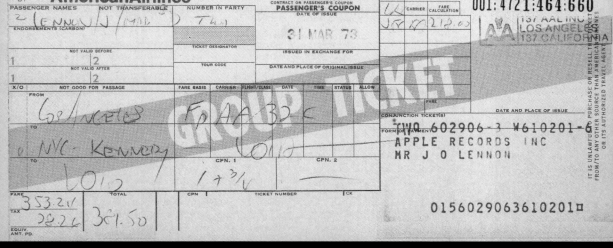

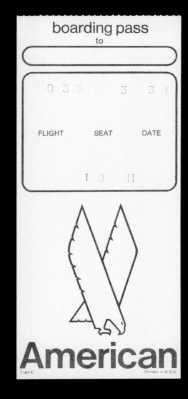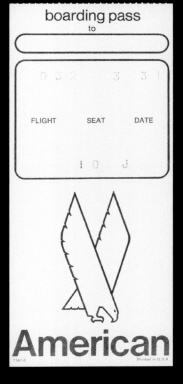

Opposite: John (wearing his Ga-den Tanka necklace and one of Yoko's FLY T-shirts) & Yoko in seats 10H and 10J on American Airlines flight AA32 from Los Angeles to John F. Kennedy Airport, New York, 31 March 1973. They were briefly returning to New York to host what would become known as the Nutopia Press Conference and visit apartment 72 at the Dakota with a view to purchase on 2 April 1973, after which they immediately went back to Los Angeles until 14 April. Above: Signed credit card charge form, group ticket and boarding passes, paid by Mr J. O. Lennon of Apple Records Inc., 31 March 1973.

The Dakota

John: I've got an apartment in the Dakota building, which is the place they made the film *Rosemary's Baby*. It's a big apartment and it's beautiful. It doesn't have grounds, but it's secure. And people can't get in and say, 'I'm Jesus from Toronto,' and all that, which was happening in the other apartment [Bank Street]. You just couldn't go out the front door because there would be something weird at the door.

Peter Brown: John & Yoko came for lunch, just the three of us. We sat in the dining room here in my apartment overlooking Central Park West and John couldn't take his eyes off the view. He was saying, 'This is so great, so great!' So, I said, 'Well….' He didn't ask me anything, but when they left he asked the doorman downstairs whether there were any other apartments available and they said no. And then he simply went to the building next door, [laughs] which happened to be the Dakota, and they said, 'No, but we may have something in the near future.'

Yoko: While we were in LA, John and I were sunbathing on the back terrace at the Beverly Hills Hotel and I just thought, 'Why not get an apartment in the Dakota?' I called my assistant, Jon Hendricks, who said, 'That's one thing I don't think we can do, because there's a two-year waiting list.' But then half an hour later I said, 'Well, try anyway,' and half and hour later he called me and he said, 'I can't believe it, because I called them and Robert Ryan was just going to put a public notice out of his apartment, and if he did that, then there would be swarms of people, so anyway, if you want to see it, they would wait.' And we came back, we saw the place, we liked it, and we took it. And it was [number] 72, which is 9. The number 9 and all that.

Jon Hendricks: John wanted a view where he could see water. We looked at a place in the building either just north or skipping one more of the Dakota, which could have been Peter Brown's place, and it was a very nice apartment; fourth, fifth floor or something like that and there was a group of people stripping paint off the woodwork. It seemed very nice. A few days later, there was an article in the paper that it all burned out from using acetone or something, so so much for that apartment! And then Yoko said, 'What about the Dakota?'

I knew about the Dakota, but I didn't know any people there. So I worked with a real estate agency, and they said there was this apartment that was for rent. I looked at it and it looked out over the park and had a sense of space but it was really dark. A lot of the woodwork around the fireplaces and doorways was really dark and the carpets were dark, so it didn't have that feeling of light that Ascot had.

I brought Yoko & John over to see it, and I remember it was early spring, and Bob Gruen was taking some photographs of Yoko & John in Central Park. Anyway, they liked it and they could buy it, but then you had to get in this co-op, so I started a campaign, like the one we were doing down at the [Immigration Service]; getting letters of recommendation from the bishop and from all sorts of people, and they got it.

Yoko: It's amazing because when first we saw the place, we didn't like because it was too huge, and John and I were saying, 'It's a bit big, isn't it?' And then, afterwards, Robert Ryan, who met us when he showed [us] his place, died, and their estate sent us a letter saying that the estate has a set price and everything, and if – 'We understand if you're interested… if you're still interested.' And so, it was just like it fell into our lap.

Bob Gruen: John & Yoko had had enough of living in a street-side home. They had arranged to look at an apartment in the Dakota building, which they eventually purchased. I had an assignment to take some pictures of them, so I suggested they stop at Central Park on the way, since the Dakota bordered the park. The shoot wasn't very long but it was spontaneous and fun, and we walked around the area now known as Strawberry Fields. It was a breath of fresh air on an early spring day after a winter indoors.

Jon Hendricks: First they put down the wonderful white carpet that they'd brought over from Ascot and then they stripped and painted all the walls and woodwork white. For John & Yoko it was very important to have the light and the lightness. So, suddenly, what's now the white room was very bright and white!

The kitchen, there's the window looking out at the courtyard straight over, where the kitchen table ends. And then there was a stove on the right. And I remember we went up to the Bronx somewhere and got these refrigerators with glass doors that John liked, so we could see the food.

There's another window over near where the counters are, and that was my office. The kitchen ended before that. And then there was a little narrow corridor up on the north side of it, and then a pantry and a walkway into the dining room. So, in the old days, it would have been people working in the kitchen, and maybe my office was a sitting room for the cooks. I had two offices. That was one office, and then what became Sean's bedroom and is now Yoko's study, that was my office.

Off the living room there was a door that lead to the library and then there was a door to the bedroom which was two rooms, one of which was John's study. There were pianos around so he was always composing.

Dakota Building Seventh Storey Floor Plan

Pages 94–95: John & Yoko after the Nutopia Press Conference and before viewing their Dakota apartment for the first time, photographed by Bob Gruen around a tree in Central Park, New York, 2 April 1973.
Pages 96–97: The Dakota building entrance, photographed by Koh Hasebe, 28 June 1973.
Page 98: John & Yoko walking down Central Park West towards the Dakota, also on 2 April 1973.

A floorplan depicting the layout in the 1970s of the seventh floor of the Dakota apartments, 1 W72nd St, New York.

Apartment 72 Floor Plan

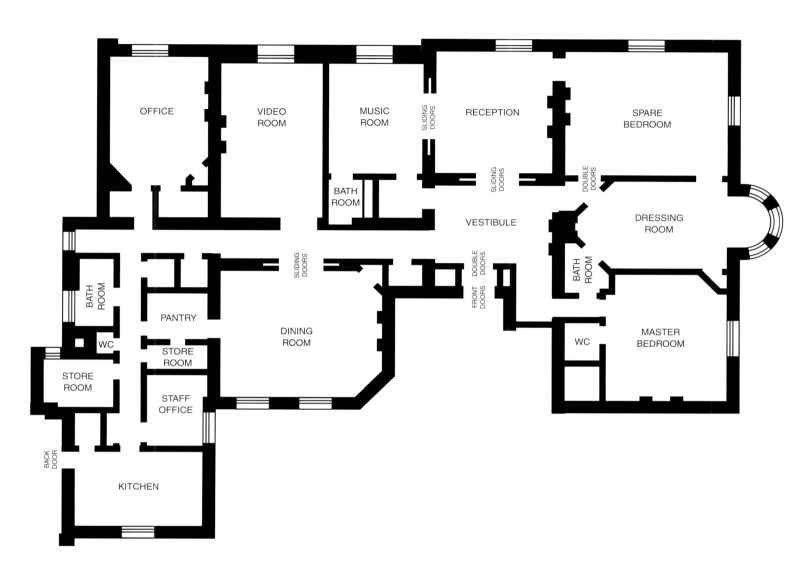

OFFICE

VIDEO ROOM

MUSIC ROOM

SLIDING DOORS

RECEPTION

SPARE BEDROOM

BATH ROOM

SLIDING DOORS

DOUBLE DOORS

VESTIBULE

DRESSING ROOM

BATH ROOM

BATH ROOM

WC

PANTRY

SLIDING DOORS

DINING ROOM

FRONT DOORS

DOUBLE DOORS

STORE ROOM

STAFF OFFICE

STORE ROOM

WC

MASTER BEDROOM

BACK DOOR

KITCHEN

When the Lennons first moved into the Dakota, the kitchen was subdivided into many smaller areas that were eventually knocked through to make the apartment feel more spacious. After the redevelopments, John affixed a brass plaque engraved 'Nutopian Embassy' to the outside of the kitchen door. After that, all the different areas of the apartment were given individual names by John & Yoko, for which brass plaques were subsequently created and installed.

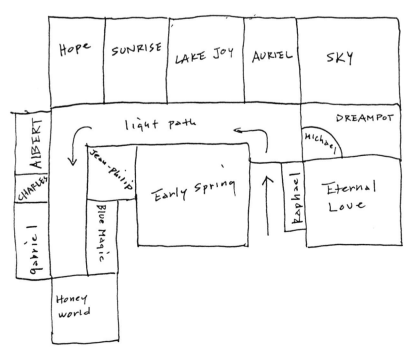

Hope   SUNRISE   LAKE JOY   AURIEL   SKY

ALBERT

CHARLES

Gabriel

light path

Jean-Philip

Blue Magic

Early Spring

DREAMPOT

Michael

Raphael

Eternal Love

Honey world

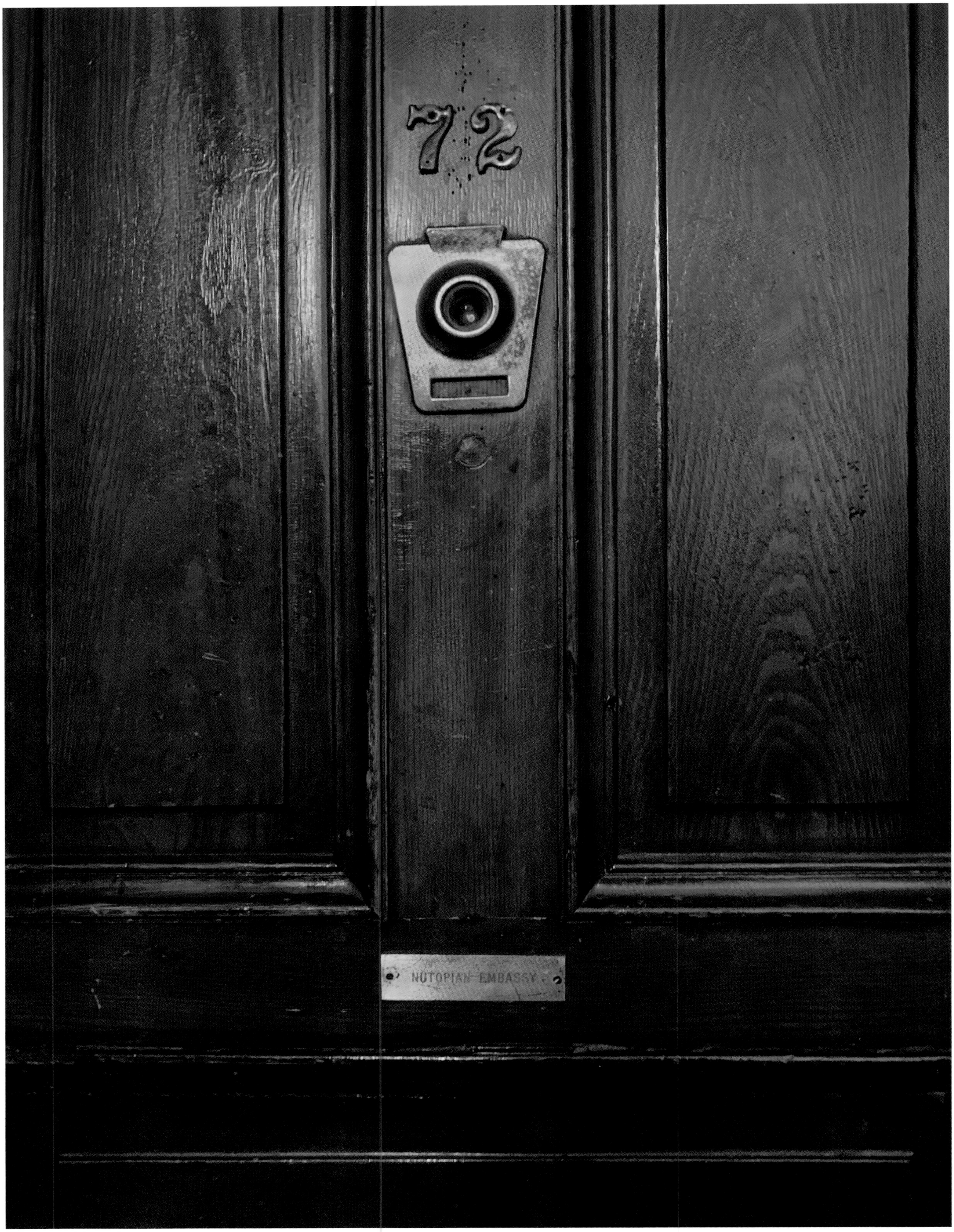
72
NUTOPIAN EMBASSY

The name plaques fixed to the doors of the rooms in the Lennons' home in apartment 72 include (opposite): 'Nutopian Embassy' on the kitchen door entrance and (right): 'Albert' – the bathroom nearest the kitchen, 'Auriel' – library, 'Dreampot' – Yoko's dressing room, 'Early Spring' – dining room, 'Eternal Love' – original master bedroom, 'Hope' – Sean's bedroom, now Yoko's office, 'Michael' – Yoko's closet, 'Sky' – White Room.

Pages 104–105: Black-and-white Portapak home video filmed by John at the Dakota apartment, soon after they had moved in, May 1973.

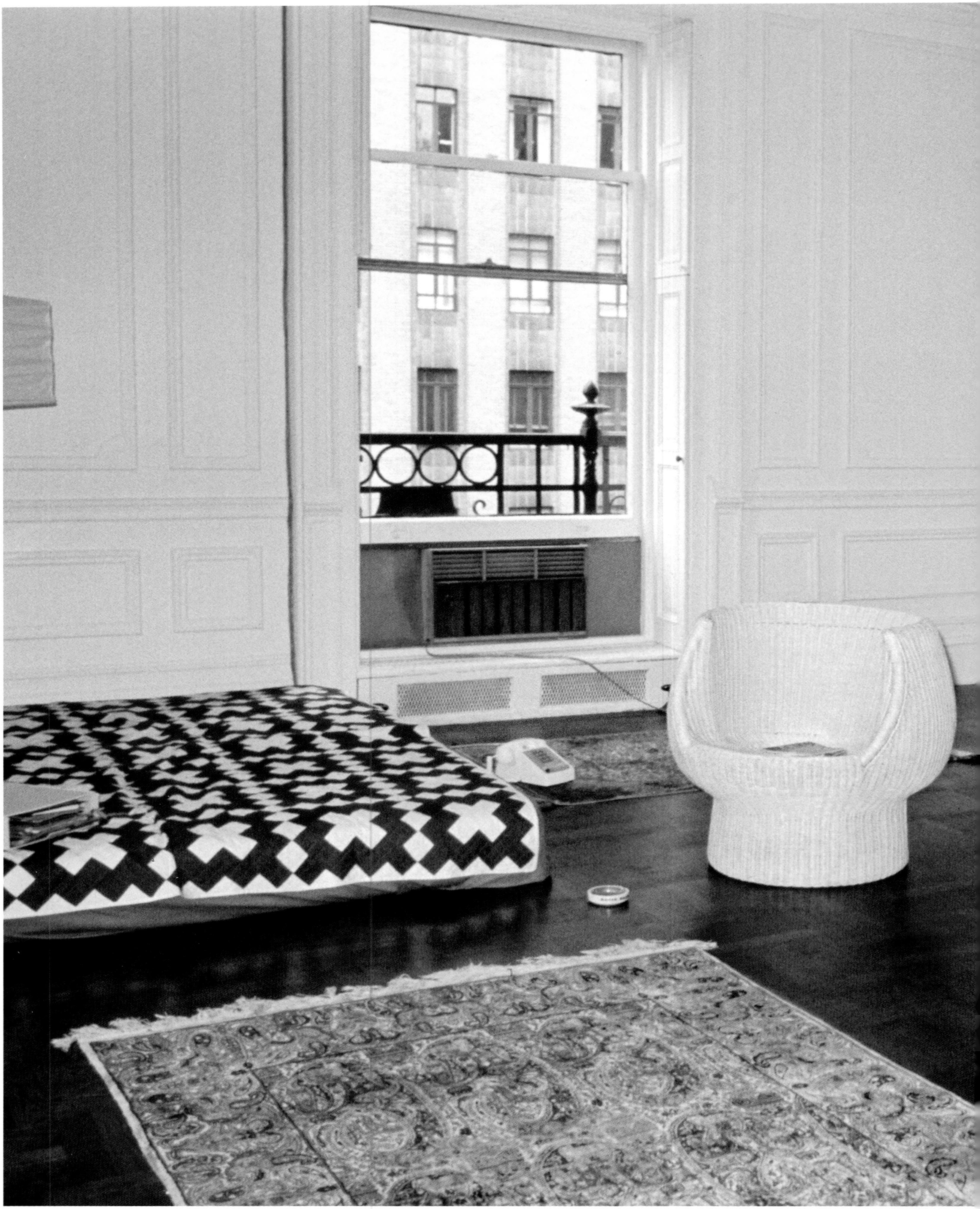

Pages 106–107: The room in the apartment that would become
known as 'The White Room', looking east. Notable items include
Yoko's artwork *Eternal Time*, 1965, on a Perspex plinth, a futon,
phone and white wicker furniture, photographed by Koh Hasebe,
apartment 72, the Dakota, 1 W72nd St, New York, 28 June 1973.

Opposite: In the old kitchen, John & Yoko are about to make a drawing for their Japanese visitors. Below: In Yoko's study with her Fender Rhodes Mark I Seventy-Three electric piano and Fender amp (top), and in the library with a WAR IS OVER headlined newspaper over the fire and John & Yoko's records and music equipment (bottom and pages 110–11). All photographed by Koh Hasebe, apartment 72, the Dakota, 1 W72nd St, New York, 28 June 1973.

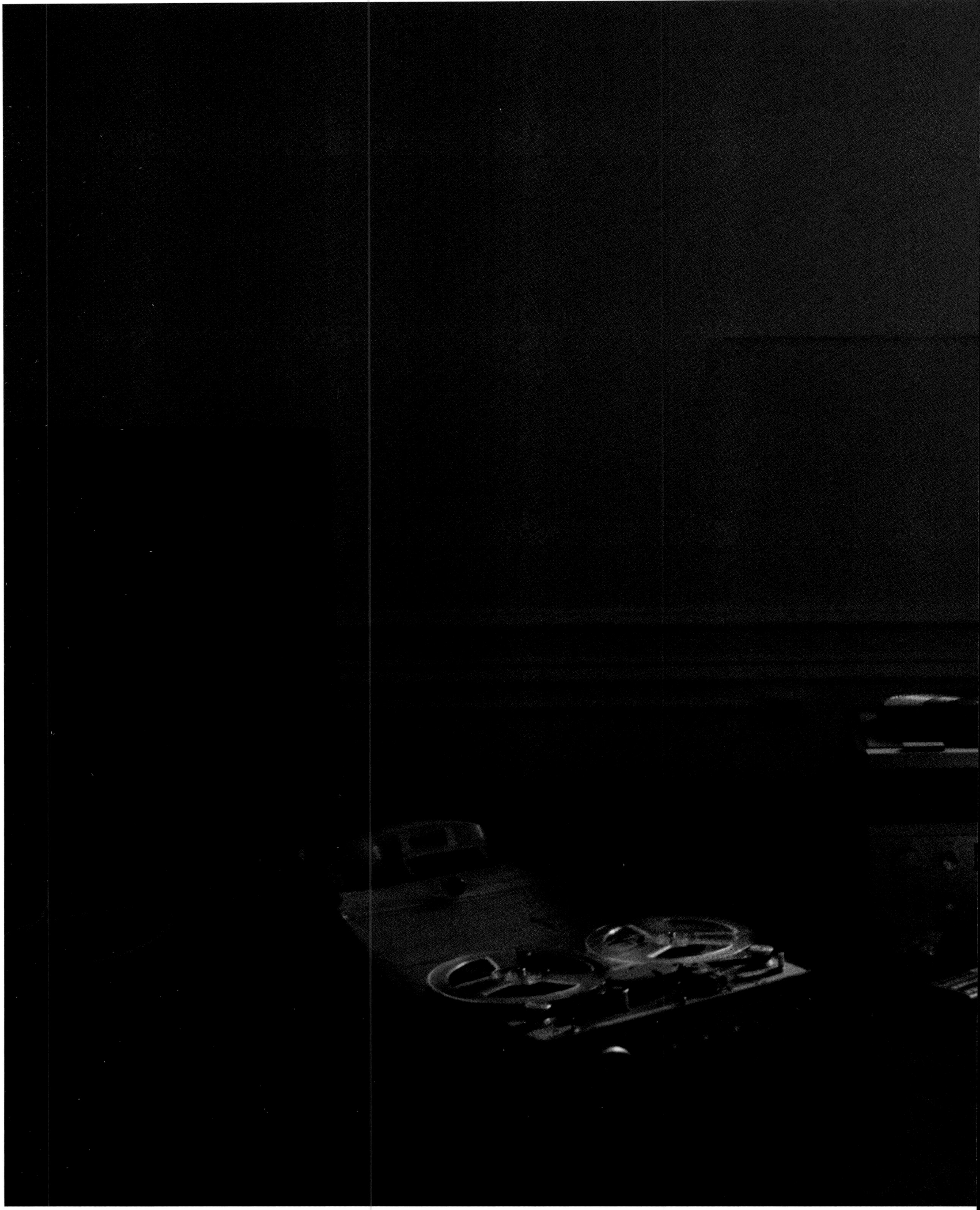

E

BRING BACK THE LUCY.(DO IT) *E.B.A.B.AE*

I
WE DONT CARE WHAT FLAG YOUR WAVING

WE DONT EVEN WANT TO KNOW YOUR NAME

WE DONT CARE WHERE YOUR FROM OR WHERE YOUR GOING

ALL WE KNOW IS THAT YOU CAME

YOUR MAKING ALL OUR DECISIONS

WE HAVE JUST ONE REQUEST OF YOU

THAT WHILE YOUR THINKING THINGS OVER

HERES SOMETHING YOU ~~(JUST BETTER~~ *can*)DO

Ch
free the people now

do it do it do it doit do it do it rightnow..

WELL WE WERE CAUGHT WITH OUR HANDS IN THE AIR

M8 DONT DESPAIR PARANOIA ~~WAS~~ EVERYWHERE

WE CAN SHAKE IT WITH LOVE ~~AND~~ *unless* *we're scared*

SO LETS ~~SHAKE IT~~ *show it aloud like* A PRAYER

free the people now

etc shake it etc

2
(WE UNDERSTAND YOUR PARANOIA) *we don't care what rules your playing*
EVEN
~~BUT~~ WE DONT WANT TO PLAY YOUR GAME
'n cos't
YOU THINK YOU, KNOW WHAT YOU ARE DOING *old*

~~666~~ ~~EVERYBODY FEELS THE~~ ~~...~~ *cause 666 is your old name*

SO WHILE YOUR JRKING OFF ~~(THE PEOPLE~~(EACH OTHER)   JUST ~~BEAR~~ *keep* THIS THOUGHT IN MIND
up *know*
YOUR TIME HAS ~~COME~~ YOU BETTER ~~FACE IT~~ (YOUR TIME IS UP..)
but maybe you can't see the sign ~~you don't read the sign~~
~~YOU CANT~~...

Ch
free thepeople now...

WELL YOU WERE CAUGHT WITH YOUR HANDS IN THE TILL (kill) ?

AND **M8** ~~BUT~~ YOU STILL GOT TO SWALLOW YOUR PILL   (Ethril)

AS YOUSLIP AND YOU SLIDE DOWN THE HILL

ON THE BLOOD OF THE PEOPLE YOU KILLED
FREE etc
Ch stop the killing now!!!....

do it doit etc.   copyright john lennon 1973.

E B A B AE

BRING ON THE LUCIE (FREDA PEEPLE)

Alright boys, this is it.
Over the hill.

We don't care what flag you're waving
We don't even want to know your name
We don't care where you're from
 or where you're going
All we know is that you came

You're making all our decisions
We have just one request of you
That while you're thinking things over
Here's something you just better do

Free the people now
(Do it, do it, do it, do it)
Do it, do it, do it, do it, do it now
(Do it, do it, do it, do it)

Free the people now
(Do it, do it, do it)
Do it, do it, do it, do it, do it now

Well, we were caught with our hands in the air
Don't despair, paranoia's everywhere
We can shake it with love when we're scared
So let's shout it aloud like a prayer

Free the people now
(Do it, do it, do it, do it)
Do it, do it, do it, do it, do it now
(Do it, do it, do it, do it)

Free the people now
(Do it, do it, do it)
Do it, do it, do it, do it, do it now

We understand your paranoia
But we don't wanna play your game
You think you're cool
 and know what you are doing
Six six six is your name

So while you're jerking off each other
You better bear this thought in mind
Your time is up, you better know it
Or maybe you don't read the signs

Free the people now
(Do it, do it, do it, do it)
Do it, do it, do it now
(Do it, do it, do it, do it)

Free the people now
(Do it, do it, do it, do it)
Do it, do it, do it, do it now

Well, you were caught with your hands in the kill
And you still gotta swallow your pill
As you slip and you slide down the hill
On the blood of the people you kill

Stop the killing (free the people) now
(Do it, do it, do it)
Do it (Do it, do it, do it, do it, do it now)

Stop the killing (free the people) now
(Do it, do it, do it, do it)
Do it, do it, do it, do it, do it now
(Do it, do it, do it, do it)

Stop the killing (free the people) now
(Do it, do it, do it, do it)
Do it, do it, do it, do it, do it now
(Do it, do it, do it, do it)

Stop the killing now
(Do it, do it, do it, do it)
Do it, do it, do it, do it, do it now
(Do it, do it, do it, do it)

Bring on the lucie
(Do it, do it, do it, do it)
Stop the killing
(Bring on the lucie now)

BRING ON THE LUCIE (FREDA PEEPLE)

John: I was disappointed at the reaction to the last album, *Some Time In New York City*. Over here they banned it and made such a fuss about the songs and it was never played. I know it was political with a capital 'P', but that was what I had in my bag at the time and I wasn't just going to throw the songs away because they were political. *Imagine* did pretty well, so after that I wanted to just do one that I felt like.

I would say *Some Time In New York City* stands as a piece of work. It sold two hundred thousand instead of half a million. The whole thing's relative. If I'd been a smaller artist I'd have been pleased to get that amount of sales. I have no regrets – only that it didn't get a lot of airplay on the so-called FM stations of the Left. The only one that really got into it was Pacifica, which has heavy programmes on politics, lesbians and things like that – anything people want to do. It's a pretty good station. Nationwide. They've even got tapes of Yoko and me from the sixties singing Japanese folk songs!

'Bring On The Lucie' – Oh, what does it mean? What the hell does it mean? I keep asking myself, but how the hell should I know? It's like 'Rainy Day Woman Number 1009' [sic]. What the hell does that mean? It's just something that came into me head. 'Lucy' is just one of those things; after 'Lucy In The Sky', 'Lucy' keeps staying in me head. I like to cross-reference myself. I enjoy it.

They [the lyrics] have been around for a long time. I just never put them on paper. It's in the Bible isn't it, the Great Beast 666 rising out of his underpants and all that. The reason it actually cropped up is because I had all me books sent from England and I had a few by Aleister Crowley that I had had for years and one of them is this little *Book of Lies*, which is beautiful poetry. He was just in my consciousness. I really write from whatever I'm doing at the time. If I were to write a song tonight, it might be about wine and photographs. It's just that simple.

Jann Wenner: Did you ever see Moratorium Day in Washington, DC?

John: That is what ['Give Peace A Chance'] is for, you know. I remember hearing them all sing it – I don't know whether it was on the radio or TV – it was a very big moment for me. That's what the song was about. You see, I'm shy and aggressive so I have great hopes for what I do with my work and I also have great despair – that it's all pointless and it's shit. How can you beat Beethoven or Shakespeare or whatever? In my secret heart I wanted to write something that would take over 'We Shall Overcome'. I don't know why. The one they always sang. And I thought, 'Why doesn't somebody write something for the people now, that's what my job and our job is.'

Pete Seeger: For those present, [Vietnam Moratorium Day, 15 November 1969] was one of the most moving days of their lives. The high point of the afternoon came, if I say so myself, when a short phrase from 'Give Peace A Chance' – a record by Beatle John Lennon – was started up by Brother Fred Kirkpatrick and me.

I didn't know if they had ever heard it before, but I decided to try singing it over and over again until they did know it. After about a minute or so, I realized that it was still growing. Sure enough, Peter, Paul and Mary jumped up to our left and started joining in on another microphone and giving us a little more instrumental and harmony background. Couple of more minutes, Mitch Miller hops up on the stage to our right and starts waving his arms. And I realized it was getting better and better, as more and more people were able to latch onto it, because it was so slow.

Soon, hundreds of thousands were singing it over and over, swaying their bodies, flags and signs from right to left in massive choreography. It was not as militant or as forceful a song as will be needed, but it united that crowd as no speech or song had been able to all afternoon. Parents had their small children on their shoulders. And it was a tremendously moving thing to realize his song was finally getting through, where not a single other song of the day had really gotten people to join in on it.

Undoubtedly some people wanted to say a lot more than that. On the other hand, history gets made when people come to the same conclusion from many different directions. And this song did hit a common denominator. There's no doubt about it.

Gloria Emerson: Where are we and what is this? What do you have to do with the Moratorium? So they sang one of your songs. Great song, sure, but is that all you can say about that – the Moratorium?

John: You were saying that in America, they're [mimicking Emerson] 'so serious about the protest movement but they were so flippant they were singing a happy-go-lucky song' – which happens to be one I wrote, and I'm glad they sang it, and when I get there I'll sing it with them. When I get in. And that was a message from me to America or to anywhere, that I use my songwriting ability to write a song that we could all sing together, and I'm proud that they sang it at the Moratorium. I wouldn't have cared if they'd sang 'We Shall Overcome' but it just so happens that they sang that, and I'm proud of it, and I'll be glad to go there and sing with 'em.

The Moratorium to End the War in Vietnam was the biggest anti-war demonstration in US history. Pete Seeger led the crowd of over five hundred thousand protestors in Washington, DC, in singing John's song 'Give Peace A Chance', with Dr Benjamin Spock interjecting 'Are you listening, Nixon? Are you listening Agnew? Are you listening in the Pentagon?'

Top left: Popular author Dr Benjamin Spock speaking at the Moratorium. Top right: Pete Seeger, accompanied by Dr Spock, Mitch Miller and Peter Paul and Mary (out of shot) leading the crowd in singing 'Give Peace A Chance' in front of the National Cathedral, Washington, DC. Bottom and pages 116–17: Anti-war protestors marching in Washington, DC, 15 November 1969.

Trials and Tribulations
The Senate Watergate Hearings
Washington, DC, 2 July 1973

John: I only went once to see Watergate, but it made the papers because I was recognized straight away. I thought it was better on TV anyway because I could see more. When it first came on I watched it live all day, so I just had the urge to actually go. I had other business in Washington, anyway. The public was there and most senators have children, so every time there was a break in the proceedings I had to sign autographs. I was looking like a Buddhist monk at the time with all my hair chopped off, and I thought nobody would spot me. They spotted Yoko before me, and assumed, rightly, that I must be with her. It was quite a trip.

One haircut every two years is about right. It gets a little hot in New York and, after all, all of you have your hair long now, even the police have long hair. I don't have any status. Put me down as a Martian.

Last time I planned to play live, the government attacked me, so I'll do it on impulse if I do it. If they can separate all the big names in pop, they effectively cut off the 'revolution' at its source. No more Woodstocks. No more mass gatherings. The real changes aren't gonna come from politicians. It's going to come from the artists and musicians. Even Bowie is a threat in a way. If you get Bowie on TV and somebody switches on in Ohio or Bradford and they see this person looking out at them, it's going to affect their whole way of life. He doesn't have to say 'Power To The People, Right On!' He is the message in himself.

It's like holding a mirror up to society. It makes people react in a specific way that's better than having them half-dead listening to Sandy MacPherson. I just think it's all great. I'm not saying I'd do it, but people like Bowie are an extension of rock 'n' roll. He still rocks like shit and keeps us going until the next phenomenon, ho ho, which is going to be this year, isn't it?

I had to keep going to court, and it got to be a way of life as court cases do. It was hassling me, because that was when I was hanging out with Elephant's Memory, and I wanted to rock – to go out on the road. But I couldn't do that because I always had to be in New York for something and I was hassled. I guess it showed in my work. But whatever happens to you, happens in your work. So while on the surface I tried to make it appear as if I were making a game out of it, trying not to take it seriously, there were periods of paranoia. Even my friends would say, 'Come on John, what do they want with you?'

When I'm not talking about it, I think about it occasionally. I mean, it's on my list of lawsuits. I was just talking about it with Yoko last night – there seems to be an awful lot of lawsuits involved with rock 'n' roll. Allen Klein – that's about twenty – he's suing me, and Yoko, and all the ex-Beatles, and everybody that ever knew them. And he's suing me individually, me collectively, any version of me you can get hold of is being sued. Ask any rock star about lawsuits. The more money there is, the more lawsuits there are. The bigger the artist, the more suits. I mean, people sue for anything. People sue you if you bump into them on the street. But immigration is the important one – the others are all just money, somehow a deal will be made. Immigration, that's the one. I mean, if they can take Helen Reddy, they can take me.

I always liked Liverpool and London – places like that had a lot of different races living in them. You could go to Soho and see all kinds of races on Earth and I like that, but there's even more of a mixture here. My ideal is to be able to travel, that's the thing I really miss most. I miss England, Scotland, Wales, all that sentimental stuff…but I also miss France, Holland… Germany I haven't been to for years.

I'd like to go to South America. I've never been. I'd like to be based here, and just travel.

It keeps all the conservatives happy that they are doing something about me and what I represent. And it keeps the liberals happy that I am not thrown out. So, everybody is happy but me. I am still being harassed. Liberals don't feel too bad because I am still here. It keeps all the other pop stars in line. In case they get any ideas about reality. Keep them in their place. They also hassle Paul, George, Mick Jagger, obviously Keith Richards. Elton John has a clean image. David Bowie's image – they probably haven't realized what it is yet. It takes them a bit of time. Bowie – they probably just think he's something from the circus. He's never been busted and he didn't get mashed up with lunatics like Jerry Rubin and Abbie 'my boy' Hoffman. I never see them now. They vanished in the woodwork. Jerry has been nothing but trouble and a pain in the neck since I met him. I decided – as he didn't lead the revolution – I decided to quit answering the phone.

I'm still appealing and my lawyers call me when they need me. Otherwise I just carry on normally. It was a matter of showing them we were not dope freaks and that we were not ogres or martyrs with bombs, but just a couple with a leaning towards socialism and it's had its effect. There are all sorts of things popping up with the immigration case and the whole thing is like a little teeny Watergate. I think things are looking up because the old guard have left and there's been change in politics. But it's still down to a political decision from the White House to let me off the hook.

I try not to miss England and I make myself not get sentimental about it. I say to myself that I'm gonna get this Green Card, and when I do I'll be on the next plane. I want to see Aunt Mimi again and I miss my son Julian.

Apple

MEMORANDUM

To: Date:

From: Subject:

Dear Hall Smith,

Thank you very much for your kindness in arranging our visit. to the historic Watergate Hearings. We have been following it on T.V. — but there's nothing like the 'real thing'. We apologize for leaving without saying good bye — we had to "escape" rather quickly! We would have loved to have met Senator Ervin, but thought his time was occupied with more serious matters! perhaps another time... peace and love

John Lennon
Yoko Ono

Opposite: John Lennon drawing and photocollage using the cover of *TIME* magazine, 4 June 1973.

Below: Postcard of the 'Western White House', Nixon's home in San Clemente, California, with a press clipping glued on the back by John, 1973.
Pages 124–25: John & Yoko's guest information folder from the Watergate Hotel, Washington, DC, 1973.

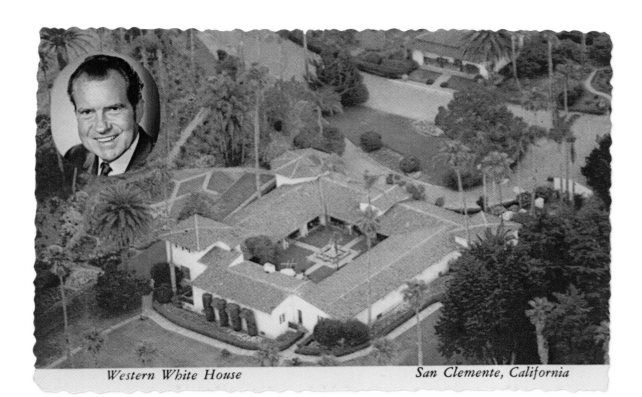

Western White House   San Clemente, California

This whole anti-nuke movement has become yet another excuse for the bleeding hearts to crawl out from under their dirty little rocks.

HOME OF RICHARD M. NIXON
37th President of the United States
San Clemente, California
Photo by Mark Rader
P302571

The Watergate H[otel]

2650 VIRGINIA AVENUE, N.W.

WASHINGTON, D.C.,

The Watergate Hotel

W

MEMBER PREFERRED HOTELS WORLDWIDE

The Watergate Hotel

IN THE WATERGATE COMPLEX

What Do You Do If You're Caught In a FIRE ?

John & Yoko wearing straw coolie hats join a demonstration with
Kay Camp and the Women's International League for Peace and
Freedom, requesting the release of Mrs Ngo Ba Thanh, a 44-year-
old law professor held as a political prisoner in Thu Duc since
September 1971, outside the South Vietnamese Embassy,
Dupont Circle, Washington, DC, 27 June 1973.

DECLARATION OF NUTOPIA

We announce the birth of a conceptual country, NUTOPIA.

Citizenship of the country can be obtained by declaration of your awareness of NUTOPIA.

NUTOPIA has no land, no boundries, no passports, only people.

NUTOPIA has no laws other than cosmic.

All people of NUTOPIA are ambassadors of the country.

As two ambassadors of NUTOPIA, we ask for diplomatic immunity and recognition in the United Nations of our country and its people.

John Ono Lennon
Yoko Ono Lennon

Nutopian Embassy
One White Street
New York, N.Y. 10013

April 1st, 1973

NUTOPIAN INTERNATIONAL ANTHEM

Yoko: In 1973 in New York City, John and I invited the press to announce the founding of a conceptual country called Nutopia. Anybody could be a citizen of this country. Citizens were automatically the country's ambassadors. The country's body was the airfield of our joint thoughts. Its constitution was our love, and its spirit, our dreams. Its flag was the white flag of surrender. A surrender to peace. We wished that one day we would take the flag to the United Nations and place it alongside the other flags as Nutopia was just another concept, as were concepts such as France, United States and the Soviet Union. It was not a concept founded to threaten any other.

At the time, the idea of 'surrender' did not go down too well. A radical friend of ours expressed that he, too, disliked the term. 'Surrender sounds like defeat,' he said. 'Well, don't you surrender to love, for instance?' I looked at him. 'No, he wouldn't,' I thought. 'Are women the only people who know the pride and joy of surrender?' I wondered. 'It's a waste of time to explain to a macho radical, didn't I tell you?' said John, a man who surrendered to the world, life and finally to [the universe]. 'Anyway, don't worry, Yoko. One day we'll put it up there. You and I. I promise.' I still believe we will.

We created our own country. We announced the birth of a nation called Nutopia. Like the new Utopia. And there's an embassy in New York [that] people can write to. Everybody – if they decide that they are the member of Nutopia, they are a member of Nutopia. And automatically become an ambassador.

John: It's a conceptual country. When we first announced it, it was the first of April, and it was our answer to the immigration people's press conference the week before. It came out of Yoko's conceptual art, where the idea is more important than the object. And this is something she had around for years. We were just waiting for the right time to bring it out. And you see, the concept, it has no land, there's nothing to fight for, there's no boundaries, there's no lines to be drawn, no passports, only people. We've got a flag but there are no laws. All the people of Nutopia are ambassadors and citizenship is available by declaring your awareness of Nutopia. It is about – once you say it, that's it. America? Oh yeah, but that's physical. That won't go on forever. Que sera, sera. The world changes so fast you can't keep up with it anyway. So I'm sure a little piddly thing like my immigration won't go on forever. It's like Leonardo drawing a submarine, it's no good saying, 'Oh look, it's going to take a thousand years before they build it.' That's not the point. Nutopia was Yoko's trip. I agree with her, so I wanted to put it on and do it as just another John & Yoko event. We mean it, it's not naive or anything like that. It'll happen when it happens. If you say it enough, it'll happen. If you don't say it, it won't.

Yoko: Nutopia is a country that exists in all of us. In 1973, John and I created this imaginary world. We called a press conference and produced a white handkerchief from our pockets and said 'This is a flag to Surrender to Peace.' Not Fight for Peace, but Surrender to Peace was the important bit. All of us represent Nutopia. John had said that we were all ambassadors of Nutopia. And so we are.

When you come to our apartment, you'll see that there is a gold plaque on the kitchen door that says 'Nutopian Embassy'. John put it there. Strangely enough, now friends just like to come in from that door, and not the front door. It seems the plaque made the kitchen door our front door.

Ambassadors of Nutopia, Think Peace, Act Peace, Spread Peace and let people know to IMAGINE PEACE. Pretty soon, the whole world will realize that we all belong to Nutopia. Together, we will let the other planets know that that's what's happening here on our planet – that we are all together, and living life in peace.

We have to understand we're human. And we have, as people, an immense part of us that we don't even know about, and it goes beyond social systems and institutions. For example, John and I are residents here, we're not citizens. But then we're not really citizens of any country. Just like with women, we don't have any country or state. That's a very strong thing to be, someone without any country or state. Because if you have the rights of a society, then you are limited by those rights as well.

From that point of view, for women to have equal rights with men might be a step down. Women are a very strong race. That's one of the reasons we are persecuted. It just came to me that it could be compared to the fact that the Jews always had to wander, they never had a country. They really wanted a country, but when they got Israel, that was a headache, too. When you get something like that, you're limited. But when you don't have a country, then the whole world is your country.

The human race is pretty aware by now. All the things they use in an advert sound like philosophical statements. One line comes to mind: 'Sometimes we talk for hours without saying anything.' Now that's an ad. That's beautiful.

What I mean is, it's that kind of age. You turn the TV on and then you see all these people saying something, then you turn the channel and some guest is saying something, but not any special guest, just people sort of saying things. It's that kind of age.

Statement from the National Committee for John & Yoko regarding the upcoming press conference on 2 April 1973, which would become renowned for their Declaration of Nutopia announcement.

Opposite: John & Yoko with attorney Leon Wildes (left) and assistant Jon Hendricks (right) at the press conference.
Pages 132–33: John & Yoko waving white handkerchiefs representing the flag of Nutopia, having just read out the Declaration of Nutopia. All at the Association of the Bar of the City of New York, 42 W44th St, New York, 2 April 1973.

NATIONAL COMMITTEE FOR JOHN AND YOKO
ONE WHITE STREET, NEW YORK, N.Y. 10013 ·

contact Helen Seaman
(212) LU9-5144
966-4062

John Lennon and Yoko Ono will be present at a press conference

10:00 A.M. Monday, April 2nd, at the Association of the Bar of

the City of New York; 42 West 44th Street; Room 10, Main floor.

The Lennons, and their attorney Leon Wildes, will discuss their

current immigration status, and will be available for comment

at that time.

NATIONAL COMMITTEE FOR JOHN AND YOKO CONSISTS OF MEMBERS OF THE AD HOC COMMITTEE FOR ARTISTIC FREEDOM, JUSTICE FOR JOHN AND YOKO COMMITTEE AND CONCERNED CITIZENS.

Opposite: Bob Gruen's contact sheet of John & Yoko at the Nutopia press conference at the Association of the Bar of the City of New York, 42 W44th Street, New York, 2 April 1973.
Below: News clipping of the Nutopia press conference mounted on board and signed by some of the members of the National Committee for John & Yoko, who included: Ken Dewey, Jon Hendricks, Patty Oldenburg, Helen Seaman, May Pang, Rev. Ralph David Abernathy, Joan Baez, Leonard Bernstein, Dick Cavett, William Sloane Coffin, Ornette Coleman, John Coplans, Robert P. Cross, Charles De Carlo, Willem de Kooning, Bob Dylan, Jim Elliot, Jane Fonda, Allen Ginsberg, Joseph Heller, Thomas Hess, Jasper Johns, Elia Kazan, John V. Lindsay, Norman Mailer, Kate Millett, the Right Reverend Paul Moore, Richard Oldenburg, Joseph Papp, Dr Stephen Prokopoff, Robert Rauschenberg, Rex Reed, Ned Rorem, Dore Schary, Nina Simone, James Taylor, Mary Temple, Jean Toche, Rip Torn, John Updike, Jon Voight, Irving Wallace, Andy Warhol, Edmund Wilson, Stevie Wonder and Leonard Woodcock.

"Imagine all the people"

Birth of a Nation: Nutopia

NEWS photo by Richard Corkery

John Lennon and Yoko announce creation of a new country.

The segment of the Beatles known as John Lennon asked the government to quash a federal deportation decision and announced the birth of a new country.

Sporting a lapel button bearing the affirmation, "Not Insane," Lennon dubbed the new nation Nutopia. Lennon declared that Nutopia has no passports, no boundaries, no land, only people.

Sitting with his wife, Yoko, Lennon told a somewhat bemused press conference that citizenship of the infant country could be obtained by the simple declaration of awareness of it.

Turning to the affairs of the more formal United States, Lennon said he had appealed against the ruling that he must leave the country in less than two months.

This plea, filed with the Board of Immigration Appeals, could take up to a year to resolve, during which time deportation would be halted. If unsuccessful with the board, Lennon said he would appeal to the courts, which could take a number of years.

—Anthony Burton

Notes written by Jon Hendricks at John's instruction, regarding the fabrication of the rubber stamp for the Great Seal of Nutopia.

Opposite: Typewritten letters by John to Elephant's Memory, his father Freddie and to Harold and David, which he imprinted using the Great Seal of Nutopia rubber stamp.

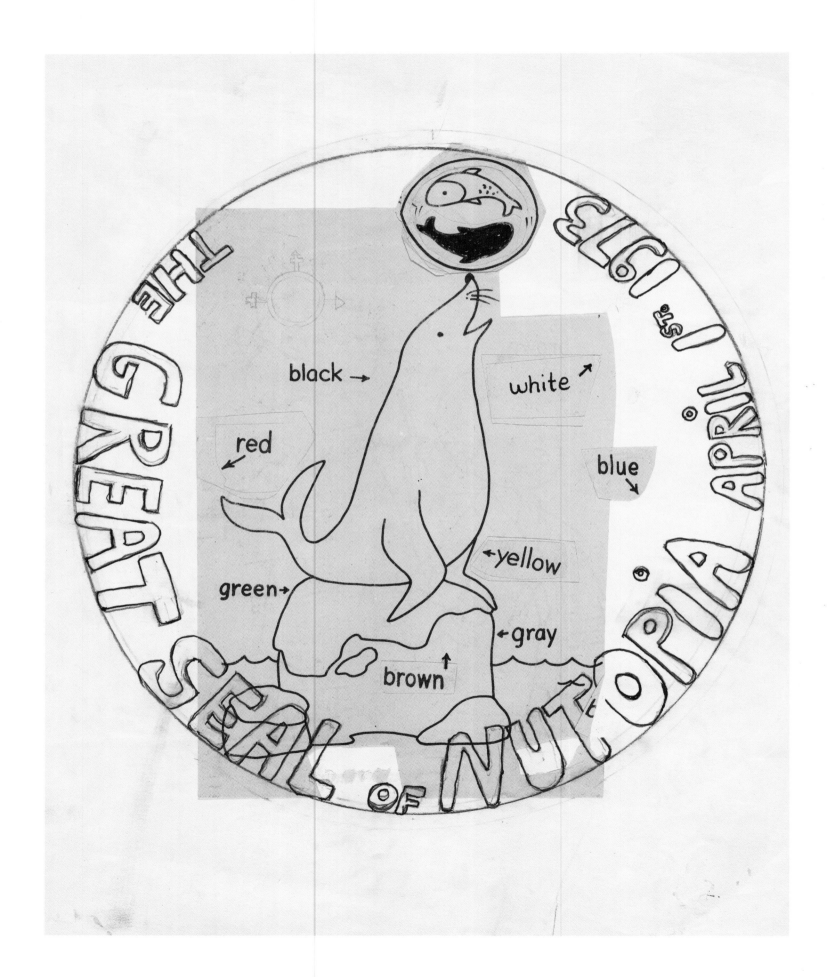

july;I.W.72.ny

dear elephants,

        i/we thought it about time to comunicate.as you might have noticed
apple went away!ive been (still am)wrapped in it.looks like the final deal comes
any day now...i,personally,dont know what to do about the eqipment you have,
i know apple will a)come for it b) hit me for it.c)BOTH (the) MY lawyers get back
from england tomorrow with the "final solution",which will then be taken bak
to the other three(when ive OKd it)what do you want done about that record you
made?it could be in the can for ever..drop me a line if you got any suggestions.
i hope your all alright ,dont be depressed cause we never got it on the road,
what ever it was it was ok with me.i dont think our relationship harmed either
of our'careers',it was a short trip ..BUT FAST!

        life is long and so is an elephants memory

        i dont like goodbyes,so this is a hello.

        ps....i never knew what i was doing myself so i could nt begin to tell you!
ya cant keep a good band down believe it.

        all the best to all of you,

            with love,
                john(yoko)

---

july n.yy

                                        I.W 72nd ST.

dear freddie and   apt.72.N.Y.N.Y.I0023.

        i decided to turn the other check,as it were,so here i am writng
to you and yours.were living in america now and the view is better!if your syill
living at this address let me know.i wont say much now,you might never see it!
i hope your all well(hoever many of you there is).julian is in practically the same
boat i was in,so understanding comes easier.it dont make you a saint,it just makes
me a HUMAN too...

            love to youse

                the other lennons

        ps.the wonderfull typing is mine.......

---

dear harold,   the following monday;

                                julightfull;24?I973.

            this is a circular;O;

i think dolgenis wastes a lot of mine his time;he arrived today with his daughter!
and mike graham,to ask,yet again what i wanted to do about 'the settlement;i remind
ed him that wed spent four hours on it two days before!nothing that was brought up
couldnt have been handled on the phone or by letter;eg;payment of comart via u.k.etc
big 7;next sept;which ive been told every time i see them;etc etc;im hoping he'll
soom get over his exbeatle mania!

            by the way we wernt very pleased to receive an e
equally useless phone call on our PRIVATE LINE(presumably given to him by you,as i had already
refused to part with it)in which he informed us that he WOULDNT be seeing us over the week
end!now we'll have to change the number again,otherwise one never knows WHO is going to be
on the other end of the line; business is business,but weekends are weekends.i will probably
have to publish ALL your phone numbers in an effort to HELP your KARMA!its o.k. paying in
$ but time and space are priceless...even maccartney seems to manage to get thru on the
OTHER phone lines..

            all the best to you and yours;

                yer old pal lennon.

ps i always have a ps.its not that i dont like david,its just that he's in a mirror.

---

                                        monday 24? I973.

dear david;

        please pay following bill;

                sghtseeing admittance charge;$200.0.0(childrens special)

YOU CAN PAY IN CASH:$ or £;

                yours faithlessl;
                    j.w.lennon.

MAYBE

URGENT

BULLSHIT

PERSONAL

REPLY

FILE

LATER

Pages 138–39: Timesaving secretarial rubber stampers designed and used by John & Yoko. Below and opposite: Drawings by John Lennon using their ink stampers and pen, 1973.

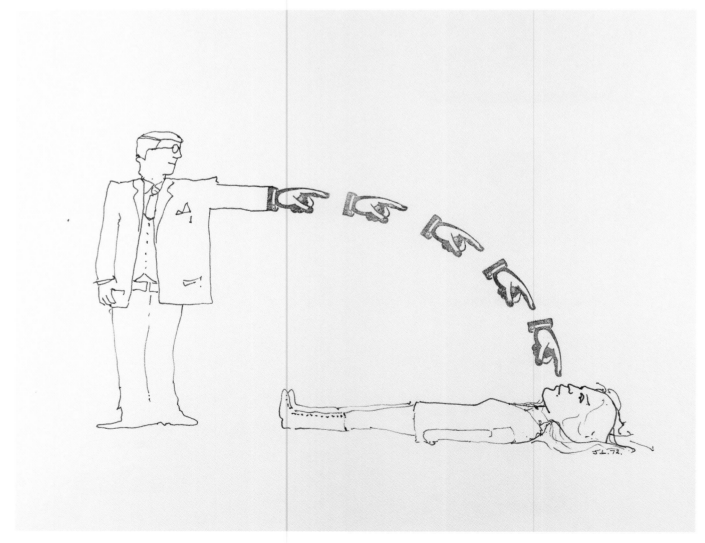

remember Bush Butterflie/Klein: also Re Beato Film. H.S. Beatlemania
priced.

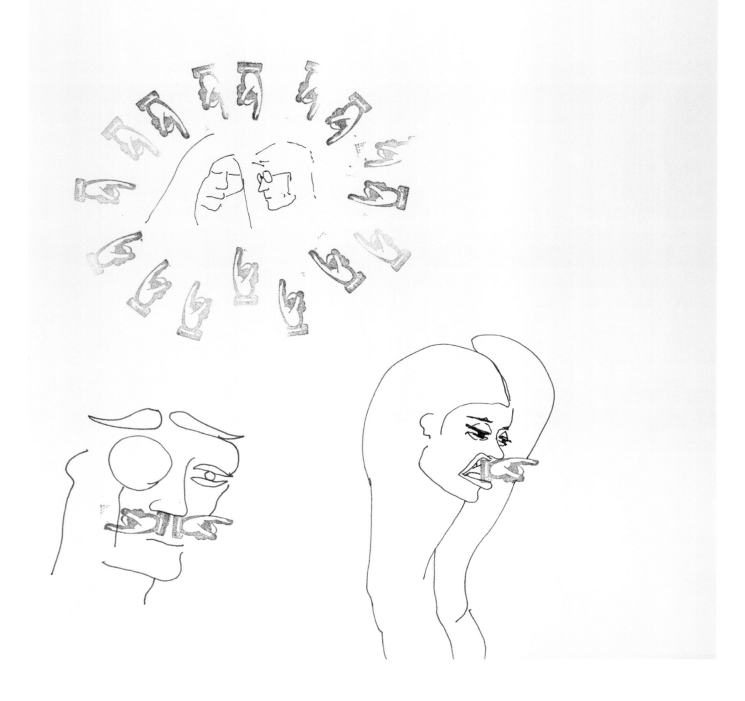

NOW International Feminist Planning Conference, 1–4 June 1973

Yoko: After we went to LA to plug *Approximately Infinite Universe*, John and I went right back into the feminist work. John was extremely warm to me, as usual, but I often thought of that night when I felt that I had a good glimpse of his intense emotion.

It was easy to just dispense with it as a 'primal scream', as John put it. But, as a woman, and a wife who was very close to him, I could not disregard the fact that the expression was very sexual. I compared John's intensity that night and our warm relationship. Isn't that, in fact, what I had wanted? If not sexual, an incredibly intense relationship.

I knew that I still had that thirst in me, which I transformed into songs, as I usually did. In LA I had written many songs about women which later became the *Feeling In Space* album.

As soon as we went back to New York, we went to a feminist meeting held by the National Organization for Women at Lesley College and Harvard Divinity School in Cambridge, Massachusetts.

The purpose of the conference was 'to state the solidarity of feminists throughout the world in their mutual attempt to institute changes that will transform the consciousness of their respective societies in making them aware of the oppressed condition and inferior status of women throughout the world'.

John and I took this very seriously. I made a booklet of my songs and statements specially for the occasion and carried copies of them with me. John carried his guitar. He was to be my band.

I sang some of the songs from *Approximately Infinite Universe* and some that I had written in LA just before. John played the guitar to

accompany me. For John it was an incredibly exciting experience to be the only male feminist of the group.

For me it was a complex experience. Most sisters wanted to talk to John, the most famous feminist: they were polite enough to talk to me but we both felt that it was a politeness covering a restraint underneath of wanting to talk to John, the accompanist.

Because of 'Sisters O Sisters', the song for sisters that I had written and put out on the album *Sometime In New York City* the year before, some sisters genuinely wanted to talk to me about their life. They were the unknown sisters. I was surprised and deeply impressed by their courage in their own lives.

When some sisters gathered to have coffee, I met a woman who had come from Middle America. She said she had left her husband and her children and was not intending to go back to them. She was a sweet girl with large frightened eyes. Those eyes have seen stuff our mothers never taught us to be part of the deal in life, I thought.

I asked her how she felt. She said she missed her children, and sometimes she heard them crying in her dreams, but she felt okay because she knew her husband was not bad to her kids. She also said she was having a hard time finding a job because she had no skills. A classic case. That was how 'Angry Young Woman' came to me.

There was a big conference of all sisters in the lecture hall, which John and I attended. I was surprised that in the election of the Women's Committee some sisters voted for me, enough for me to be considered as a candidate. John was very proud of it and kept whispering to me that I should accept. I stood up and declined their kind recommendation and promised that I would work for them

outside the Women's Committee in my own way as best I could.

I realized that the committee's work would separate me from John too often and, in the end, John would not appreciate it and most possibly would make it difficult for me. I was not particularly sure which of the many complex elements of me they were voting for and I sincerely believed that I could do more for them outside of the Women's Committee.

John and my concert, in a separate small hall, was attended by approximately fifty to a hundred sisters. I played the piano and John played the guitar. There were no platforms and the sisters just made a circle around us.

When I sang 'Woman Power', which was the final song, representative sisters from over fifty countries all stood up and joined me. It was a very powerful scene. So powerful that the flashbulb of the only camera refused to work, a video camera stopped and the sound tape went bonkers.

John, who immediately wanted to know if the big moment was recorded, was very disappointed to find out about this. This was not the first time that had happened. The same thing had happened in some of my early avant-garde concerts. That's the most dramatic moment not to have been recorded.

Pages 142–43 and opposite: John & Yoko attend the First International Feminist Planning Conference. The four-day event, staged by NOW, the National Organization for Women, drew 300 feminists from 28 countries, including New Zealand, India and Russia, and attracted women of every age and political viewpoint; Lesley College and Harvard Divinity School, Cambridge, Massachusetts, 1–4 June 1973.

John: There were five women in my family and all my male relatives were weak. I thought that to be strong I had to have power over women. Yoko showed me that power comes only through love…. Every man should have a chance to take some time off and think about things. The women's movement means we can forget about roles and be people…women are people and not objects to manipulate.

Opposite: John at the conference and his name badge with three Japanese pro-feminist stickers added.

JOHN LENNON

N.O.W.
Int. Femenist Planning Conf.

NOW Concert, 'Coffin Car' Introduction
by Yoko Ono

While John is setting up the amp....

What happened to me was that I was living as an artist who had relative freedom as a woman and was considered the bitch in the society. Since I met John, I was upgraded into a witch...and I think that that's very flattering. Anyway, what I learned from being with John is that the society suddenly treated me as a woman, as a woman who belonged to a man who is one of the most powerful people in our generation. And some of his closest friends told me that probably I should stay in the background, I should shut up,

I should give up my work and that way I'll be happy.

And I got those advices. I was lucky, I was over thirty and it was too late for me to change.

But still – still – this is one thing I want to say to the sisters, because, I really wish that you know that you're not alone. Because the whole society started to attack me and the whole society wished me dead, I started accumulating a tremendous amount of guilt complex and [as a] result of that I started to stutter. And I consider myself a very eloquent

woman and also an attractive woman all my life and suddenly, because I was associated to John, that was considered an ugly woman, ugly Jap, who took your monument or something away from you.

And that's when I realized how hard it is for women. If I can start to stutter, being a strong woman – and having lived thirty years by then, learn to stutter in three years of being treated as such – it is a very hard road. Now, the next song is called 'Coffin Car' and this is a song [about something] that I observed in myself and also in many sisters who are riding on coffin cars....

Opposite: Yoko performing a concert at NOW accompanied by John on guitar, Old Cambridge Baptist Church, Cambridge, Massachusets, 2 June 1973.

Lyrics for Yoko's song 'Coffin Car' from a booklet John & Yoko made and printed for the event.

4

COFFIN CAR

COFFIN CAR   YOKO ONO '73
                                     ONO MUSIC ©

COFFIN CAR
SHE'S RIDING A COFFIN CAR
SHE LIKES TO RIDE A COFFIN CAR
PEOPLE WATCHING HER WITH TENDER EYES
FRIENDS WHISPERING IN KINDLY WORDS
CHILDREN RUNNING, WAVING HANDS
TELLING EACHOTHER HOW PRETTY SHE IS

COFFIN CAR
SHE'S RIDING A COFFIN CAR
SHE LIKES TO RIDE A COFFIN CAR
PEOPLE THROWING KISSES FOR THE FIRST TIME
FRIENDS MAKING WAY FOR THE FIRST TIME
SHOWERING FLOWERS, RINGING BELLS
TELLING EACHOTHER HOW NICE SHE IS

COFFIN CAR
SHE LIKES TO RIDE A COFFIN CAR
SHE'S RIDING A COFFIN CAR
WIVES SHOWING TEARS FOR THE FIRST TIME
HUSBANDS TAKING THEIR HATS OFF FOR THE FIRST TIME
CRUSHING THEIR HANDKERCHIEF, RUBBING THEIR NOSE
TELLING EACHOTHER HOW GOOD SHE IS

HALF THE WORLD IS DEAD ANYWAY
THE OTHER HALF IS ASLEEP
AND LIFE IS KILLING HER
TELLING HER TO JOIN THE DEAD

SO EVERY DAY
SHE LIKES TO RIDE A COFFIN CAR
A FLOWER COVERED COFFIN CAR
PRETENDING SHE WAS DEAD

COFFIN CAR
A FLOWER COVERED COFFIN CAR
A FLOWER COVERED COFFIN CAR
A FLOWER COVERED COFFIN CAR

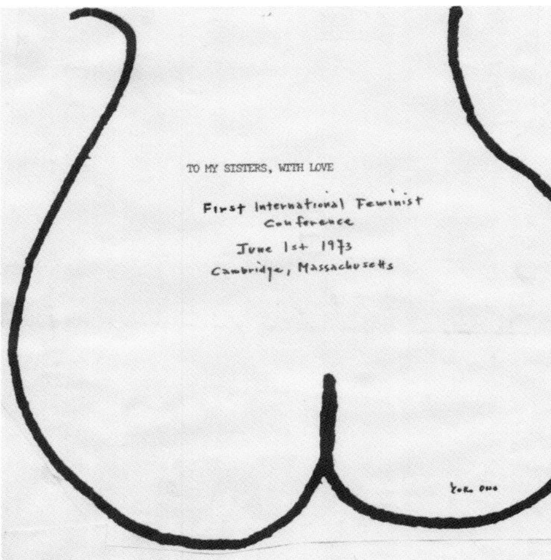

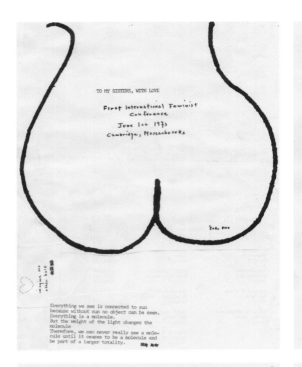

TO MY SISTERS, WITH LOVE

First International Feminist Conference
June 1st 1973
Cambridge, Massachusetts

Yoko Ono

Everything we see is connected to sun
because without sun no object can be seen.
Everything is a molecule.
But the weight of the light changes the
molecule
Therefore, we can never really see a molecule until it ceases to be a molecule and
be part of a larger totality.

1.

FROM SOMETIME IN NEW YORK CITY
ALBUM ON APPLE RECORDS

O SISTERS O SISTERS

WE LOST OUR GREEN LAND
WE LOST OUR CLEAN AIR
WE LOST OUR TRUE WISDOM
AND WE LIVE IN DISPAIR

O SISTERS O SISTERS
LETS STAND UP RIGHT NOW
ITS NEVER TOO LATE
TO START FROM THE START

WISDOM O WISDOM
THATS WHAT WE ASK FOR
AND YES MY DEAR SISTERS
WE MUST LEARN TO ASK

MIDDLE 8 .... WISDOM O WISDOM
THATS WHAT WE ASK FOR
THATS WHAT WE LIVE FOR NOW

O SISTERS O SISTERS
LETS WAKE UP RIGHT ON
ITS NEVER TOO LATE
TO SHOUT FROM OUR HEARTS

FREEDOM O FREEDOM
THATS WHAT WE FIGHT FOR
AND YES MY DEAR SISTERS
WE MUST LEARN TO FIGHT

MIDDLE 8 .... FREEDOM O FREEDOM
THATS WHAT WE ASK FOR
THATS WHAT WE LIVE FOR NOW

O SISTERS O SISTERS
LETS GIVE UP NO MORE
ITS NEVER TOO LATE
TO BUILD A NEW WORLD

NEW WORLD O NEW WORLD
THATS WHAT WE LIVE FOR
AND YES MY DEAR SISTERS
WE MUST LEARN TO LIVE

MIDDLE 8 .... NEW WORLD O NEW WORLD
THATS WHAT WE LIVE FOR
THATS WHAT WE MUST LEARN TO BUILD

NEW WORLD O NEW WORLD
THATS WHAT WE LIVE FOR
THATS WHAT WE MUST LEARN TO BUILD

YOKO ONO '71
ono music ©

2

LOOKING OVER FROM MY HOTEL WINDOW — YOKO ONO '72 ONO MUSIC ©

AGE 39 LOOKING OVER FROM MY HOTEL WINDOW
BLUE DOTS AND RED DOTS SKATING AWAY IN THE PARK
I USED TO BE THERE TWENTY YEARS AGO
HUFFING OVER A MUG OF HOT CHOCOLATE DRINK

AGE 39 LOOKING OVER FROM A HOTEL WINDOW
WONDERING IF ONE SHOULD JUMP OFF OR GO TO SLEEP
PEOPLE TELL YOU UP IS BETTER THAN DOWN
BUT THEY NEVER TELL YOU WHICH IS UP AND WHICH IS DOWN

AGE 39 LOOKING OVER FROM A HOTEL WINDOW
95 POUND BUNDLE BUT ITS TROUBLE WHEN THERES NOWHERE TO LEAVE
PEOPLE SAY STARDUST AND GOLDUST ARE IT
BUT THEY NEVER TELL YOU IT CHOKES YOU JUST AS SAWDUST DOES

AGE 39 FEELING PRETTY SUICIDAL
THE WEIGHT GETS HEAVIER WHEN YOUVE BLED THIRTY YEARS
SHOW ME YOUR BLOOD JOHN AND I'LL SHOW YOU MINE
THEY SAY ITS RUNNING EVEN WHEN WERE ASLEEP

NO TRACE OF RESENTMENT NO TRACE OF REGRETS
ONE BLOOD'S THINNER BUT BOTH LOOK RED AND FRESH
IF I EVER DIE PLEASE GO TO MY DAUGHTER
AND TELL HER THAT SHE USED TO HAUNT ME IN MY DREAMS
(THAT'S SAYING A LOT FOR A NEUROTIC LIKE ME)

AGE 39 LOOKING OVER FROM A HOTEL WINDOW
TRYING TO TACKLE AWAY WITH HEART OF CLAY
THE WEIGHT GETS LIGHTER WHEN THERES NOWHERE TO TURN
GODS LITTLE DANDRUFF FLOATING IN THE AIR

AGE 39 LOOKING OVER THE WORLD
AGE 39 FLOATING OVER THE WORLD
AGE 39.... FLOATING ALONG

FROM APPROXIMATELY INFINITE UNIVERSE
ALBUM ON APPLE RECORDS

6

NOW OR NEVER — YOKO ONO '72 ONO MUSIC ©

ARE WE GONNA KEEP PUSHING OUR CHILDREN TO DRUGS
ARE WE GONNA KEEP DRIVING THEM INSANE
ARE WE GONNA KEEP LAYING EMPTY WORDS AND FISTS
ARE WE GONNA BE REMEMBERED AS THE CENTURY THAT FAILED

PEOPLE OF AMERICA
WHEN WILL WE LEARN
ITS NOW OR NEVER
THERE'S NO TIME TO LOSE

ARE WE GONNA KEEP SENDING OUR YOUTH TO WAR
ARE WE GONNA KEEP SCARRING RICEFIELDS AND INFANTS
ARE WE GONNA KEEP WATCHING DEAD BODIES OVER DINNER
ARE WE GONNA BE KNOWN AS THE CENTURY THAT KILLS

PEOPLE OF AMERICA
WHEN WILL WE STOP
ITS NOW OR NEVER
THERES NO TIME TO WASTE

ARE WE GONNA KEEP PRETENDING THINGS ARE ALRIGHT
ARE WE GONNA KEEP OUR MOUTH CLOSED JUST IN CASE
ARE WE GONNA KEEP PUTTING OFF UNTIL ITS TOO LATE
ARE WE GONNA BE KNOWN AS THE CENTURY OF FEAR

PEOPLE OF AMERICA WHEN WILL WE SEE
WHEN WILL WE SEE
ITS NOW OR NEVER
WE'VE NO TIME TO LOSE

ARE WE GONNA KEEP DIGGING OIL WELLS AND GOLD
ARE WE GONNA KEEP SHOOTING THE ONES THAT TRY TO CHANGE
ARE WE GONNA KEEP THINKING IT WONT HAPPEN TO US
ARE WE GONNA BE KNOWN AS THE CENTURY THAT KILLS

PEOPLE OF AMERICA
PLEASE LISTEN TO YOUR SOUL
WE CAN CHANGE THE TIMES
TO CENTURY OF HOPE

'CAUSE

DREAM YOU DREAM ALONE IS ONLY A DREAM
BUT DREAM WE DREAM TOGETHER IS REALITY

FROM APPROXIMATELY INFINITE UNIVERSE
ALBUM FROM APPLE RECORDS

7

LET ME COUNT THE WAYS — YOKO ONO '73 ONO MUSIC ©

LET ME COUNT THE WAYS IN WHICH TO DIE
EACHTIME YOU DONT SAY WHAT YOU WANT TO SAY
THATS WHEN YOURE DYING INSIDE
LET ME COUNT THE WAYS IN WHICH TO DIE
EACH TIME YOU CLOSE YOUR MIND TO HOW YOU REALLY FEEL
THATS WHEN YOURE DYING INSIDE

CHORUS

LET ME COUNT THE WAYS IN WHICH TO LIVE
EACHTIME YOU DARE TO DO WHAT YOU REALLY WANT TO DO
THATS WHEN YOURE ALIVE INSIDE
LET ME COUNT THE WAYS IN WHICH TO LIVE
EACHTIME YOU OPEN YOUR MIND TO WHAT YOU SEE AND HEAR
THATS WHEN YOURE ALIVE INSIDE

CHORUS

LET ME COUNT THE WAYS IN WHICH TO LIVE TOGETHER
THINK OF YOURSELF AS AN EYE TO SEE THE WORLD
AND THEN YOU'LL KNOW THAT A PAIR CAN SEE CLEARER
LET ME COUNT THE WAYS IN WHICH TO LIVE TOGETHER
THINK OF YOURSELF AS A HAND TO MAKE A SOUND
THEN YOU'LL SEE THAT A PAIR CAN MAKE IT BETTER
(THINK OF YOURSELF AS A LEG TO TAKE YOU AROUND
THEN YOU'LL FIND THAT A PAIR WOULD TAKE YOU FURTHER)

CHORUS

WE ALL EXIST IN THE GHETTOS OF OUR MINDS
BUT ITS TIME TO GIVE AND LET GIVE
LETS UNLEASH US ALL FROM OUR FEARS AND BINDS
TOGETHER WE CAN LIVE AND LET LIVE

8

WOMEN POWER — YOKO ONO '73 ONO MUSIC ©

TWO THOUSAND YEARS OF MALE SOCIETY
LAYING FEAR AND TYRANNY
CLINGING TO GRADES AND MONEY
SEEKING VALUES VAIN AND PHONY

DO YOU KNOW THAT ONE DAY YOU LOST YOUR WAY, MAN
DO YOU KNOW THAT SOME DAY YOU HAVE TO PAY, MAN
HAVE YOU ANYTHING TO SAY, MAN, EXCEPT

MAKE NO MISTAKE ABOUT IT
IM THE PRESIDENT, YOU HEAR
I WANNA MAKE ONE THING PERFECTLY CLEAR
IM THE PRESIDENT, YOU HEAR

YOU DONT HEAR THEM SINGING SONGS
YOU DONT SEE THEM LIVING LIFE
CAUSE THEYVE GOT NOTHING TO SAY, BUT

MAKE NO MISTAKE ABOUT IT
IM THE PRESIDENT, YOU HEAR
I WANNA MAKE ONE THING PERFECTLY CLEAR
IM THE PRESIDENT, YOU HEAR

YOU MAY BE THE PRESIDENT NOW
YOU MAY STILL BE A MAN
BUT YOU MUST ALSO BE HUMAN
SO OPEN UP AND JOIN US IN LIVING

THE COMING AGE WILL BE A FEMININE SOCIETY
WE'LL REGAIN OUR HUMAN DIGNITY
WE'LL LAY SOME TRUTH AND CLARITY
AND BRING BACK NATURES BEAUTY

EVERY WOMAN HAS A SONG TO SING
EVERY WOMAN HAS A STORY TO TELL

AND MAKE NO MISTAKE ABOUT IT, BROTHERS
WE WOMEN,
HAVE THE POWER
TO MOVE THE MOUNTAINS

BUT WAIT, WAIT, SISTERS
WE DONT HAVE TO MOVE THE MOUNTAINS CAUSE THEYRE MOVING ANYWAY
THE POWER WE NEED IS THE POWER OF TRUST
THAT THE MOUNTAINS MOVING AND WE'RE COMING, AND

THERE'S NO MISTAKE ABOUT IT, SISTERS
WE WOMEN,
HAVE THE POWER
TO CHANGE THE WORLD

WE'LL TEACH YOU HOW TO COOK, BROTHERS
WE'LL TEACH YOU HOW TO KNIT
WE'LL TEACH YOU HOW TO CARE FOR LIFE
INSTEAD OF KILLING

WOMEN POWER, WOMEN POWER, THE MOUNTAINS MOVING (REPEAT)

12

WHAT IS THE RELATIONSHIP BETWEEN THE WORLD AND THE ARTIST?

Many people believe that in this age, art is dead. They despise the artists who show in galleries and are caught up in the traditional art world. Artists themselves are beginning to lose their confidence. They don't know whether they are doing something that still has value in this day and age where the social problems are so vital and critical. I wondered myself about this. Why am I still an artist? And why am I not joining the violent revolutionaries? Then I realized that destruction is not my game. Violent revolutionaries are trying to destroy the establishment. That is good. But how? By killing? Killing is such an artless thing. All you need is a coke bottle in your hand and you can kill. But people who kill that way most often become the next establishment after they've killed the old. Because they are using the same method that the old establishment used to destroy. Violent revolutionaries' thinking is very close to establishment-type thinking and ways of solving problems.

I like to fight the establishment by using methods that are so far removed from establishment-type thinking that the establishment doesn't know how to fight back. For instance, they cannot stamp out John and Yoko events *Two Virgins*, *Bed Peace*, *Acorn Peace*, and *War is Over* Poster event.

Artists are not here to destroy or to create. *Creating* is just as simple and artless a thing to do as *destroying*. Everyone on earth has creativity. Even a housewife can create a baby. Children are just as creative as the people whom society considers artists. Creative artists are just good enough to be considered children. Artists must not create more objects, the world is full of everything it needs. I'm bored with artists who make big lumps of sculpture and occupy a big space with them and think they have done something *creative* and allow people nothing but to applaud the lump. That is sheer narcissism. Why don't they at least let people touch them? Money and space are wasted on such projects when there are people starving and people who don't have enough space to sleep or breathe.

The job of an artist is not to destroy but to change the value of things. And by doing that, artists can change the world into a Utopia where there is total freedom for everybody. That can be achieved only when there is total communication in the world. Total communication equals peace. That is our aim. That is what artists can do for the world!

In order to change the value of things, you've got to know about life and the situation of the world. You have to be more than a child.

That is the difference between a child's work and an artist's work. That is the difference between an artist's work and a murderer's work. We are artists. Artist is just a frame of mind. Anybody can be an artist. It doesn't involve having a talent. It involves only having a certain frame of mind, an attitude, determination, and imagination that springs naturally out of the necessity of the situation.

Message is the medium. There are only two classes left in our society. The class who communicates and the class who doesn't. Tomorrow I hope there will be just one. Total communication equals peace.

Men can destroy/Women can create/Artists revalue.

Y.O., Cannes Film Festival, May, 1971

Mirror becomes a razor when it's broken.
A stick becomes a flute when it's loved. *

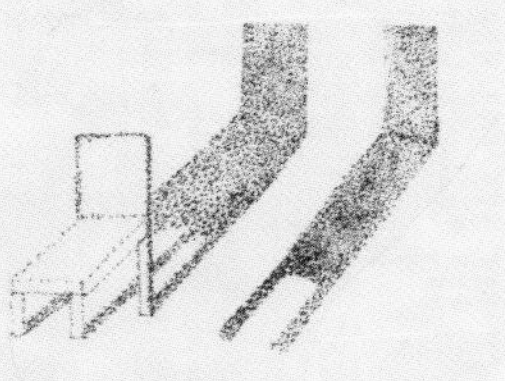

We believe in God instead of believing in ourselves.

All words are verbs.

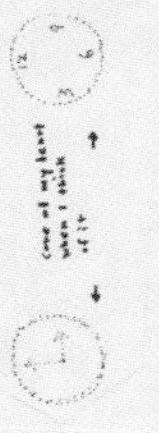

AIR TALK

It's sad that the air is the only
thing we share.
No matter how close we get to each other,
there is always air between us.

It's also nice that we share the air.
No matter how far apart we are,
the air links us. *

13

We Can Work It Out

Dear Sir;

To Jill Johnston on attending Female Liberation Movement: Thank you for allowing me to attend the meeting. It was a bit sad to see the age-old intellectualism and idealism almost killing the movement. I thought if the movement would never get too specialized on its organizational problems and intellectualized in its activities, so that newcomers could feel that they are instantly part of the movement, there is a chance of the movement getting big. Getting big doesn't mean becoming establishment, it means getting to reach a lot of women and eventually all the women who need help. And all women do need help.

Something simple and unwordy, like "Let's get together" and "What's your story?" should be the pass words for the Female Lib meetings, and the movement should always work on that level, instead of getting to be a word game among the female intellectuals.

Don't ask questions, let in anybody regardless of their color, way of living (married or not), or way of thinking (intellectual or not). For instance, I think there may be a great deal of truth in one of the girl's statement that lesbianism is a major issue of Female Lib, but the sad thing is that all statements when they are stated immediately limit the issue and alienate women who think differently. I think our job is not to seek truth and make statements to that effect, but just to get together to communicate—women who think and live differently but who have one definite thing in common, and that is being a woman.

—Yoko Ono Lennon
Manhattan
July '71

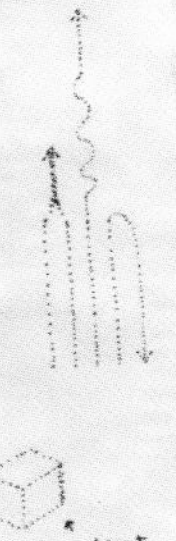

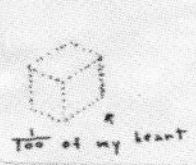

SENSE PIECE *

Common sense prevents you from thinking.
Have less sense and you will make more
sense.

Art is fart. Fart more and you will fart
less.

Screaming is a voice never loud enough
to reach. Scream more and you will scream
less.

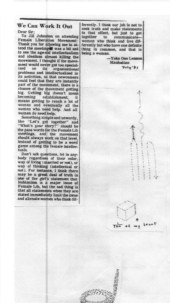

water talk *

you are water
I'm water
we're all water in different containers
that's why it's so easy to meet
someday we'll evaporate together

but even after the water's gone
we'll probably point out to the containers
and say, "that's me there, that one."
we're container minders

* LET'S PIECE

500 Noses are more beautiful than
one nose. Even a telephone no. is more
beautiful if 200 people think of
the same number at the same time.

a) let 500 people think of the same
telephone number at once for a
minute at a set time.
b) let everybody in the city think
of the word "yes" at the same time
for 30 seconds. Do it often.
c) make it the whole world thinking
all the time.

* Copyright GRAPEFRUIT

14

Yoko ono / john lennon
1972.
from 'Sometime in New York City' album.

Apple

WOMAN IS THE NIGGER OF THE WORLD

WOMAN IS THE NIGGER OF THE WORLD
YES SHE IS-THINK ABOUT IT
WOMAN IS THE NIGGER OF THE WORLD
THINK ABOUT IT DO SOMETHING ABOUT IT

WE MAKE HER PAIN HER FACE AND DANCE
IF SHE WONT BE A SLAVE WE SAY THAT SHE DONT LOVE US
IF SHES REAL WE SAY SHES TRYING TO BE A MAN
WHILE PUTTING HER DOWN WE PRETEND THAT SHES ABOVE US

WOMAN IS THE NIGGER OF THE WORLD
YES SHE IS-IF YOU DONT BELIEVE ME LOOK AT THE ONE YOURE WITH
WOMAN IS THE SLAVE OF THE SLAVES
AH YEH BETTER SCREAM ABOUT IT

WE MAKE HER BEAR AND RAISE OUR CHILDREN
AND THEN WE LEAVE HER FLAT FOR BEING A FAT OLD MOTHER HEN
WE TELL HER HOME IS THE ONLY PLACE SHE SHOULD BE
THEN WE COMPLAIN THAT SHES TOO UNWORLDLY TO BE OUR FRIEND

WOMAN IS THE NIGGER OF THE WORLD
YES SHE IS_IF YOU DONT BELIEVE ME TAKE A LOOK AT THE ONE YOURE WITH
WOMAN IS THE SLAVE TO THE SLAVES
YEH THINK ABOUT IT

WE INSULT HER EVERY DAY ON TV
AND WONDER WHY SHE HAS NO GUTS OR CONFIDENCE
WHEN SHES YOUNG WE KILL HER WILL TO BE FREE
WHILE TELLING HER NOT TO BE SO SMART WE PUT HER DOWN FOR BEING SO DUMB

WOMAN IS THE NIGGER OF THE WORLD
YES SHE IS_IF YOU DONT BELIEVE ME TAKE A LOOK AT THE ONE YOURE WITH
WOMAN IS THE SLAVE TO THE SLAVES
YES SHE IS IF YOU BELIEVE ME YOU BETTER SCREAM ABOUT IT

WE MAKE HER PAINT HER FACE AND DANCE
WE MAKE HER PAINT HER FACE AND DANCE
WE MAKE HER PAINT HER FACE AND DANCE

'Woman is the Nigger of the World' is a quote from Yoko which was on the cover of NOVA (an english 'womans' magazine; March 1969.) In 1972, we wrote and recorded it, it was redeased as a single (45rpm) with 'sisters o sisters' on the other side. The record was banned on most (80%) radio stations, the reason given was the use of the word 'nigger'; N.O.W. said it was the word 'woman' that offended them – they were right! (D.J.s are mainly white/men.)

J.L.
June 1. 73.

APPROXIMATELY INFINITE UNIVERSE YOKO ONO '72
ONO MUSIC ©

IN THIS APPROXIMATELY INFINITE UNIVERSE
I KNOW A GIRL WHO'S IN CONSTANT HELL
NO LOVE OR PILL COULD KEEP HER COOL
CAUSE THERE'S A THOUSAND HOLES IN HER HEART

AND THE WIND OF THE PAST
BLOWS THROUGH HER HEART
REMINDING HER OF THE PEOPLE SHE KILLED
WIND OF NOW
BLOWS OFF HER COOL
TELLING HER THERE'S SOMETHING SHE'S MISSED

YOU KNOW THE TOWN OF SAPPORO, SHE SAYS
WHERE MEN TALK ROUGH AND NEVER SING
TWO BOTTLES OF LONELINESS
PATCHING THE HOLES IN HER DREAM

IN THIS APPROXIMATELY INFINITE UNIVERSE
I KNOW A GIRL WHO'S RAISING CONSTANT HELL
NO LOVE OR BOTTLE COULD FIX HER GOOD
CAUSE THERE'S A THOUSAND HOLES IN HER HEAD

AND THE WIND OF THE FUTURE
BLOWS THROUGH HER HEAD
SAYING THERES NO POINT OF RETURN
THE WIND OF THE UNIVERSE
BLOWS OFF HER SOUL
TELLING HER THERE'S NOWHERE TO GO

I WANNA SLEEP WANNA SLEEP, SHE SAYS
AND TAKE HER FIX TO BED
TWO BOTTLES OF LONELINESS
PATCHING THE HOLES IN HER DREAM

FROM APPROXIMATELY INFINITE UNIVERSE
ALBUM ON APPLE RECORDS

COFFIN CAR YOKO ONO '73
ONO MUSIC ©

COFFIN CAR
SHE'S RIDING A COFFIN CAR
SHE LIKES TO RIDE A COFFIN CAR
PEOPLE WATCHING HER WITH TENDER EYES
FRIENDS WHISPERING IN KINDLY WORDS
CHILDREN RUNNING, WAVING HANDS
TELLING EACHOTHER HOW PRETTY SHE IS

COFFIN CAR
SHE'S RIDING A COFFIN CAR
SHE LIKES TO RIDE A COFFIN CAR
PEOPLE THROWING KISSES FOR THE FIRST TIME
FRIENDS MAKING WAY FOR THE FIRST TIME
SHOWERING FLOWERS, RINGING BELLS
TELLING EACHOTHER HOW NICE SHE IS

COFFIN CAR
SHE LIKES TO RIDE A COFFIN CAR
SHE'S RIDING A COFFIN CAR
WIVES SHOWING TEARS FOR THE FIRST TIME
HUSBANDS TAKING THEIR HATS OFF FOR THE FIRST TIME
CRUSHING THEIR HANDKERCHIEF, RUBBING THEIR NOSE
TELLING EACHOTHER HOW GOOD SHE IS

HALF THE WORLD IS DEAD ANYWAY
THE OTHER HALF IS ASLEEP
AND LIFE IS KILLING HER
TELLING HER TO JOIN THE DEAD

SO EVERY DAY
SHE LIKES TO RIDE A COFFIN CAR
A FLOWER COVERED COFFIN CAR
PRETENDING SHE WAS DEAD

COFFIN CAR
A FLOWER COVERED COFFIN CAR
A FLOWER COVERED COFFIN CAR
A FLOWER COVERED COFFIN CAR

WARRIOR WOMEN YOKO ONO '72
ONO MUSIC ©

I WENT THROUGH A LONG BATTLE
IT WAS A HEAVY STRUGGLE
WHEN I LOOKED AROUND
I SAW MOST OF US WERE DEAD

THEY KILLED US IN EVERY WAY
TRY TO ROB OUR SOUL AWAY
I LOST MY VOICE FROM FEAR
AND MY LEGS WOULD NOT MOVE AHEAD

MANY OF US WERE BLEEDING TO DEATH
MANY OF US WERE REACHING FOR BREATH
AND IN A DISTANCE I SAW OUR BROTHERS CHANTING
KILL ALL WARRIOR WOMEN

WARRIOR WOMEN, WARRIOR WOMEN
WARRIOR WOMEN, WARRIOR WOMEN

THERES NO WAY TO GET AWAY
THEYRE GETTING CRAZIER EVERY DAY
STAMPING ON OUR MINDS
AND TIGHTENING OUR BLINDS

I HEAR MY DAUGHTER SCREAM
IN HER BRIEF AND SHALLOW DREAM
I CRUTCH HER IN MY ARMS
AND TRY TO CLEAR MY HEAD

SOME OF US ARE SLAUGHTERED IN CAVES
SOME OF US ARE CAPTURED AS SLAVES
AND IN THE DISTANCE I SEE A SIGN SAYING
END OF ALL WARRIOR WOMEN

WARRIOR WOMEN, WARRIOR WOMEN
WARRIOR WOMEN, WARRIOR WOMEN

THERES NOT VERY MANY OF US
LEFT IN THE WORLD
BUT OUR BLOOD WILL FEED THE FLOWERS
AND CARRY OUR WORD
SO I SAY TO MY SISTERS
REMEMBER THE SHAME
THE MASSACRE OF WARRIOR WOMEN
SO I SAY TO MY SISTERS
REMEMBER OUR NAMES
AND THE PRIDE AND JOY OF WARRIOR WOMEN

Yoko Ono
Victims of the Phantom Society

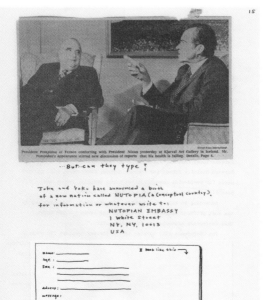

...But...can they type?

John and Yoko have announced a birth
of a new nation called NUTOPIA (a conceptual country).
for information or whatever write to:
NUTOPIAN EMBASSY
1 White Street
NY, NY, 10013
USA

Name:
Age:
Sex:
Adress:
message:

I look like this →

← and think like this

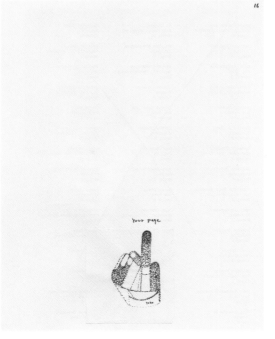

Your page

First International Feminist Planning
Conference booklet pages.
Pages 152–53: Selected stills from Portapak
video footage of the conference filmed by
John, Yoko and their assistants Jon Hendricks
and Nadja Gruen at Lesley College, Harvard
Divinity School and Old Cambridge Baptist
Church, Cambridge, Massachusetts,
1–4 June 1973.

The Feminization of Society
by Yoko Ono, February 1972

The aim of the feminist movement should not just end with getting more jobs in the existing society, though we should definitely work on that as well. We have to keep on going until the whole of the female race is freed.

How are we going to go about this? This society is the very society that killed female freedom: the society that was built on female slavery. If we try to achieve our freedom within the framework of the existing social set-up, men, who run the society, will continue to make a token gesture of giving us a place in their world. Some of us will succeed in moving into elitist jobs, kicking our sisters on the way up. Others will resort to producing babies, or being conned into thinking that joining male perversions and madness is what equality is about: 'Join the army,' 'Join the sexist trip,' etc.

The major change in the contemporary woman's revolution is the issue of lesbianism. Lesbianism, to many, is a means of expressing rebellion toward the existing society through sexual freedom. It helps women realize that they don't necessarily have to rely on men for relationships. They have an alternative to spending ninety per cent of their lives waiting for, finding and living for men. But if the alternative to that is finding a woman to replace the man in her life, and then build her life around another female or females, it isn't very liberating. Some sisters have learned to love women more deeply through lesbianism, but others have simply gone after their sisters in the same manner that the male chauvinists have.

The ultimate goal of female liberation is not just to escape from male oppression. How about liberating ourselves from our various mind trips such as ignorance, greed, masochism, fear of God and social conventions? It's hard to so easily dismiss the importance of paternal influence in this society, at this time. Since

we face the reality that, in this global village, there is very little choice but to coexist with men, we might as well find a way to do it and do it well.

We definitely need more positive participation by men in the care of our children. But how are we going to do this? We have to demand it. James Baldwin has said of this problem, 'I can't give a performance all day in the office and come back and give a performance at home.' He's right. How can we expect men to share the responsibility of childcare in the present social conditions where his job in the office is, to him, a mere 'performance' and where he cannot relate to the role of childcare except as yet another 'performance'? Contemporary men must go through major changes in their thinking before they volunteer to look after children, and before they even start to want to care.

Childcare is the most important issue for the future of our generation. It is no longer a pleasure for the majority of men and women in our society, because the whole society is geared towards living up to a Hollywood-cum-Madison Avenue image of men and women, and a way of life that has nothing to do with childcare. We are in a serious identity crisis. This society is driven by neurotic speed and force accelerated by greed, and frustration of not being able to live up to the image of men and women we have created for ourselves; the image has nothing to do with the reality of people. How could we be an eternal James Bond or Twiggy (false eyelashes, the never-had-a-baby-or-a-full-meal look) and raise three kids on the side? In such an image-driven culture, a piece of reality, such as a child, becomes a direct threat to our false existence.

The only game we play together with our children is star-chasing; sadly, not the stars in the sky, but the 'STARS' who we think have achieved the

standard of the dream image we have imposed on the human race. We cannot trust ourselves anymore, because we know that we are, well… too real. We are forever apologetic for being real. Excuse me for farting, excuse me for making love and smelling like a human being, instead of that odourless celluloid prince and princess image up there on the screen.

Most of us, as women, hope that we can achieve our freedom within the existing social set-up, thinking that, somewhere, there must be a happy medium for men and women to share freedom and responsibility. But if we just took the time to observe the very function of our society, the greed-power-frustration syndrome, we would soon see that there is no happy medium to be achieved. We can, of course, aim to play the same game that men have played for centuries, and inch by inch, take over all the best jobs and eventually conquer the whole world, leaving an extremely bitter male stud-cum-slave class moaning and groaning underneath us. This is alright for an afternoon dream, but in reality, it would obviously be a drag.

Just as the blacks have in the past, women are going through an initial stage of revolution now. We are now at a stage where we are eager to compete with men on all levels. But women will inevitably arrive at the next stage, and realize the futility of trying to be like men. Women will realize themselves as they are, and not as beings comparative to or in response to men. As a result, the feminist revolution will take a more positive step in the society by offering a feminine direction.

In their past two thousand years of effort, men have shown us their failure in their method of running the world. Instead of falling into the same trap that men fell into, women can offer something that the society never had before because of male dominance.

Journalist, activist and co-founder of the National Organization for
Women, Betty Friedan (top row, fourth from left) at her New York
apartment across from the Lincoln Center with attendees from
the International Feminist Planning Conference, including (top row)
Cecilia L. Negrete and Susan Kedgley (2nd and 3rd from left),
Berit Ås and Bitten Modal (6th and 7th from left), and (second row)
Gilda Grillo (2nd from left) and Yoko Ono (4th from left), 7 June 1973.

President Pompidou of France conferring with President Nixon yesterday at Kjarval Art Gallery in Iceland. Mr. Pompidou's appearance stirred new discussion of reports that his health is failing. Details, Page 4.

United Press International

...But...can they type?

That is the feminine direction. What we can do is to take the current society, which contains both masculine and feminine characteristics, and bring out its feminine nature rather than its masculine force which is now at work. We must make more positive usage of the feminine tendencies of the society which, up to now, have been either suppressed or dismissed as something harmful, impractical, irrelevant and ultimately shameful.

I am proposing the feminization of society; the use of feminine nature as a positive force to change the world. We can change ourselves with feminine intelligence and awareness, into a basically organic, noncompetitive society that is based on love, rather than reasoning. The result will be a society of balance, peace and contentment. We can evolve rather than revolt, come together, rather than claim independence,

and feel rather than think. These are characteristics that are considered feminine; characteristics that men despise in women. But have men really done so well by avoiding the development of these characteristics within themselves?

Already, as I catch a glimpse of the new world, I see feminine wisdom working as a positive force. I refer to the feminine wisdom and awareness which is based on reality, intuition and empirical thinking, rather than logistics and ideologies. The entire youth generation, their idiom and their dreams, are headed in a feminine direction. A more advanced field of communication, such as telepathy, is also a phenomenon which can only be developed in a highly feminine climate. The problem is that feminine tendency in the society has never been given a chance to blossom, whereas masculine tendency overwhelms it.

What we need now is the patience and natural wisdom of a pregnant woman, an awareness and acceptance of our natural resources, or what is left of them. Let's not kid ourselves and think of ourselves as an old and matured civilization. We are by no means mature. But that is alright. That is beautiful. Let's slow down and try to grow as organically, and healthfully as a newborn infant. The aim of the female revolution will have to be a total one, eventually making it a revolution for the whole world. As mothers of the tribe, we share the guilt of the male chauvinists, and our faces are their mirrors as well. It's good to start now, since it's never too late to start from the start.

Abridged version:
New York Times, February 1972
Unabridged version:
Sundance Magazine, May 1972

Opposite: Newsclipping of Presidents Nixon and Pompidou with handwritten annotation by Yoko: '...But...can they type?' Below: 'But can she type?' – a 1970s feminist poster calling attention to gender stereotypes and sexism in the workplace. It featured Golda Meir (1898–1978), the prime minister of Israel (1969–74), the first female head of government in the Middle East, and the fourth elected female head of government or state in the world.

Pages 158–59: Guests of co-founder Gloria Steinem, John & Yoko photographed at *Ms.* magazine's first birthday party aboard the Circle Line tour boat *Ms Liberty*, Hudson River, New York, 26 June 1973.

But can she type?

Seattle-King County National Organization for Women

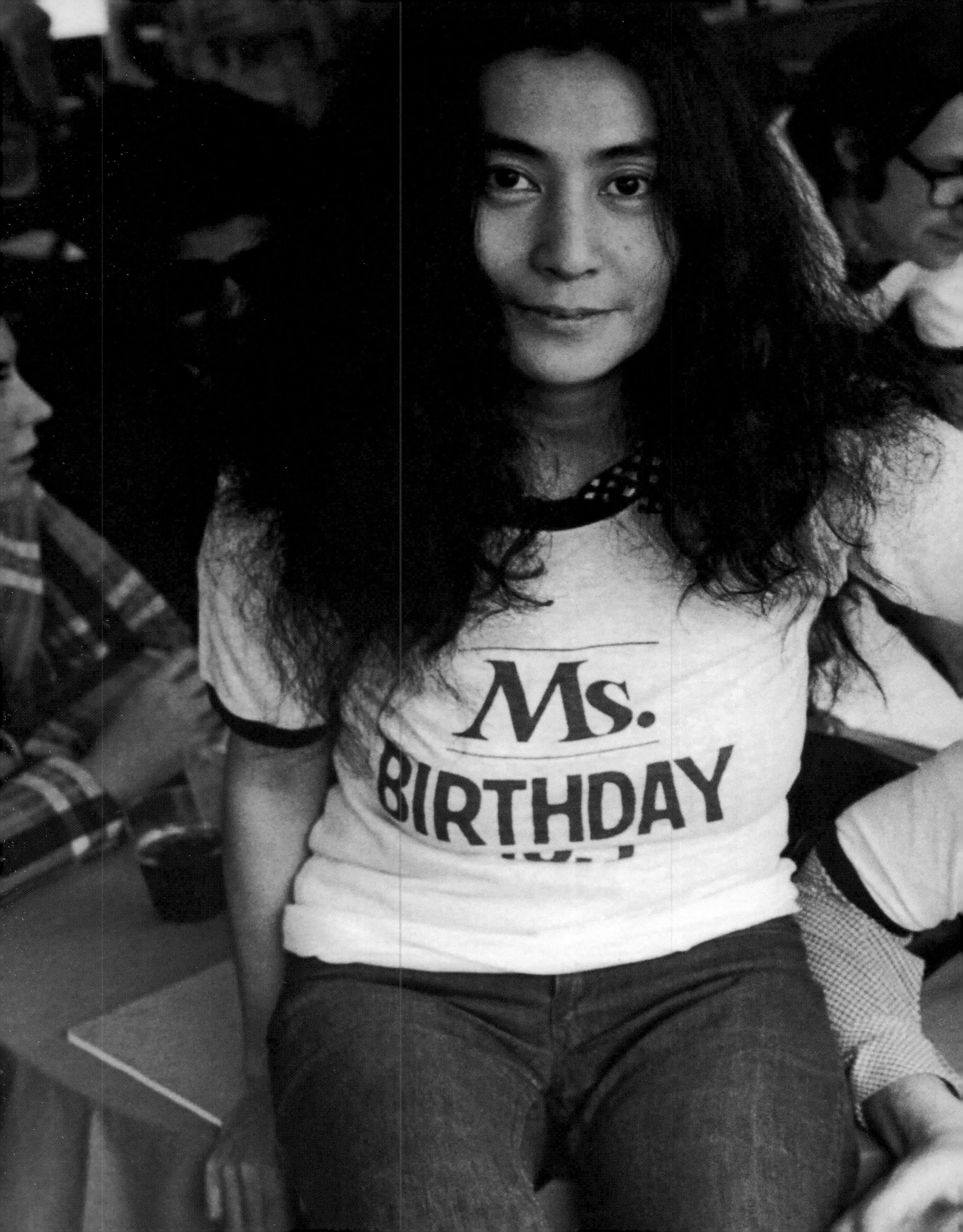
Ms.
BIRTHDAY

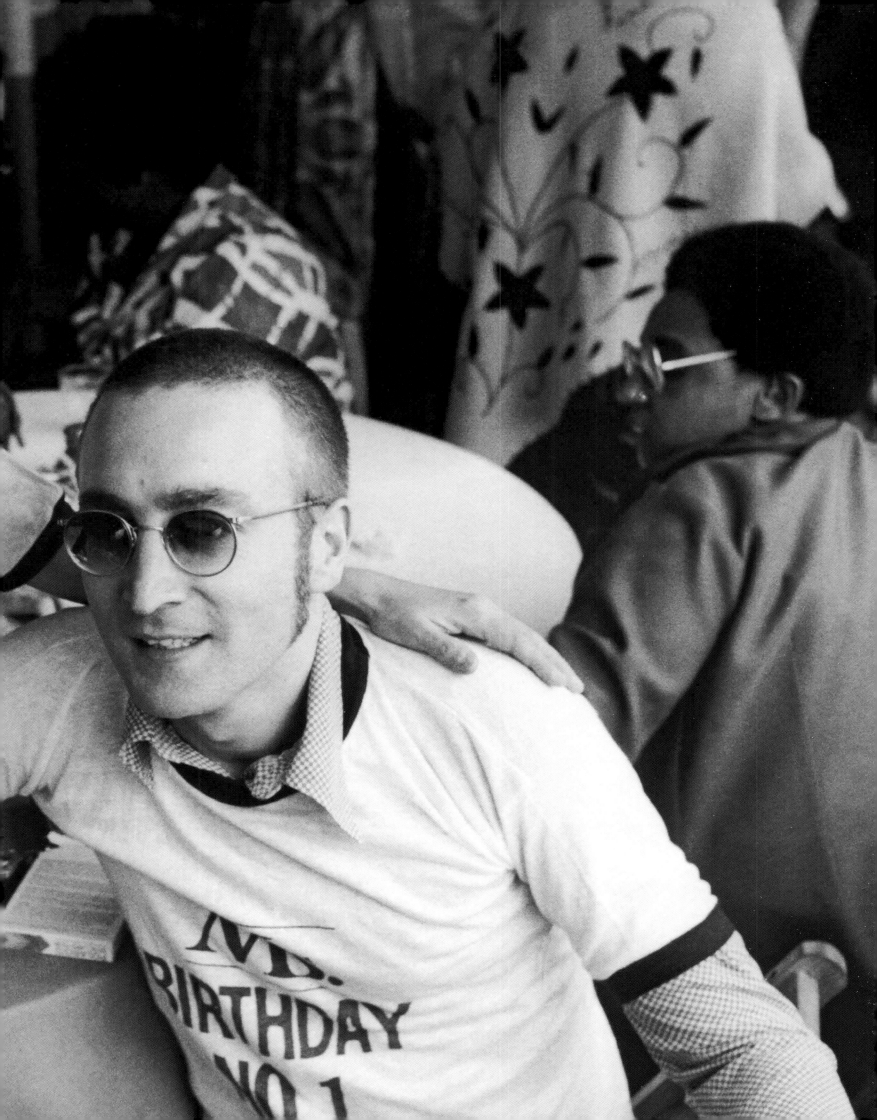

But Can He Type?

Yoko: In May 1973 we moved into the Dakota building. Some of the sisters from the conference visited us in our new apartment – Berit and Bitten from Norway. I mean, it was the days when all the women complained – you know, Jerry Rubin is very radical, Abbie's radical, but they all wanted the women to type their thesis or articles.

John: With the Jerry Rubins and the Tariq Alis and that, we'd always comment to them, and after they'd left, 'Well, where's the women?'

Where's the women running *Red Mole*? Where's the women socialists? Where's the women left wingers? Where's the women in on the meeting about how they're going to overthrow the government or whatever the hell they were talking about? They're all going to liberate the world, but they're all doing the typing and making the coffee. Come on, this is garbage. It took us time to see through it all.

Yoko: And John was saying, 'Look, I'm going to learn typing.' And Bitten said, 'I can teach you how to type.' And she came here and taught him how to type.

So John said he would be playing with his new found toy, the typewriter, while I made the *Feeling The Space* album – and he did – it was the beginning of *Skywriting by Word of Mouth*.

He got really into typing and he wrote some interesting, artsy prose with James Joycean wordplay, puns, using typing mistakes, or, you know, just going 'x x x' and then suddenly writing.

And he was sending letters out to people. I would come home and he would say, 'Look at this! I wrote this thing. How do you like it?' and all that. And it was just a very, sort of, peaceful time.

In the course of making *Feeling The Space* I cherished my own space.

I hadn't realized how much I missed being alone. It was good to work alone. When I came home, John used to read me funny letters and little word games that he had written while I was out. Every day I would bring back a cassette of what I had done that day and play it for him. He would comment on it.

He started to say he wanted to play on a couple of my songs. 'You should call me in when you're ready, just like you would call in a session guitarist and I'd come and play.' I knew that I could not get a better guitarist than John so he did an overdub guitar on 'Woman Power' and 'She Hits Back' that afternoon.

One day I came home and heard John playing a beautiful song which was later to become 'Steel And Glass'. 'It's great that you're doing this [recording] because now I feel like I want to go in and make mine,' he said. After *Feeling The Space* was done, John went into the studio and made *Mind Games* with the same session musicians. He did not want to go alone so I was there with him.

A journalist described the way I was living in the Dakota with virtually no furniture as if it was an artist's loft. Well, I was an artist. And, because of my extreme pride, which was accelerated by the fact that I was married to a rich man, I had been driven to an extreme minimalism in terms of living conditions.

John and I used to say that our apartment at the Dakota is a conceptual monastery, just for the two of us. When we go out of the Dakota, we get so many people communicating with us, so it's very important that we had silence and quietness. The apartment is a very small space compared to the world, and we needed that for our peace of mind.

I could not bring myself to buy furniture like a middle-class housewife. Therefore, we had a kitchen table, a working table and a bed. That was about it. When I read the article I had to laugh. Yes it was true. I was still visualizing myself as that young artist who lived in a downtown loft doing my own thing.

John and I were very similar that way. John would be equally frightened by the thought of becoming middle class. In our minds we associated that vaguely with getting old, though it didn't necessarily have to mean that. This was the seventies. It was a different age.

I went out to Columbus Avenue and started to shop for bric-a-brac to make the apartment more homelike. I cannot be acting like a jailbird in solitary confinement. I have to learn to have friends and invite them to a comfortable place that they can enjoy.

I looked at myself and realized that I was wearing jeans and a black sweater. I should change this too, I thought. And I bought some dresses that I could live with, a few trinkets.

Through the effort of establishing my mental balance and doing what I could, as a person in my position at the time, I finally felt that a lot of things became right in my life. I was doing my work. I was helping others. And I even had decorated my apartment to a point where it was presentable. I even liked the way I looked in my new image wearing long art deco dresses and a silly hat.

There was one room that I had decorated the way John would have liked. It was a bit jazzier than the other rooms, with mostly black things – black furniture, black carpet and white walls. For meditation or reading or whatever. I put his favourite typewriter in there too. He was very happy about that.

Pages 160–61: John employing his typewriting skills at Lou Adler's house, 800 Stone Canyon Road, Bel Air, California, 14 November 1973.

Below: 'This Could Be the Start of Something, Pig', written and typewritten by John, 10 May 1973.
Pages 164–65: 'A Tale of Two Titties', perhaps the sequel to 'Wonsaponatime', May 1973.

This Could Be The Start of Something, Pig

I always thought the highlight of my career as a Rock-n-Roll Reviewer, was cleaning Chick Jagger's pants after he had come all the way from england to score some goals. Was I wrong! Yes, I was! I've seen it all, but was not prepared for the oral roberts I was going to get from the Alice Pudding/ Pudding Alice; It's Only A Normal Thing Show! My was I horny as I watched him snake thru the greatest rock and roll heavy happening event type THEATRICKLE awe inspiring completely spontaneously rehearsed phsycadyllic horrorshow brotherly hate type lighthouse helen heady heavenly blissfull teenage trousers set yer mom on fire ridiculously simply entitled four letter nippled positively nineteen seventy three with overt tones of early masochismo de/slade errogeniusly zone deaf ambiguously bi/sickle celled anemick wonderfully co/ordinary run of the mills brother you should have been there to beleaving your mind that dog if you know watts good for tuna fish sandwitched betweeny boppers and buddy holly did I have one helluva good boy when I got home and realiza minnelliphants mammery in between thirty fourth street and rob dylatant at his best, not to mention those self indulgentlemen who split write before my eyes before we gave them permission impossible and even if they did get back to back again like we did last summer who'd want to know anyway you want me that's how I will be.....he....he.

Next week I'll be sucking you in all the old familiar places, until then keep yerroxoffthegrass, get the kinks outya hair, and long may you rainbow,

Mel Torment.

P.S. Jam Whenna is always IN THE PINK when in the BIG APPLE. (source).......

© Copycat JOHN LENNON
May 10, 1973

abcdefghijklmnopqrstuvwxyz

A TAIL OF TWO TITTIES.

Oncne upon a womb,in a farout land,way beyond the call of duty,there lived

Two Titties,called Fred and Ada.they hadapad in the center of the universe

overlooking Central Fish and the Poor;but being yang,jaded,and blank they sau

ght THE ANSWER TO LIFE,which was a full time ocupation.Liberal did they

know what strange admen awaited themas theystruggled onward ever onward

towards a HIGHER SELF(as advocado by Renta Davies,the well knownradicule.)

They had heard a rumortis that a 3 yr old tibetan,

from O.T.B. ("one at a time boys") was coming/had come was about to be

having had cme to the west to "put them straight about not eating horses."

Also he was aparently jesuS,or a close relatively harmless yong dude

with an apptitude for DIVINE RIGHTS.Any way 3 weeks with WOPBOPALOOMAH,

(WOP to his admirers) and one was INCLINED TO KNOW EVERYTHING,or at worst,

MOST OF IT.Now Fed and Radar were always looking for a/thier match,wasnt*t

everybodyquestion mark.This fast growling rumorgue was geting under their ski

ns,itching for knowledge as it were,thirsting for the Lip of the Gods.

Suddennly theyre not half the man they usedacar theres a shithouse hanging

over me,oh i beiling you now sir.(beileave in chesterfields.)Why, she,had

a go,i dont know,she wooden leg .

When asked why he smoked 60 cigarettettes ad

y the RIGHT HOLY BAMALAMA said "I know what i like", which got

a look of knowledge from his fellowers.one well known former radicule who sh

ll remain faceless to prtect the identity of his crisis ,said I was in

Hindia with RAMALAMADINGDONG and he blinded me with a sudden flash of

light,i coudnt believe my eyes,are the eyes,of a woman in bed,and o how

they give me away.""From then on iNEW that He wasnt just another starving

Hindulooking for a ficks,becuase as i lay there these FLYING FROGS kept singing"La viende rare supreme"which ruffly handled means,'This Way',and you

know,they were right, i never looked back in fact i couldnt see a thing i was

so full of the rites of spring.

                Well you can unnerstan how this news affectated

Red und Frada...they were hysteriuos with inquiry ,they imediately backed

their pags and were orf on another adventure which we*ll get to sometime

in de future if not sooner you than me boy.Until next time this is your old pal

Egnog signig of with a miracle of modern scifi.

        hope your coming soon,

                  to the Isle of Pras(in the springbok)

           effectively,

                Kaptain Kundalini.

                        May.73.be with you.

As Good As Swimming
by Berit Ås

In 1973 there was a terrible tumult for me in Norway. I had been suspended from the Labour Party and became leader of a new small political party of democratic socialists, over a difficult political issue. Then came an invitation from America, from the National Organization for Women, to the First International Feminist Planning Conference. They had come across an article that I had written in the sixties about the strong invisible women's culture that men are so dependent on, but which they actually understand nothing about. For some reason, the American women had picked up on this and asked me to give a lecture on the same subject.

I went with the journalist and New Feminist Bitten Modal. The conference mainly consisted of lectures and conversations. There were all sorts of women who told stories about the countries they came from. Both Kate Millett and Gloria Steinem were there, with whom I later wrote a paper in 1974 to present at the UN Women's Conference in Mexico in 1975. I also met Robin Morgan.

It was at the conference that we also met Yoko Ono and her husband John Lennon, who together with three others recorded all the lectures on tape. When the conference was over,

the two of us were invited to join them at their Dakota apartment in New York and listen to the tapes so that I could get the transcripts. I told him that Bitten could type it out, as she could 'touch type'. John asked if she could teach him.

It was terribly hot. John & Yoko had rented the apartment in the winter and they had taken away the big air conditioner that blocked the view of one of their windows. Now it was June and terribly hot! In the street outside, the children had opened the fire hydrants and were running lightly clothed or almost naked through the cooling jets of water. In the apartment, some other guests walked wrapped in wet sheets. To cool off, they dipped the sheets in a bathtub filled with water and ice cubes.

We were quite surprised when we got to the apartment because there was only one chair. And on that chair sat the secretary who answered the phone with, 'No they are unfortunately not at home,' 'No they are unfortunately not at home' – and finally we realized that they were very much in demand. Otherwise, everyone else sat on mattresses on the floor or in the kitchen where we were served raw fish. I remember Bitten sitting down and teaching John how to touch type.

I slept in a room full of glass cases and drawers filled with beautiful dresses, suits, trousers, shoes and glasses. There were a great many headdresses and jewelry. But the hostess herself walked around in cut-off jeans and was by no means adorned with jewelry and only wore one of the many pairs of sunglasses that were also on display.

What kind of person was she? I felt there was more to her than I was able to detect at the time. Eventually I learned that she was the daughter of one of Japan's richest men. I tried to talk to her a bit about whether she might think that she was a bit in

Lennon's shadow? Perhaps she was also exposed to what many women become, who are with famous men? I later learned what a great artist she was. At that time, I wrote poems in newspapers in Denmark, Sweden and Norway to earn some money. They weren't world literature, but at least I was able to sell them. So, I mentioned it to Yoko and she said, yes, I also write poetry and here is one of mine. She gave me a copy of *Grapefruit*, a collection of her poems, with a dedication in it. I promised to talk about it in Norway.

My children were angry when I came home with it. 'Didn't I even get a signature from John Lennon? What kind of fool was I to not know the Beatles?' In retrospect, I have often thought that she was worth much more than just being 'John Lennon's wife'.

John and I didn't talk about anything other than everyday things that you talk about when you live together somewhere. Then suddenly they were going travelling. They asked if Bitten and I could look after the house. We did so with pleasure, and we had time to look around more. I remember we found an exhibition room. Eventually I began to understand something more about her artistic ambitions.

The exhibition room was a white-painted room where all objects were divided in two: a divan split in the middle so that it became a narrow shelf. A half-telescope mounted on a half-stand. And the stove? It was also split in two. And then there were several half-objects. But the most beautiful was the bed, which was in another room. It was not split but made of beautiful wood material, including a built-in radio. It was as if it were singing, 'Make Love, Not War!'

One could live in that bed. I decided that I would sleep in this great bed one night while we were babysitting their house.

Below: Typewritten letter from John to Bitten Modal, 24 July 1973.
Pages 168–69: 'On Being Inclined But Not Having the Wherewithal'
and letter to R. P. Bagguley, *Sun Time*, 27 May 1973.
Pages 170–71: Letters to and from Elliot Mintz, June 1973.

```
                                                       I.W.72.stapt.72.ny ny.I0023

                                                 julightfull
                                                    24?

       dear bit͡ĉn  !                                       I973.

              yes its me typing!pretty good huh?how are you and your norway?n.y. is still b

eutiful;very hot;ive been typing  letters to every one i know,even if i dont know them!!

its as good as swimming!!i type something,and then decide who to send it to...!(not always

but often).thanks for the final shove.we went to gloria steinems M.S. birthday party,met h

er,breifly,she was very nice to us both.its a tough scene;

                         how is NORWOMENs moving?are you s

                         still buzzing from cambridge?i thought id change

                         the size of the page,o what fun!there is a black

                         friend of ours gonna be hung in trinidad,with the

                         'help' of the british,how about writing to their

                         embassy in norway,it might help save his life.?!

it would give them the feeling THE WHOLE WORLD IS WATCHING;kate millets been helping in lond

on (oxford universtile),and here in u.s.michael x is his name,and his trial was 'fixed.he ma

y or may not have done what they say he has,but its no reason to kill him,they hounded him o

ut of britain,and he went back home(trnd),eric williams P.M.of trinidad didnt want nomuslim

black power typs causing trouble in 'his little (touris)t paridise..'anyway were all writing

like mad ,wher thers a will theres relatives.

                   as you can see,the typing aint perfect,but im always in to much of

a hurry to bother with correct spellings /grammer or whatever.as long as the message isCLEAR

                   lots of love to you and yours from ustwo;

                         johnyoko.

ps say high to 𝘉𝘦𝘳𝘪𝘵 if/when you see her.
```

ON BEING INCLINED,BUT NOT HAVING THE WHEREWITALL.
_____

MANY ARE THE APROACHES,YEA MANIFOLD,TO WIT YOUR HUMBLE SERVANT IS BEQUESTED,NAY

BESEECHED TO,AMONGST OTHER MORE PRESSING THINGS ,"save the world,with a concert,

or a small donation of aproximately 100,000."AND"by the way,you must know SIMPLY

EVERYBODY in the business,coudnt you just CALL THEM ALL ON THE PHONE? plus,"of

course,we know nothing about rock concerts,thats YOUR BUSINEES,we*re just VERY

SINCERE PEOPLE,looking for a way to promote our cause."

and brothers and sisters,do not think it is SO SIMPLE,and why must we always follow

the path of THOSE WHO HAVE GONE BEFORE,have we no MINDS OF OUR OWN?,is tomorrow

just an INSTANT REPLAY of days gone by? these and other questions must be answered.

1.the artist.KNOW NOTHING FROM PUTING ON THES THINGS*

@.the money.THE HORSE KNOWS NOTHING FROM THE O.T.B.hexxxhexgeksxhayxandxroofx

$.the taxman cometh and turn one into an mickey rooney /joe louis.to work for

greys is bad enough, but to work for debts is anHELL.

so beleive not your potted dreams,scheme not from what you*ve read,

think hard before you make amove,and USE YOUR FUCKING HEAD...................._...

                    yors in spirit of themselves,

                              those two,

6th June 1973

R. P. Bagguley: Sun Time, May 27, 1973

Re: Reading

Instead of blaming or competing with T.V. - as if it wasn't run by people,
why not use it - it is an instrument. How do you expect children who
have - EXPERIENCED - T.V. to be interested in 'old nursery rhymes' ?!
(which aren't exactly 20th century english.) American Public Televisions'
Sesame Street is teaching children to read - they use jingles in a positive
way - with music as the 'mind bait', just as the old nursery rhymes did.
"TRY IT, YOU'LL LIKE IT." (Alka Seltzer ad.)

JOHN LENNON

N.Y.C.

dear elliot,

      as you can see.I'm learning to type.you ars receiving a letter.

I am writing it.That makes two of us.anyway que pasa ?as they say in

prison.I see SAL did it again!we might be down your way soon for the

dykes balls.meaning yoko id going to prison.(to perform)aI will be s

upporting her like a bra,(but not as a master musiker),meanimg I.ll

be hanging around looking serious with me portapak video which reveals

ALL.(beware the lennon)I wonder if one has freudian slips on a typeweiter?

Iwonder if one has freydian lips on an afghan hound?all thede questiond

and more will be answered a somertime in the future.(which is judt around

the corner.)

      Yoko has just woken up.someone has stopped practising in

ca central park.thesw two things happened at the same time.upi.you will

inf undwer stand the deeper meaning behind thedsw two appwarantly yyu

unrelated occurances,.The massage is simple,

      que sera aaaa"!

         youxxinkexedxx

         your interesting friead,

            j.f .lennonononono.

            (jog)john.

ps. im having a ps. because i'm enjoying himself.;

nb.i'mlooking over the l park.pweople aerd rowing,trees aeare greening.

for me am muy gal.

Mr. Elliot Mintz
8522 Oak Court
Los Angeles, Calif. 90046

File: Mintz

Mr. John Lennon
The Dakota
I West 72nd Street
New York City

PERSONAL   AIR MAIL

25 June '73

Dear John;

Received your letter today. Your typing is coming

along quite nicely. But the real way to do it is

without looking at the keys. I'm not looking at my

keys and see how perfectly this is coming out......

What is this about you and Yoko coming out here to

go to prison ??????? How long will you stay ?

Maybe I should go out and start looking at houses

again. You know how lovely summer at the sea shore

can be and..........and.......

Everything is just fine with me. Ups and downs you

know but mainly stable. The real problem with the

world is that nobody takes any chances anymore.

Well I must go now to pick up my car.......I'm

having some work done on the door !!!!!!!

All my love to Yoko.

                    your quiet, unassuming, sipping, pal.

                    Elliot 'Ragga' Mintz

C) Dm / / / /   INTUITION.
MY INTENTIONS ARE GOOD,

I USE MY INTUITION _IT TAKES ME FOR A RIDE Am -8

BUT I NEVER UNDERSTOOD

OTHER PEOPLES SUPERSTITION,IT SEEMED LIKE SUICIDE Am

AND AS I PLAY THE GAME OF LIFE

I TRY TO MAKE IT BETTER,EACH AND EVERY DAY Am

AND WHEN I STRUGGLE IN THE DARK NIGHT

THE MAGIC OF THE MUSIC SEEMS TO LIGHT THE WAY!

INTUITION,TAKES ME THERE

INTUITION,TAKES YOU ANYWHERE!

WELL MY INSTINCTS ARE FINE

I HAD TO LEARN TO TRUST THEM,IN ORDER TO SURVIVE.

AND TIME AFTER TIME

CONFIRMED AN OLD SUSPICION,ITS GOOD TO BE ALIVE!

AND WHEN IM DEEP DOWN AND BLUE OUT

AND LOSE COMMUNICATION,WITH NOTHING LEFT TO SAY

ITS THEN I REALIZE

ITS ONLY A CONDITION OF SEEING THINGS THAT WAY!

INTUITION,GETS YOU THERE!

INTUITION,GETS YOU EVERYWHERE!

Solo

my intentions are good......etc

Play 4x's
|: Em / / / | A⁷ / / / | Bm / / / | / . :||

|| Em / / / | A⁷ / / / | 2½ ||

| Em / / / | A⁷ / / / | D / C# B | A / / |

Play 2x's
|: Em / / / | A⁷ / / / | Bm / / / | / . :||

|| Em / / / | A⁷ / / | 2½ |

| Em / / / | A⁷ / / / |: D / C# B | A / / / :|

Play 2x's
|: Em / / / | A⁷ / / / | Bm / / / | / . :||
Ad. infinitum
|: Em / / / | A⁷ / / / :||

INTUITION

Hey, hey, hey. Alright
Hey, hey, hey. Alright

My intentions are good
I use my intuition
It takes me for a ride
But I never understood
Other people's superstitions
It seemed like suicide

And as I play the game of life
I try to make it better each and every day
And when I struggle in the night
The magic of the music
Seems to light the way

Ahh
Intuition takes me there
Intuition takes me everywhere

Well my instincts are fine
I had to learn to use them
In order to survive
And time after time
Confirmed an old suspicion
It's good to be alive

And when I'm deep down and out
And lose communication
With nothing left to say
It's then I realize it's only a condition
Of seeing things that way

Ahh
Intuition takes me there
Intuition takes me anywhere

Takes me anywhere
Alright

Ahh
Intuition takes me there
Intuition takes me there

Intuition takes me there
Intuition takes me there

Intuition takes me there
Intuition takes me there

Intuition

INTUITION

John: I have a good intuition, which has saved me from many a disaster.

I was talking to myself really. I was a bit confused then, and I was thinking, 'Well, I'll just have to rely on my intuition to get out of this confusion.' Well it didn't work, did it? Eventually I had to get away from the music [in 1975] to get some light into my life!

I always took the songs personally, whether it was 'In My Life' or 'Help!'. To me, I always meant it. I always wrote about myself. Very few of the completely Lennon songs weren't in the first person. I'm a first-person journalist. I find it hard, though I occasionally do it, to write about, you know, 'Freddie went up the mountain and Freddie came back.' And even that is really about yourself.

Some Time In New York City was done in a different way. It wasn't a planned album. It was just that at that period people were asking for songs. Someone suggested I write a song about John Sinclair, then someone asked for something for Angela Davis. So what I was doing in a sense was being commissioned to write songs about certain people. Yoko and I did it together and it was about other people. It wasn't about me. That's the difference.

I'm going through a change. It seems like little parts of me are left over from the 'New York City' period, if you could call it a period, and half sort-of thinking about where I am now.

I never have a lot [of songs] left over. I have some left over that I occasionally forget, and then remember them, and just use bits of them. I just scribble on a bit of paper. And then leave it in a sort of pile. And when it begins to be more interesting, I venture on to the typewriter and type it out. And the typewriter adds things, too. I change it as I type it. It's usually the third draft when I get to the typewriter. Depending on how easy it came. If it just all came it's just like 'write it and type it'. But if it's a general song, I'll type it a few more times. But the final version is never until we've recorded it. I always change a word or two, at the last minute.

Lyrics first, then the music. Usually. It's better. I like that. The music is sort of easy. I sometimes envy Elton John. Bernie Taupin sends him a big stack of words, and he writes all the songs in five days. I could do that. But I am too egocentric to use other people's words. That's the problem. So it's my own fault. I still like black music, disco music…'Shame, Shame, Shame' or 'Rock Your Baby', I'd give my eyetooth to have written that. But I never could. I am too literal to write 'Rock Your Baby'. I wish I could. I'm too intellectual, even though I'm not really an intellectual. I feel as though I am a writer, really. And the music is easy. The music is just all over the place.

I have the ability to cry if I am upset or feel something deeply. Therapy was valuable to me and useful to get it out of my system, instead of bottling it up the way I used to. I'm not saying I'm not neurotic anymore but I can handle it better and I don't need to get ulcers and a heart attack. If I'm at a sad movie I'll cry. Women cry, but men are not supposed to show their emotions.

I'm a survivor. My instinct is to survive and I came through everything – Beatlemania, the Maharishi, therapy, American immigration – it's all water off a duck's back and I put it down to experience.

Part of [the therapy with Janov] was not to self-control yourself, in any way. That included anything so I would just eat and eat and eat. And it was all very well for the mind, but for the body it was terrible. But the idea was, 'Well, I am an artist, not a model, so fuck it.' I wonder who I try to please? It was me I was trying to please, I found out; too late, after I'd got about five million pounds. And I wore the same clothes for two years. I had two things: a jumpsuit – not a fashionable one; one you get to do the plumbing in. I had two of them. And that's all I wore for almost two years. In the middle of the Janov thing I got fat as hell. I was living on chocolate and Dr Pepper. I mean, Janov was an idiot, but he was not bad. His therapy was good. It was just he was a pain in the neck. So I got big and I wore the same clothes. I got used to it. I didn't feel terrible about it, but I didn't enjoy it. I was a slob.

I was in the therapy with Yoko, and we both were as fat as hell. And in the dark it feels great. We both would roll around…. It's when you wanna go somewhere else, or when someone else sees you, that you are conscious of it.

Sometimes I don't like dressing up. And I don't dress up for months, or almost a year. Just wear a T-shirt and jeans. And someday I just get an urge to get dressed. And then you can't wear anything – nothing looks good, nothing… you always look like an asshole.

The two books I wrote in my twenties I started writing as children's books. But something nasty would happen in the story that would make it not child-like. I'm always in that frame of mind – 'Once upon a time…' – that's where I'm at. I'm still in Alice in Wonderland. But something nasty would happen in the story, though I never planned them. I always do them free form. But that's another thing I would like to do when I'm older, you know. Sit on a mountainside and write children's books.

Oh, I can't wait. I'm looking forward to it. Being old, yeah. I mean I can wait, I don't have the dread of it. I mean if I'm

Portrait of John standing next to an empty chair, photographed by Michael Brennan at Lou Adler's house, 800 Stone Canyon Road, Bel Air, California, 14 November 1973.

Notes on yellow notepad in John's handwriting, 1972.

healthy and all that and there's no pain. I think it's great. Yoko and I'll be sitting in a nice cottage in New England either looking through our press clippings or writing stories for children. I'd like it to look a little like Scotland or Ireland or Cornwall, but still have twenty-four channels for New York within an hour or two hours. Well, at sixty-four, who's going to care about how many hours away we are?

I'm not stopping. That's a myth about slowing down and becoming senile. That's bullshit. I know lots of old people who are really swingers. It just depends on how you think about it. It's like all your friends when you left school, you know the ones who took a bank job. They passed all the exams. Well, they all turned into thirty-year-olds by the time they were twenty-one. I ain't twenty-one yet. There's no doubt about it. I'm not going to miss anything. I don't want to be regretting anything. Do it all once. That's my motto, at least once.

I reckoned Klein was alright because of the Stones. I thought Mick was together – see, this is the fallacy. Everyone always thinks everyone else is together. You're either together yourself or forget it. I remember asking Mick what Klein was like, and he said, 'He's alright, but it's hard to get your hands on the money.' And even though my instincts were screaming, my intellect thought: that must mean that he doesn't allow you to waste it or spend it, maybe that's good.

It's a hard thing to learn after being programmed for life not to use your instincts. Women use them a bit more than men – you're allowed. One benefit you got from slavery was that you were emotional…that's cool. But men were supposed to make decisions on reason and intellect, so it interfered with your instinct. But my instinct is what has always saved me from lots of dragons.

Yoko: If you want something, wish for it; if you don't get it, it's because part of you is resisting, possibly for your own good.

John: Many, if not all, great men and women were 'mystics' in a sense: Einstein, who at the end of his life remarked that if he had to do it over, he would have spent more time on the spiritual; Pythagoras and Newton were mystics. In order to receive the 'wholly spirit', i.e. creative inspiration (whether you are labelled an artist, scientist, mystic, psychic, etc.), the main 'problem' was emptying the mind. You can't paint a picture on dirty paper; you need a clean sheet. Van Gogh's 'going crazy', Dylan Thomas's 'drinking himself to death', etc., were just efforts on their behalf to break out of the straitjacket of their own minds. I include myself and my generation's so-called 'drug abuse'. Self-abuse would be a more apt expression.

John: Dick Gregory gave Yoko and me a little kind of prayer book – *The Game of Life and How to Play It*, by Florence Scovel Shinn. It is in the Christian idiom, but you can apply it anywhere. It is the concept of positive prayer. If you want to get a car, get the car keys. Get it? If you can imagine a world at peace, then it can be true.

Yoko: You should find how to play the game of life. It can be a very serious game but it is a game. Find out how you would play it. However you do it, do it well. I enjoy getting up in the morning and looking from my window I see the delicate change of weather. Every season is so beautiful. Seeing that first thing in the morning lets me know how lucky I am! And then I learn all day. It shows to me how little I know. And how much I still have to learn. That is an action that is not open handed, beautiful and joyous like looking over from my window and seeing the beautiful sky. It humbles you to realize there is so much you don't know. But at the same time, it gives me a great feeling that I am learning. Learning the game of life. There is no such thing as the 'other side'. It's all what you are creating in your head to play the game of life as such. We are on the same side. All of us, and always.

OUT THE BLUE:

(1) EVERY DAY I THANK THE LORD AND LADY

FOR THE ~~DAY~~ *way* YOU CAME INTO MY LIFE

ANYWAY IT HAD TO BE:TWO MINDS ONE DESTINY°

OUT THE BLUEetc...

(2) ALL MY LIFES BEEN A LONG SLOW KNIFE

I WAS BORN JUST TO GET TO YOU°

ANYWAY I SURVIVED LONG ENOUGH TO MAKE YOU MY WIFE:

OUT THE BLUE etc..

         (1) OUT THE BLUE YOU CAME TO ME

             AND BLUE AWAY MY MISERY

             OUT THE BLUE LIFES ENERGY

             OUT THE BLUE YOU CAME TO ME.

(2) out the blue

(3) Like a U.F.O

OUT THE BLUE

Out the blue you came to me
And blew away life's misery
Out the blue life's energy
Out the blue you came to me

Every day I thank the Lord and Lady
For the way that you came to me
Anyway it had to be two minds one destiny

Out the blue you came to me
And blew away life's misery
Out the blue life's energy
Out the blue you came to me

All my life has been a long slow knife
I was born just to get to you
Anyway I survived long enough to make you my wife

Out the blue you came to me
And blew away life's misery
Out the blue life's energy
Out the blue you came to me

Like a UFO you came to me
And blew away life's misery
Out the blue life's energy
Out the blue you came to me

OUT THE BLUE

John: I remember a beautiful acid trip in Ireland in the pre-Maharshiti period when I ended up in the bathroom of some hotel for six hours or so (it was the only room in which one could be al/one).

Anyway I 'discovered' 'myself' in the mirror...apart from finding out what the Temple on the side of the forehead is, I discovered eyes (I/s)...before that I always looked them in the mouth, so to speak!

After using any word that took my fancy as a 'mantra'...Jesus for one...Bridget...for another...I changed the 'mirrored' reflection of myself and the small bathroom into a giant Taj Mahal...the bridge of my nose dissolving and becoming marble pillars of the Temple....

Well to cut a long trip short I finally re/cognized (dis/covered) MYSELF. I turned in/out to be a SHIMMERING BLUE ENERGY...sort of like the filament in a light bulb...a 'soul' which was 'occupying' this 'body'...the shock of recognition was a beautiful 'revelation'!!

I found I could get 'higher' and 'higher' by 'focusing' on the eyes until they drifted into ONE...take a deep breath and go up to the 'next' floor then back to two eyes, then one ($\triangle$) ← the w/holey trinity)...it was exhausting but fantastic!

The other trippers (in the bedroom)...thought I was having a 'bad trip'. I was making either too much (crying/talking) noise or not enough.

The thing that brought this to mind was that I was recently re-reading some Wilhelm Reich and came across his 'explanation' of his Orgone (cosmic) energy...the colour was blue! (I forgot to say how dark...not navy...but DEEP 'ELECTRIC' BLUE.)

Later on when I was 'taught' to meditate...I noticed this same colour was evident at certain 'levels' of the mind on the 'way down'. Usually after the first minute or two.

'Out the Blue you came to me and blue away life's misery...' *Mind Games* circa seventies.

By the way...I never met ANYONE who even heard of anyone jumping out of windows on acid...not until the suggestion was 'planted' in the media...I got that info from the government...remember *The Consumer Guide to Drugs?*...that thing set up by Nexxon...which they didn't like 'cause the findings didn't agree with their own nightmares....

Anyway it got pretty hard to get Realacid, 'they' were mixing it with all kinds of shit...think about it...the stuff was doing

a GOOD JOB...then 'all of a sudden'...anyway it's easier to deal with ORGANIC 'ACID'. I.E. PEYOTE...MUSHROOMS...oh yeh...what about the CIA making that guy jump out of the window...in the FIFTIES...so that's the story Gerry....

We 'abused' the gift...and it hit us in the head in the form of paranoia/fear...helped along by International Patriots, etc., etc.... Well I for one have learned that lesson well, Jeeze if I don't look out I'll end up like Donald Sutherland and all the other 'nouveau butch' 'hard drinking' 'men o' the world'...you know...the ones that wanna replace Errol Flynn/Bogart/Tracy...and drink themselves to death? I'd sooner go out like Huxley....

There are still a lotta HEADS, new and old...who keep it cool. LONG LIVE THE R/EVOLTION. And up yours cynic slaves of the imaginary masters. Oh yeh...at the end of the Bathroom Revelations I 'took' my friends 'up'...using only my own energy (at first) all they had to do was trust me, look me in the eyes...and bob's yer uncle hope!

Of course it got better when we did it in UNI/SUN...HEADS TWOGETHER...BREATHING TWOGETHER...Two heads are better than one...even when they're your OWN!!!

∴ ∵ ∴

...there's so much going on around here...anyway, now it gets a bit dramatic...somehow...or other...I find I've now lost one pants leg (I'm still wearing them) apart from the shoes and socks, etc...it's a grey flannel pair...this sems to be the straw that broke the camel's hump...I break down and cry...I'm completely exhausted, exsacperated...humiliated and fucking human...I immediately recognize the feeling...which I had on the Irish acid trip...I gotta ask for help...humbly...and mean it! Well, I mean it alright...'Dear, sweet Christ...get me out of this...' etc., etc.... It only works if you're really at the end of your tether...seems like the only way one 'lets go'...for real.

However it works...it took me to that 'place'...'reality'...'nirvanna'...whatever the fuck it's called.... THAT MOMENT IN 'TIME'/SPACE WHEN YOU SEE AND KNOW EVERYTHING...AND IT IS O-FUCKIN-K....

∴ ∵ ∴

Opposite and pages 184–85: Bob Gruen's contact sheet of John & Yoko on a house-viewing trip with Bob and his wife Nadja, showing them viewing the house, walking in the woods and rowing a dingy in the grounds; Greenwich, Connecticut, 5 January 1973.

John: I keep thinking that people are gonna say to me, 'Why are you writing only about Yoko?' But I write about what's happening at the time. I write love songs because I'm in love.

It's hard to put my finger on. But it's affected my whole being. Yoko's not just a lover and a wife. It's also mentally. She opened a part of my life that wasn't opened. Whether it would have happened without her, I don't know. She changed my life completely. Not just physically. The only way I can describe it is that Yoko was like an acid trip or the first time you got drunk. It was that big a change, and that's just about it. I can't really describe it to this day.

Yoko: Naturally, my life also changed. Mainly what we give each other is energy, because we're both energetic people and when we're in the company of other people who we might feel are less energetic, then we have to give more. For instance, if we're on stage and John is reading a song really good, and I have to come after him, then that means that I've got to do my very best. So then I do a screaming piece or something, and then John does a screaming piece after that, and then he has to top me. That's precisely what was happening during our concert at Madison Square Garden. Many of our close friends noticed we were really sparking off each other.

My life was extremely exciting and we had so much love between us. I'd never had that kind of situation where a guy was putting so much intense attention on me. Maybe other women might have really felt terrible about it. I thought, 'Well, it's nice.' We were so open and we felt so thankful that we had a great life together, so we wanted to be nice to other people too.

John: I was too scared to break away from the Beatles, which I'd been looking to do since we stopped touring. I was vaguely looking for somewhere to go, but didn't have the nerve to really step out into the boat by myself, so I hung around. And when I met Yoko and fell in love: 'My God! This is different than anything before. This is more than a hit record. It's more than gold. It's more than everything!'

Being with Yoko makes me free. Being with Yoko makes me whole. I'm a half without her. Male is half without a female. Before Yoko and I met, we were half a person. There's an old myth about people being half, and the other half being in the sky or in heaven or on the other side of the universe or a mirror image. But we are two halves, and together we're a whole.

Yoko taught me about women. I was used to being served, like Elvis and a lot of the stars were. Always just being

served by women, whether it was my Aunt Mimi, God bless you, or whoever – served by females, wives, girlfriends. You just flop in drunk and expect some girlfriend at college to make the breakfast the next morning. You know she'd been drunk as a dog too, with you at party, but the female is supposed suddenly to get on the other side of the counter. It was quite an experience, and I appreciated what women have done for me all my life. I'd never even thought about it.

Yoko didn't buy that. She didn't give a shit about Beatles: 'What the fuck are the Beatles? I'm Yoko Ono! Treat me as me.' From the day I met her, she demanded equal time, equal space, equal rights. I didn't know what she was talking about. I said, 'What do you want, a contract? You can have whatever you want – but don't expect anything from me, or for me to change in any way.'

'Well,' she said, 'the answer to that is that I can't be here. Because there is no space where you are. Everything revolves around you, and I can't breathe in that atmosphere.'

I'm thankful to her for the education. I was used to a situation where the newspaper was there for me to read, and after I'd read it, somebody else could have it. It didn't occur to me that somebody else might want to look at it first.

I think that's what kills people like Presley and others of that ilk. The king is always killed by his courtiers, not by his enemies. The king is over-fed, over-drugged, over-indulged; anything to keep the king tied to his throne. Most people in that position never wake up. They either die mentally or physically, or both.

And what Yoko did for me was to liberate me from that situation. And that's how the Beatles ended. Not because Yoko split the Beatles, but because she showed me what it was to be Elvis Beatle and to be surrounded by sycophants and slaves who were only interested in keeping the situation as it was. She said to me, 'You've got no clothes on.' Nobody had dared tell me that before.

With us, it's a teacher–pupil relationship. That's what people don't understand. She's the teacher and I'm the pupil. I'm the famous one, I'm supposed to know everything – but she taught me everything I fucking know. The lessons are damned hard and I can't take it sometimes because those lessons are hard. And that's why I'm the one that freaked out.

When we were separate, it was me making an asshole of myself in the clubs and in the newspapers. It wasn't her. Her life was ordered. She missed me as a human being and she loved me, but her life was ordered. I went back to her life, it wasn't the other way around.

ONLY PEOPLE:

ONLY PEOPLE KNOW JUST HOW TO TALK TO PEOPLE

ONLY PEOPLE KNOW JUST HOW TO CHANGE THE WORLD

ONLY PEOPLE REALIZE THE POWER OF PEOPLE

A MILLION HEADS ARE BETTER THAN ONE SO COME ON !

(repeat?)

well i know how we tried and the millions of tears that we cried

but now we are hipper we been thru the trip

and we cant be denied with woman and man side by side

make no mistake its our future were making bake the cake and eat it too!

we dont need no pig brother scene!

ONLY PEOPLE...ETC

well its long over due and there aint nothing better to do

now we are hipper we been thru the trip

we can fly right on thru there's nothing on earth we cant do

fish or cut bait its our future were making all together now pull the chain!

we dont want no pig brother scene!

ONLY PEOPLE ...ETC

ADD TAPE

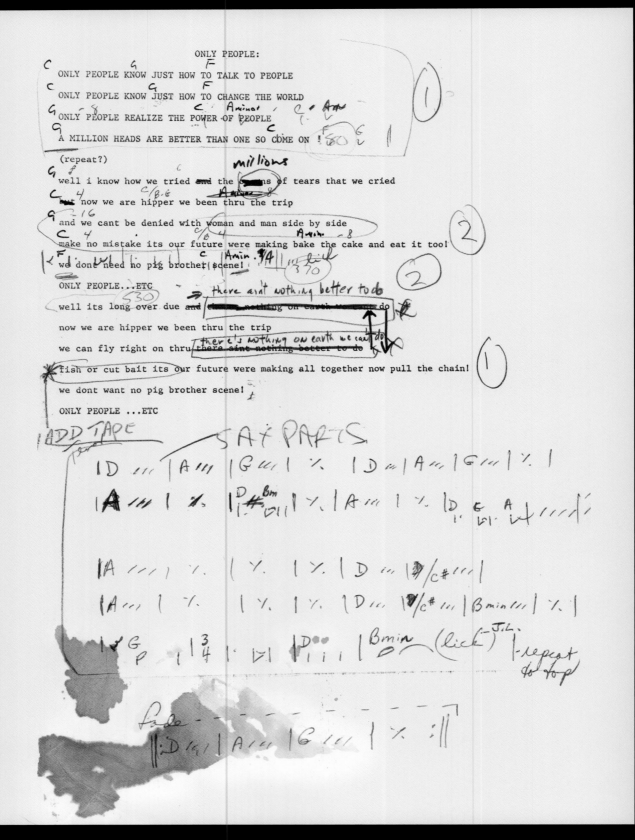

ONLY PEOPLE

Only people know just how to talk to people
Only people know just how to change the world
Only people realize the power of people
A million heads are better than one, so come on, get it on

Well I know how we tried
And the millions of tears that we cried
Now we are hipper we've been thru the trip
And we can't be denied
With woman and man side by side
Make no mistake it's our future we're making
Bake the cake and eat it too
We don't want no pig brother scene

Only people know just how to talk to people
Only people know just how to change the world
Only people realize the power of people
Well a million heads are better than one
So come on, get it on

Well it's long overdue
There ain't nothing better to do
Now we are hipper we've been thru the trip
We can fly right on thru
There's nothing on Earth we can't do
Fish or cut bait it's our future we're making
All together now pull the chain
We don't want no pig brother scene

Hey, alright
Boogie baby, yeah
Let's go, hey, hey, hey, alright
Keep on keeping on
Evey day's a Sunday for a yellow girl
Alright
Keep on keeping on

John & Yoko: Nutopia has no land, no boundaries, no passports, only people.

Yoko: Only people can change the world.

John: The big problems are the only ones to handle! It's no good changing the local post office when the government is the thing responsible for it. We're all responsible for what happens. We don't have to live with ten cars. We don't need those things, but it's no good writing to me and saying, 'Well, you've got them!' Until I, or people like me, change society, I'll work within the framework and try and change it or build around it rather than smash it.

People are believing in projecting their own power, visualizing goals, visualizing positiveness and doing these things that are changing the world. It all takes time, you see. I think the bit about – [in] the sixties we were all full of hope and then everybody got depressed and the seventies were terrible – that attitude that everybody has, that the sixties was therefore negated, for being naive and dumb, and the seventies is really where it's at, which means putting make-up on and dancing in the disco – which was fine for the seventies.

But I don't negate the sixties. I don't negate the seventies. The seeds that were planted in the sixties and possibly they were planted generations before, but the seed, that whatever happened in the sixties, the flowering of that is in the feminist feminization of society, the meditation, the positive learning, that people are doing in all walks of life – that is a direct result of the opening up of the sixties.

Now maybe in the sixties we were naive and like children. Everybody went back to their room and said, 'Well we didn't get the wonderful world of just love and peace and happy chocolate and it wasn't just pretty and beautiful all the time.' And that's what everybody did. We didn't get everything we wanted, we just acted like babies and everybody went back to their rooms and sulked and I'm just gonna play rock 'n' roll and not do anything else, we're gonna stay in our rooms and the world's a nasty, horrible place cause it didn't give us everything we cried for, right?

Crying for it wasn't enough. The thing the sixties did was show us the possibility and the responsibility that we all had. It wasn't the answer, it just gave us a glimpse of the possibility and the seventies everybody's going, 'Na na na,' and possibly in the eighties maybe everybody will say, 'OK, well let's project the positive side of life again,' you know, the world's been going on a long time, right? It's probably gonna go on a long time.

Yoko: But also the sixties was really going out and communicating and expanding, but in the seventies people think that nothing happened. In a way, we went back inside us. [There are] a lot of very interesting magical, psychic things that happened and people got tuned into.

And so with the seventies expansion and seventies knowledge, I think the eighties is going to be another step up. It will be beautiful, you know? We really believe in the message of peace and love, which sounds corny but we do still need peace and we do need love in this world a lot, and to change the world all together with everybody, the people have to change. Nobody else is going to change.

John: Only people can save the world.

Yoko: If we can't solve our own personal problems, we can never solve a big problem. All we have to do is convince one person and if everyone convinces one person, the whole world is going to be convinced, you see? It's that simple.

John: People tend to think that somebody will save them, whether it's a president or whoever you hear it might be – somebody's going to come out to save you. And only people can save us. Only us deciding to do something. Any of us. It's just even making that decision – that 'I want to do something' – is a start.

Yoko: The people that you're really responsible to are the people around you. If you can start to convince people around you, and if we all take care of our friends around us, then the whole world will be fine.

John: Just enough of us. Just everybody that prefers peace – and I know you're a bit cynical and so even while you're cynical, you can still make positive moves. If you're cynical about the clothes you wear, you're still going to wear [them] because [they suit] the job you do, so be cynical but still make a positive move and play the game. Have a game of chess with me and be cynical about chess because it's a game. But let's have the game and let's have some fun and let's work towards something good rather than being cynical and saying, 'I told you [there's going to be] another war,' 'cause that's the choice you have.

We put them in power, man. It's our kids [that] are going to put the next lot in power, if they're not told there's an alternative. Because they're all people. They're only people in government. They're only somebody that we chose. We gave them the responsibility of telling us how many roads we could have, because we're so insecure we don't believe we could manage our own road system. So we have [the attitude of] 'that's his responsibility' and we can blame

John & Yoko speak at the Troops out of SE Asia rally, Times Square, New York, 22 April 1972.

John: Okay! We all know why we're here. It's great that you came in the rain, and I read somewhere that the war movement was over; he-he! We're here to bring the boys home, but let's not forget the machines. Bring the machines home, and then we'll really get somewhere! The people are the only people that can do it.

Whether it's rain, snow, hail, you've got to get that out every time. Right?

Yoko: We have invaded Vietnam long enough. Why don't [we] try to understand them? We have to learn to understand people who speak different language[s] from us.

John: Okay, so basically [leads the crowd in singing], 'All we are saying, is Give Peace a Chance!' Let's hear it in Washington!

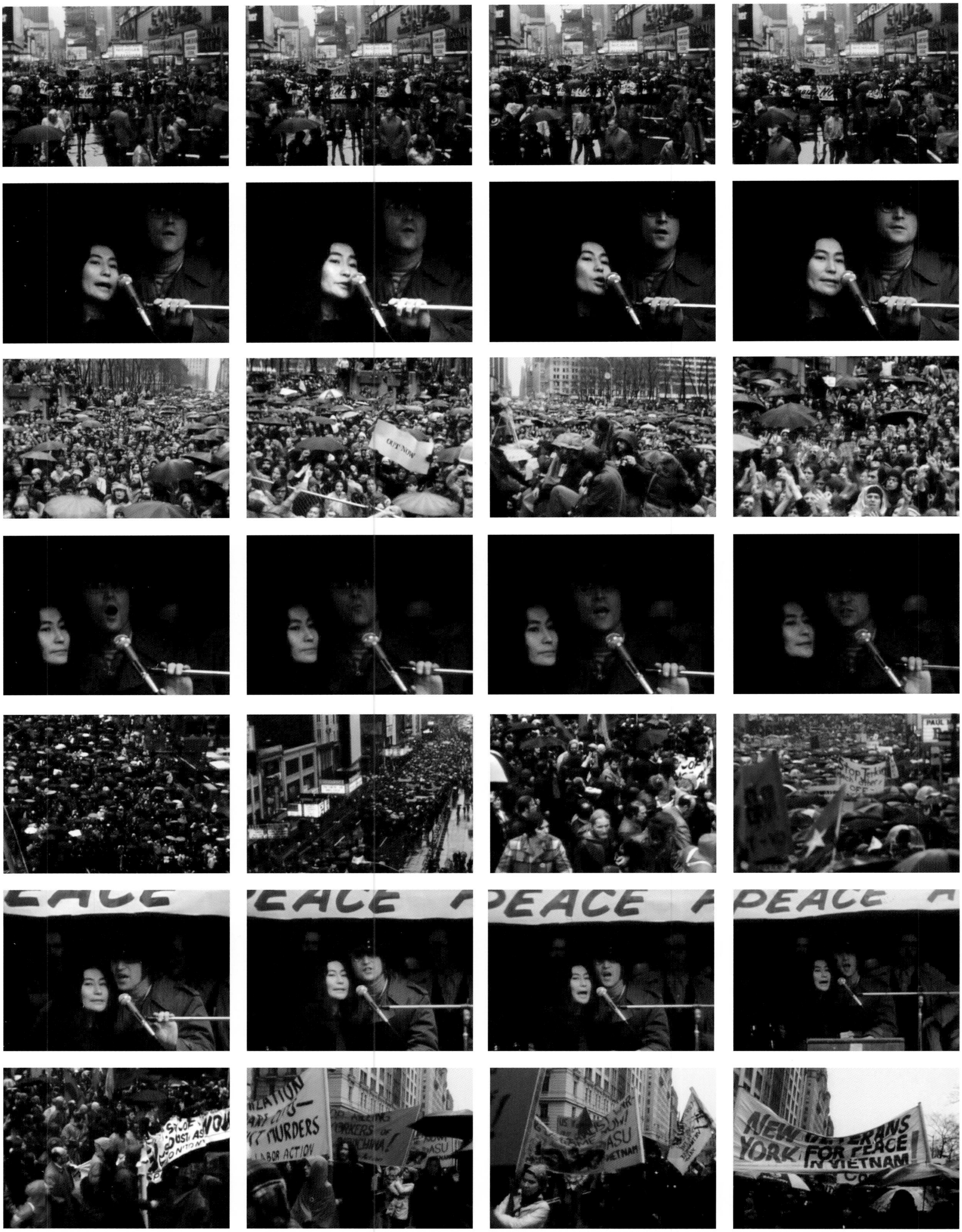
PEACE
OUT NOW
LABOR ACTION
FOR PEACE
IN VIETNAM

him every time we fall off the road or every time the bridge falls down.

I know how I felt when I was at college at nineteen and twenty – I would have been for complete destruction.

I always hoped for it anyway, just as a happening, just to go on the loot, to destroy it. I would have done then, but I don't know whether I would now – I still like stealing things; but I don't, because I can't be bothered. That's how I felt then, but if there was somebody like me I might listen.

If you want peace, you won't get it with violence. Please tell me one militant revolution that worked. Sure, a few of them took over, but what happened? Status quo. And if they smash it down, who do they think is going to build it up again? And then when they've built it up again, who do they think is going to run it? And how are they going to run it? They don't look further than their noses.

The system-smashing scene has been going on forever. What's it done? The Irish did it, the Russians did it and the French did it – and where has it got them? Nowhere.

It's the same old game. Who's going to run this smashing-up? Who's going to take over? It'll be the biggest smashers. They'll be the ones to get in first and they'll be the ones to take over. I don't know what the answer is, but I think it's down to people. What I said in 'Revolution' – in all the versions – is 'change your head'.

These people that are trying to change the world can't even get it all together. They're attacking and biting each others' faces, and all the time they're all pushing the same way. And if they keep going on like that, it's going to kill it before it's even moved. It's silly to bitch about each other and be trivial. They've got to think in terms of at least the world or the universe, and stop thinking in terms of factories and one country.

The point is that the Establishment doesn't really exist, and if it does exist, it's old people. The only people that want to change it are young, and they're going to beat the Establishment.

If they want to smash it all down, they have to be labourers as well, to build it up again.

The Establishment can't last forever. The only reason it has lasted forever is that the only way people have ever tried to change it is by revolution. And the idea is just to move in on the scene, so they can take over the universities, do all the

things that are practically feasible at the time. But not try and take over the state, or smash the state, or slow down the works.

All they've got to do is get through and change it, because they will be it. If you think of the Establishment or whoever 'they' are, the Blue Meanies, you've got to remember that they're the sick ones. And if you've got a sick child in the family you don't kick it out the door – you've got to try and look after it or extend a hand to it.

So somewhere along the line we've got to make a meeting point with whoever 'they' are, because even amongst them there are some human beings. In fact they're all human, but there's some that even look like it and respond like it. So it's up to us, if we're the 'aware' generation, to extend a hand.

The only way to ensure a lasting peace of any kind is to change people's minds. There's no other way. The Government can do it with propaganda, Coca-Cola can do it with propaganda – why can't we? We are the hip generation.

These left-wing people talk about giving the power to the people. That's nonsense – the people have the power. All we're trying to do is make people aware that they have the power themselves and the violent way of revolution doesn't justify the ends. All we're trying to say to people is to expose politicians and expose the people themselves who are hypocritical and sitting back and saying, 'Oh, we can't do anything about it, it's up to somebody else. Give us the answer, John.'

People have to organize. Students have to organize voting. We have to be the Monday Club, only in a different way.

When it gets down to 'having to use violence' then you're playing the system's game. The Establishment irritate you, pull your beard and flick your face to make you fight, because once they've got you violent, then they know how to handle you. The only thing they don't know how to handle is non-violence and humour.

The thing they sure-as-hell know is how to handle you if you're violent.

Because they'll irritate you and knock you and do this to you and keep doing that, until they make you fight.

And then they know how to fight you.

But if you fall for that, then you've lost.

IKNOW

~~(title)~~ (i know) I KNOW

A the years have passed so quickly

one thing i've understood C

A I'm ~~i am~~ only learning F#m

C to tell the trees from wood,

TO

A   I)I KNOW WHATS COMING DOWN E

D AND I KNOW WHERE ITS COMING FROM A

A AND ~~YES~~ I KNOW AND IM SORRY E (yes i am)

D BUT I NEVER COULD SPEAK MY MIND. A

2)AND I KNOW JUST HOW YOU FEEL

AND IKNOW NOW WHAT I HAVE DONE

AND I KNOW AND ~~THAT~~ IM GUILTY (yes i am)

BUT I NEVER COULD READ YOUR MIND.

i know what i was missing

but now my eyes can see

i put myself in your place

as you did for me...

                         E   A (D FIRST F#m)
            D TODAY I LOVE YOU MORE THAN YESTERDAY
                         E   A (Aflat F#m)
            D RIGHT NOW I LOVE YOU MORE RIGHT NOW.

3)NOW I KNOW WHATS COMING DOWN

...I CAN FEEL WHERE ITS COMING FROM

AND I KNOW ITS GETTING BETTER(ALL THE TIME)

AS WE SHARE IN EACH OTHERS MINDS

            TOAY I LOVE YOU MORE THAN YESTERDAY

            RIGHT NOW I LOVE YOU MORE RIGHT NOW.

            OOH HOO NO MORE CRYING

            OOH HOO NO MORE CRYING...

I KNOW (I KNOW)

The years have passed so quickly
One thing I've understood
I am only learning
To tell the trees from wood

I know what's coming down
And I know where it's coming from
And I know and I'm sorry (yes I am)
But I never could speak my mind

And I know just how you feel
And I know now what I have done
And I know and I'm guilty (yes I am)
But I never could read your mind

I know what I was missing
But now my eyes can see
I put myself in your place
As you did for me

Today I love you more than yesterday
Right now I love you more right now

And I know what's coming down
I can feel where it's coming from
And I know it's getting better (all the time)
As we share in each other's minds

Today I love you more than yesterday
Right now I love you more right now

Ooh hoo no more crying
Ooh hoo no more crying

Ooh hoo no more crying
Ooh hoo no more crying

I KNOW (I KNOW)

John: I would love to take the band from *Mind Games* on – getting it together where we really got off, not to just show me singing 'Imagine' again, would really be something else. It's more likely for me to think about that after this album because I know I'm not going to go back in again soon. I've gotta take a break.

I would have been on tour last year when I had Elephant's Memory together, but all that government business threw me off…just the pressure of the immigration business. They hung me up so much I just couldn't do anything.

I've been thinking about touring again now that we've got all these fantastic musicians on this session. I thought, 'Let's go out now. Let's do it now.' But there are so many hassles to it. There's all that money and organization. If you could just do it without 'JOHN LENNON GOES ON THE ROAD'. That sort of inhibits you.

At one time, I didn't think I ever wanted to sing again for money. I thought that whatever I did was going to be for free. Money seems to be the reason for all the problems. All the fighting was about money. War between people and the Beatles. The thing it came down to [with the Beatles] was who spent what and why. And Allen Klein and Lee Eastman and who was going to get what. It seemed to be all about bloody money.

But then all these free things…I learned years ago, when the Beatles did a few charities and we said we'd never do them again because there was always chaos and the artists would always get ripped off or treated badly.

The *One to One* benefit at Madison Square Garden was exactly the same. I don't mean the screaming and all that because that has nothing to do with how I feel…I'm up there and there are people miles away and I look around and the only difference is that I didn't see George Harrison. Someone else was standing over there. That's the only time I remembered it wasn't the same.

Otherwise, I'm just doing it on the microphone. I sort of cut off from what is happening. I only wake up when I come off. And I have trouble remembering the words. I was making them up at the *One to One* concert…. Like 'Come Together', I couldn't remember a damn thing except the chorus.

People want to hear old stuff. When I did that charity at Madison Square Garden, I was still riding high on *Imagine* so I was OK for material. But when I did 'Come Together', the house came down, which gave me an indication of what people wanted to hear. At the time I was thinking that I didn't want to do all that Beatles [stuff] – but now I feel differently.

I've lost all that negativity about the past and I'd be happy as Larry to do 'Help!'. I've just changed completely in two years. I'd do 'Hey Jude' and the whole damn show.

All people ever talk about in the business or around us about getting the Beatles together is to make some money, because all the other money was either stolen or lost or wasted. And the only talk about Beatle reunions comes from people at the side of Beatles who want to put us together and make millions and millions of dollars. And I'm not interested in that or in playing with the old team again…. When you do something just because the public wants you to do it you become something else. You become Muzak.

The Beatles might play together again if they ever could get together in the same country at the same time. It's the only real problem. Paul still has legal problems about entering the States, and I have just finished three years of fighting for the right to stay in the States, but I'm not too sure if I ever left whether or not I'd be let back in. There's no bitterness between us anymore. Whenever we talk, it's always about unfinished business, like what we are going to do about Apple Corps. But if we did get together, it probably would be a one-time thing. I mean, I can't believe Bob Dylan is going back on the road with the Band. I think he's crazy to do it. Yet I'll wait to see what he's like after his thirty days of playing are over.

Apple is now a well-run, well-organized and very powerful record company. And that wasn't what we set out to make. We set out to make an artists' haven like a Westbeth [artist housing centre in New York] with money and it just didn't work. See, it's a real problem many people will understand. Anyone who's even tried to run a newspaper or even when you make the decision to live as a community, whatever it is, suddenly you have that hassle of owning this property. Somebody's gotta hire and fire the people that are working for you. Somebody's gotta be in charge and it always grows into a monster. Whenever you try to do something it sort of grows on its own and becomes something that you can't control that takes you more time to control than it does to live your own life. It evolves and it's very hard even to start a little thing.

We still like to say Apple is high and rising. I speak to Paul on the phone and someone told me Paul said we were only a decimal point from settling everything. But I wish he would just send me a letter now and then…with all the legal stuff we'll be tied together for a long time to come.

If you had asked me last year, I would have said, 'No. No way. I'm not going back one step'…but I just think anything is possible now. It's not like it's in the offing or anything, but

Apple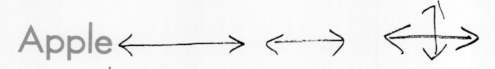

MEMORANDUM

To: Paul McCartney and Linda

From: J. &. Y.

Date: Feb. 7, 1972

Subject: Telegram to Paul

Right on brother and sister!' Now what do we do with "The Luck
of the Irish"!? and "Sunday Bloody Sunday"!? Would you do a
Madison Square Garden with Wings, Plastic Ono, and Stones?!
We've already talked to Mick!(⬛⬛⬛⬛⬛). Also, in three weeks
actually go to Ireland (again Possibly with Stones!) let's forget our past
and save some people! Good luck anyway, xxxxx we're proud of you.
                                    Love,
                                        Sonny and Cher O'Lennon
P.S. No A.K. at M.S.G. if it's uncool.

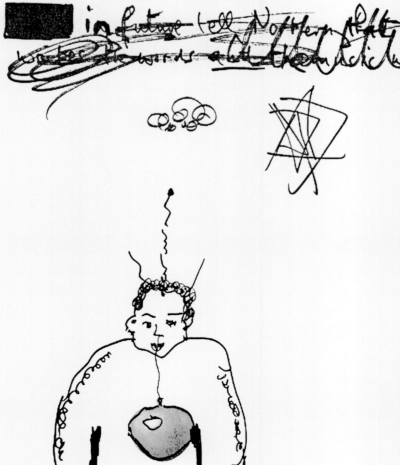

Lyrics for John's song 'I'm The Greatest' in John's handwriting.
Opposite: John recording 'I'm The Greatest' with producer Richard
Perry, Ringo Starr and George Harrison (pictured) together with
Klaus Voormann and Billy Preston; Sunset Sound Recorders,
Hollywood, California, 13 March 1973.

when i was a little boy
way back home in liverpool
my mama told me i was great
then when i was a teenager
i knew that i got something going
my mama told me i was great

now i'm a man
i took a woman by the hand
and she told me i was great

I'm not ruling it out. Que sera, sera. If it happens, I'm sure we'll all do something wonderful and I'm just as sure that everybody would say it wasn't good enough…that we were better separate or something.

We called George the other day and [he] said he was having a great time and wish you were here. George said he was on his way and hasn't been heard of since. I miss Paul a lot. It's been a year since I've seen him. He came over with Linda to my place in New York. Of course I'd like to see him again. He's an old friend, isn't he? At least we're talking and we're all happy with each other. If we got back together it wouldn't be for one last show, right? If we ever got together, my instincts tell me it would be more sensible to sit in a studio and get relaxed together and make some music before stomping out on dates. I'm not saying that's in the offing, though.

Yoko: The world was really hating me, and sending hatred vibes toward me very overtly for I don't know how many years. But in some ways I'm happy about it. It taught me a lesson. These hate vibes, they're like love vibes, they're very strong. It kept me going. When you're hated so much, you live. Hate was feeding me. It was fashionable to put me down. You don't hurt me though, because I know you, and I love you. I can take hatred, because I don't believe that people are capable of real hate. We are too lonely for that. We vanish too quickly for that. Do you ever hate a cloud? How could anyone hate people who are on their deathbeds? That's where we all are, since the day of birth.

At first I was surprised, disgusted and then frightened by the assault of people's hatred against me. I'm still frightened a little bit, but there is nothing you can do about it. I used to think I was hard done by by the press. Now I think it's something else. I mean even when they're being very nice I still think it's something else. Maybe they're getting a little tired of attacking me, but they're so relentless about it I don't think they ever really get tired. I suppose I'm the perfect scapegoat, and no one's going to complain.

People's attitude to the work John and I do is that if it's bad then it's my fault, if it's good then it's because of John, and that attitude does make it hard for us both. John and I try to protect each other as much as possible, but you can't avoid the world all the time.

Half the reporters who interviewed us ignored me completely and the other half blamed me. I could say nothing without having it distorted, put into a headline, and used against John and his friends.

At the time we did *Some Time In New York City* the hostility around us was really something else. Neither of us felt we communicated. I felt very guilty because I thought that if John had done this on his own, people would have accepted it. And John thought: if Yoko had done this on her own, people would have accepted it. We didn't feel it was fruitful at all. Now we're going to try to do things separately for a while. Maybe early next year we might do something together.

There was such anti-John-and-Yoko thing out there, and it didn't come from Middle Americans either. They [illegible] anti-John-and-Yoko at all. In fact, they said we were a cute couple, so much in love. The [illegible] came from the underground [that] was what really got to us.

John: My main education, apart from creatively, from Yoko, has been racism, education as much of the experience of being with her, because we're [an] intermarried, interracial couple, which, although we didn't realize at the time, has a lot of side effects. And a lot of people don't realize that. Racism and chauvinism. Now, the racism was an eye-opener for me, although I considered myself a liberal and whatever it was, you know, and understood these problems, but having lived it, it's a different ball game altogether. And the chauvinism was a real eye-opener, because…I didn't realize what a pig I was…I mean, one doesn't realize until somebody tells you. And it's been a slow process, and it's been hard, harder for Yoko, probably, than for me.

Yoko: Well for both of us, probably.

John: Well, whatever. I know it's harder for you, because you were suffering both. And I am aware of it, I've been aware of it for a long time, because she made me aware of it, but being aware enough to, for it to be a natural happening for me is, is, I think it's…'73 is probably the final year, I probably might be a whole human being next year. I think the final sort of whole thing's coming home to me now. And it's a delight. Although, like in therapy or anything else, you hang on to your old habits, you know, whatever they may be, because you're so…they're so internalized and computerized or whatever, you've been programmed and programmed. And now there's usually a warning light goes on whenever I become that which I don't want to be, and that's…that's where it is now…. And another thing about relationships is they always [get to a stage where] 'The bloom wears off', and all that jazz. Now, it was wonderful to be sort of in the rosy bloom of first love, and it was really an experience, but it's much better now.

Yoko: Hmm, it's good! [laughs]

John: It's so much – and it's getting better!

Yoko: Yeah, that's really true.

'Newsweakanalldowithout' was John's 23 March 1973 response to
a much-embellished article in *Newsweek* about an alleged 'Beatles
reunion' that had happened on 13 March at Sunset Sound Recorders
and all its adjacent activities.

Dear ~~Mr~~ -News -weak,

Three ex-Beatles were in Los Angeles last week, for, amongst other reasons, business meeting. (John and Yoko, Ringo and Maureen, and George.) The Lennons —who had been there for two weeks already (promoting Yoko Onos Apple Album, Approximately Infinit Universe), were happy to hear that MR + MS starr and George were arriving soon. G. Harrison to Record + visit Ravi Shankar, and Ringo to make his new album. ~~Having~~ which he was ~~trouble with,-~~ As many different songwriters - including Randy Newman - George Harrison, had already contributed material for Ringo's album, it seemed only natural that John would also. (~~He~~ in fact collaborated with Yoko ono to finish the song 'My Mama told me I was great' in time for the session the next day.) The musicians back up, "apart from the 3 ex Bs" star or otherwise who played on the session, were ~~Ringo~~ ~~George~~ Billy Preston, Klaus Voorman.

"it was an incredible evening', someone said "the vibes were great" John played Piano, George the head, Ringo Drums, and afterwards when a 'clap track" (the sound of people clapping!) was dubbed over, everyone ~~except~~ who played on the original track plus super session star Jim Keltner and ~~George~~ ~~apple~~

except Yoko – who was re-writing the third verse about Ringo's wife and ~~kids~~ staggered into the studio to join in the ~~over~~dubbed ~~~~ ~~~~ back-beat.

"Although John +Yoko and George, George and Ringo, ~~John~~ Yoko and Ringo, had played together often, it was the first time the three ex beatles had played together since, – well since they last played together" said Lennon.

As usual, an awful lot of rumors, if not down right lies was going on including the possibility of impresario Allen de "Klein playing bass for the other three in an as yet untitled album called "I was a teenage ~~fat Cat II~~. ~~And producer Perry, who planned to consult with McCartney on his upcoming~~ A→

The extreme hostility that existed between ~~John + Paul~~ seems to have evaporated, ~~said a McCarley associate,~~ "They've spoken to each other on the telephone, and in english, that's a change" said a McCartney associate. "if only ~~~~ everything were as simple and unaffected as ~~~~ McCartneys new single 'My love' the maybe Dean Martin and Jerry Lewis would be reunited with the Marx Brothers and Newsweek could get a job" said an East African Official.

yours up to the teeth

John Lennon
Yoko Ono.

~~~~ ~~Elvis is getting back together again~~
P.S. peace + love.

Below and opposite: Letters and notes by John as he made moves to uncomplicate his life, extracting himself and Apple from Allen Klein and ABKCO, and to simplify and economize his portfolio of businesses, investments and lawsuits, May–June 1973. Opposite bottom left: A 'strictly private and confusing' letter 'from a fanatic' typewritten by John to George and Patti Harrison at the Plaza Hotel, New York, 25 June 1973.

John: I don't want to be possessed by possessions, whether they come in the form of people, businesses or cash in the bank. I don't want it to possess me. And that was the danger that I was finding myself in. It was taking me over. It's the same for anybody on any level. The payments on the car or the house take their life over. How much joy are we getting out of the things we're buying?

Apple

MEMORANDUM

To: Date:

From: Subject:

Ascot. Apple 3 Savile Row. etc. 10 cars. etc.
I want to own NO PROPERTY, if I can
help it various buildings with relatives in
will be left.
Everything else I want turning into cash.
an artist cannot create when his mind is
cluttered with property and possessions
The cash, is still 'property'. I will use it
as wisely as I know how.
O.K. my records come out on Apple. let them pay.
O.K. I need some kind of publisher in '73.
but do I need ABKCO. on some other vast
company? e.g. Dave Platz: 20% on Publishing
is too much.
In America + Britain — two people could
handle Yoko / Lennon publishing. in
other countries let. Klein or someone
work it out. (if George or Ringo want this
kind of minimal office — it might be even
cheaper. I don't like this £10,000 for Ringo but.

Letter 1 (top left)

Apple

29th May 1973

Abkco Industries, Inc *R.I.P.*
1700 Broadway
New York, New York 10019

Dear Sir or Madame:

Please give all APPLE Stationary to the

bearer of this letter.

[signature: Lennon]

JOHN LENNON
President *of Apple!*

[doodle]

P.S. Hi Al!!

Letter 2 (top right)

Mr. Allen Klein
Abkco Industries
1700 Broadway
New York, New York 10019

<u>Re: SIX BAG ONE LITHOGRAPHS</u>

Dear Allen:

Thank you for your letter. We have been looking for your Glass
Hammer piece but haven't found it yet *[*]

Whoever has this letter has my authorization to pick up
the Bag Ones.

Sincerely, *love*

[signature: John]

JOHN LENNON
el President of Apple Records Inc *incapacitated!*

[*] i think it got broke — will fix and send ya!

Letter 3 (bottom left)

ANTHER (ANOTHER) LETTER FROM THE DECK OF FRED ASTAIRCASE...

dear me,

how time flyz.it seems like only yesterday that it happened.i am typing this
lettuce from agreat height.I.WEST,72nd st.ny.ny.looking over the park,which we dont
have to mow.george/pattie isare in town tho we've yet to see/hear them,theyre supposed
to arrive today mon.25 june spoon moon.i'd write to them but they keep moving about.
letthe dogs bark but the caramel tastes just as good',thats what they say!and thy coul
d be right.i'm enclosing a picture of myselves,taken an a fantastic new polaroid which
developes the pictyre inside the camera!then it leeps out all by itself.no im wrong
FIRST TI LEAPS OUT,then developes BEFORE YOUR VERY EYES! its very?small too,just thoug
ht you'd like to know,;if you enclose three thousand box tops of harry neileons rating
s i will draw you a diagram of where to find one two three fourWOPBOPALOOMA!!

if upu you dont pass this letter on a great and
curious curse will appear inthe garden.take no notice of it and you will receive
amillon japanes zen in exchange for your self!dont miss this amazing offer!!offer
expires JANUARY 209I!!(gives ya time to think)
ENOUGH OF THIS NONSENSE,hows beowolf?i think we
should give apple to the LOWEST BIDDER,or donate it to animal slaughter.if you
agree get neil to sign a will stating same and we can put it to the board of racial
equality;(theres a rumour in the city that frank cousins wants to by it for his childr
en)also we should burn whats left of saville rOW in memory of YOU KNOW WHO(its the way
HE WOULD HAVE WANTED IT)!! and how about if we each sell a different bit ofBADTAYLOR
to different record companies/?(MY BIT TO ply/records,yours to decca etc)im sure we'd
make MILLIONS MORE this way and could look forward to some lovely TAX PROBLEMSin our
OLD AGE-this would stop us getting bored in the WIFRED PICKLES MEMORIAL HOME!!!!!!!!
also to save getting in each others way ,how alout each of us realissing our records
IN ONE COUNTRY ONLY!(id like to have NORWAY)surely you can see that this is the
answer to all our problems?I'm sure I can negotiate these INTRICATE DEALS with all the
VRY IMORTANT PEOPLE concerned,all i need is a word in their ears telling them
"I'VE COME ON BHALF OF J.G.R.AND MAYBE EVEN........P!"and those fat cats will be eati
ng out of my HAMBURGER"!(how could one forget it?)

IF YOU AGREE PLEASE SONG (SIGN ON THE DOTTED LINE.
.
.
.. . .,. . . .. .
.
.
.
yors tutti,
[signature] JEOGINGO LENSTARRISON.(DIRECT DECSENDANT
OF APPLE)

c.c.rider:george harrisingle   lopsde rhampa   arther bungle&con
        apaul McCompany   slew greed   harry pinchit &dr. strachlove
    richard carkeys   sammy davish jewnear.   clive e.s.pstime
        john lemming   tarik aliphant   len faircluff   horace saliver
    frankly koala   lord goodgod   less antony   robert stickwould
        neil afterall(this time)   lois b. meyercifll   antiny forskin
    harold seidline   united arsoles   E.M,I,N,E.   petr browse
    lee eastmanforhimself   lent wood--bine   warning brothers   bill harry
david brawn;n;muscle   dame josephlock/jaw calive davisionary horst fascist
    allen klame   hilary dillary dock dougie millings   lord woodbine
    bhasket of menonly   maharisky mahash boogie jeamy socks   mrs. shitcliffe
    lord harlet   john eastmouth   jeramy wanks/rotten o'rightone
    mal content   peter ashtray   the royl mounted butterflies
    derek saveme   prik james   c cheeses christoffering tee heeth.

Letter 4 (bottom right)

30,may 73

dear jack:

thank you for your letter,your right about lawyers!(see enclosed).maybe we could
provide them with'worry beads',to keep them busy while i make a record?!...

i dont know exactly whats going on in london.re:kleins nthn action,as far as i know
nothing is supposed to be happening.all of those affected are being (about to be)informed
by lawyers about 'the merits',now that deKlein is out.i'll let you know as soon as i hear
from them,

the 'u.s.'thing(lawsuit)should not be difficult,for ALL concerned.i told my lawyers
to make a deal whereby we split the publishing 50/50(nrthn/ono),it really does seem
reasonable to me.

a)theres not that much money in it. *[*]*   *no question*

b)you/we did it before.(OH MY LOVE)(MAGGIE MAY?DIG IT)etc etc.the rcords
speaks for itself,if you'd care to check...ie.not your lawyers(who IMAGINE things!)
i was suprised when my'counter offer 'was rejected,they did tell you about it...?dint they?

please let me know what you think.it all seems so pointless.

all the best anyway,

lets make this the last round...

johnlennon.

[*] ??

YOU ARE HERE.

(1) E

FROM LIVERPOOL TO TOKYO

WHAT A WAY TO GO! B

B FROM DISTANT LANDS ~~XXXXXXXXXXXXXXXX~~ ONE WOMAN ONE MAN

E LET THE ~~OXXXXXXXXXX~~ 4 winds blow

A THREE THOUSAND MILES OVER THE OCEAN Am   Am   B♭

A THREE ~~MILLION LIGHT~~ thousand light YEARS FROM THE LAND OF THE RISING SUN!

LOVE HAS OPENED UP MY ~~MIND~~ eyes   E ... | E sus4 ... | E sus4 ... | E ... |

LOVE HAS BLOWN RIGHT THROUGH.   E ... | ... | E sus7 ... | E ... |

M8 ~~AND~~ WHEREVER YOU ARE, YOU ARE HERE   F#m ... | ". | E ... | ". |

WHEREVER YOU ARE YOU ARE HERE.   F#m ... | ". | E ... | ". |

(2) FROM MYSTICAL TO MAGICAL

WHAT A WAY TO FLY!

FROM TEMPLE SCENES TO VILLAGE GREENS

LET ~~THERE BE~~ in the light

THREE THOUSAND MILES OVER THE OCEAN

THREE ~~MILLION~~ LIGHT YEARS FROM   THE LAND OF THE SUPRISING SUN!

OUT.

M.8.

3 EAST IS EAST AND WEST IS WEST

~~AND~~ THE TWAIN SHALL MEET!

EAST IS WEST AND WEST IS EAST

LET IT BE COMPLETE

THREE THOUSAND MILES OVER THE OCEAN

THREE THOUSAND LIGHT YEARS FROM THE LAND OF THE MORNING STAR ~~XXXXXXXXXXXXXXXXXXXXXXXX~~

~~AND THE AGAIN YOU ARE HERE SAY IT AGAIN AND AGAIN AND AGAIN AND AGAINAGAINAGAINAGAINAGAINAGAIN~~

YOU ARE HERE

From Liverpool to Tokyo
It's a way to go
From distant lands one woman one man
Let the four winds blow

Three thousand miles over the ocean
Three thousand light years from the land of the rising sun

Love has opened up my eyes
Love has blown right through
Wherever you are, you are here
Wherever you are, you are here

Three thousand miles over the ocean
Three thousand light years from the land of surprising sun

Well now, east is east and west is west
The twain shall meet
East is west and west is east
Let it be complete

Three thousand miles over the ocean
Three thousand light years from the land of the morning star

YOU ARE HERE

Yoko: John had a very warm view of his past. He thought of Liverpool as a place that was incredibly wonderful. I didn't hear that from many others at the time. Some people who leave the city they were born in or grew up in say, 'Thank God I left.' But John always thought it was a great place and he loved it. In the last week of his life he was planning to go visit his England on the *QE2*. He wanted to go to Liverpool and show the city he was from to his son Sean.

John: 'You Are Here' – that's more than just a joke, I suppose. People read it and suddenly realize it's true. Yes, I'm here, they think. So are these other people. We're all here together. And that's where the vibrations start being exchanged. Good and bad ones according to who is sending out and how they feel.

I did a *You Are Here* show at the Robert Fraser Gallery. It consisted of a bare gallery and a big white canvas that was round and it just had my writing on it: 'you are here'. You had to go down the stairs and you had to get through all these different charity cans to put money in, like RSPCA, animal and cancer funds, and dogs and people – the room was full of them – and on the left side of the wall was this big, big canvas with 'you are here', a hat to put money in for the artist and a jar of teeny white badges to take that said 'you are here'. We filmed them from behind a dark window with the English *Candid Camera* team, and let balloons off with 'send your message back when you get it', and they'd write to tell me where it came from. I cut the canvas down and it's about three foot now.

A lot of people went to India to find out they were here. Like [Timothy] Leary's friend Richard Alpert [Ram Dass] went to India and saw all the gurus, chasing all over the place, and all the gurus said to him was, 'Remember, be here now'. That's all them gurus will ever tell you. Remember this moment now. I was talking to George the other day and I forgot to say to him, 'What are you searching for? You are here!'

Yoko: We're democratic. We don't believe in one person being greater than the other, we believe that everybody has godliness in themselves and it's just a matter of discovering it. So we don't believe in that, 'Well, there's just one man with a big aura or something,' you know, we all have auras. And there's no bigger or smaller aura, it's all depending on what kind of physical condition you're in at that moment. So it's not a mysterious matter at all.

John: You could also…. If you change 'pain' – because that's what I was experiencing – 'God is a concept by which we measure our joy!' So not that it or a thing may or may not exist in whatever entity one can imagine, but we're all it. It's in everything. So we're all it.

We're all God. I mean, Christ said the kingdom of heaven is within you. And that's what it means. And the Indians say that and the Zen people say that. It's a basic thing of religion. We're all God. I'm not a god or the god, not the God, but we are all God and we are all potentially divine and potentially evil. We all have everything within us and the Kingdom of Heaven is nigh and within us you know. And if you look hard enough, you see it.

I believe in life after death, without any doubt. I believe in it. In meditation, on drugs, on diets, I've been aware of soul and been aware of the power. Somebody asked a witch on TV, 'Are you a black witch or a white witch?' and she said, 'There's no such thing. There is a power which people tap and they use it for whatever ends they use it.' And God is a power which we're all capable of tapping. We're all lightbulbs that can tap the electricity. You can use electricity to kill people or to light the room, and God is that – neither one nor the other, but everything – and we use him to our best ability and it's no good blaming God for war because you can use the H bomb for cheap power throughout the world or you can use it for a bomb – the H power, whatever it is, the atomic power…. God is that.

Now, the guru trip is a declaration by Indian gurus from Baba Ram Dass to a doctor – anybody that declares their colours – they put up a shop window sign saying, 'Guru', 'Teacher', 'Physician', whatever it is. Then the people or interested parties come there and ask that entity to either entertain – if it's a rock star or pop star – or to tell them the answer. Now, that guy – simply by declaring that – has made the first game plan move, and the people then approach him and invest him with energy.

He might have a lot of energy anyway, he might be born with it, whatever! But the people, we invest each other with energy. Now if we, the three of us go somewhere and give our attention and energy to somebody because he's made a statement which has intrigued us, or had been written down two thousand years ago…which is just true, sure, and he can spout them all off. He can quote the Bible, the Gita, the Ching, all those things, the Dylan, the Beatles, whatever your trip is…

Yoko: …he becomes…

John: …what we create! We create them! I don't know what the expression means, but whatever it is, you are. The public then call you, and communicate with you. But you're receiving two hundred thousand people's attention and energy, and you have that to give back to them. Now that [may be] the way mankind or humankind works, but let's not pretend that we – you, they, these Baba Ram Dasses,

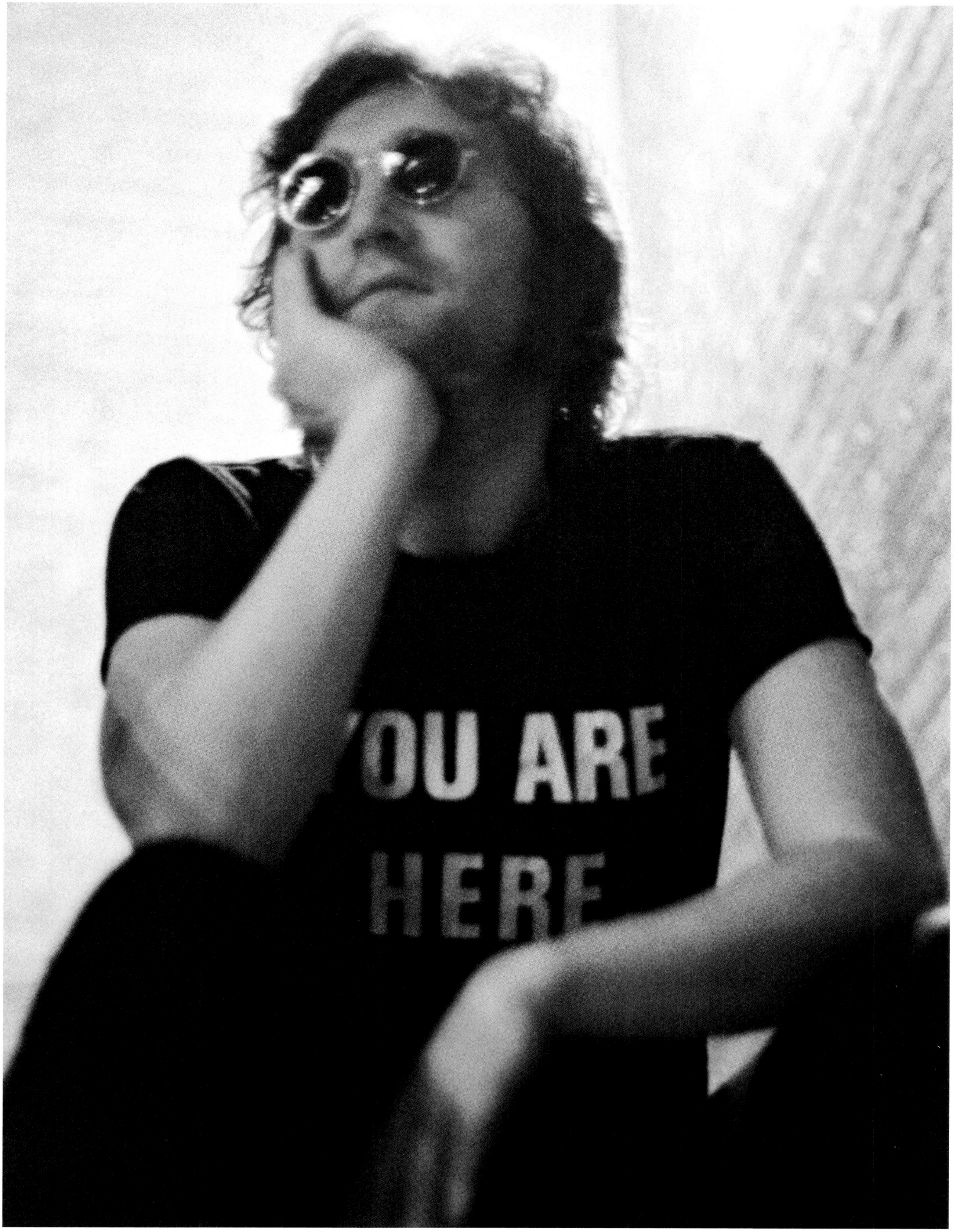
YOU ARE
HERE

these Maharishis or anything else – have anything that is not accessible to us if we want it. If you wanted to play guitar like me, all you have to do is take the time out. If you want it, you get it.

It's just a simple as that and that's all we've been saying. It's not that we don't like this and we don't like that, or we're negative about this or we're negative about that. One gets into a dialogue about these people because they're always being talked about, and we are in that position too, in a way, but we keep trying to negate that responsibility. We're responsible for what we do and what we are, but not to provide anything other…. Let's have an exchange, and don't ask us to provide something for you. We'll exchange something with you.

I was in the conspiracy being a male pig, although I wasn't in the 'revering the Beatles past' conspiracy, and maybe in my way I tried to break it, in, maybe in rather a negative way, but that's what I had to go down. But I noticed that [Yoko] was changing into that which I was not originally… I didn't know her! I saw her becoming somebody else, not the person I met.

I fell in love with an independent, eloquent, outspoken, creative genius, for me; whatever a genius is, right? To me it was a revelation. And then I saw through this process

of not just the press comments, but the general thing, that's what made me see the chauvinism – not just on my behalf, on everybody's behalf!

Not that people, you know, we all looked at Rod Steiger or something, we didn't look at the guy sitting next to him. We understand that. But…from all points of view, she was becoming somebody else. She was killing herself, like we all do, but women especially.

And I was in the conspiracy, subconsciously out of naivety, and [for] the same reason most men are: ignorance. And I can see that that's how those marriages grow apart, because the man might get a fresh young girl who hasn't been programmed that much at twenty or whenever they marry, younger or something, and then she [turns] into that thing which they find themselves less attracted to after ten years.

Yoko: Because we have to adapt ourselves.

John: Yeah! If she'd gone through so many changes in two years, I thought, 'God, what, you know, what's going to become of us in the future, if it goes on like this?', and with that and with her basic optimism and [her strength to cling] onto herself as an individual, I started waking up…. At least she could face it on the outside if I was helping on the inside, if I was aware of it; once I was aware of it, then slowly that damage [could be] undone again. And for us '73 is our year, we just know it and we feel it…. We've been through a cycle, [and] the whole ball game changes now.

And she is becoming herself again and it's beautiful. It's an extraordinary thing and we both experienced it and we both saw it, and that's what happened and we know it…. I don't know if we've expressed it well, but that's what goes down. George has a statement [that] he keeps quoting – Gandhi or something – 'We make and become the image of our choice,' but it also goes round to the people all around us.

And if I can just ramble on, 'Power To The People' means investing that energy in all of us. There will always be people that can do one thing conveniently more well for society's sake. It doesn't mean we all have to be headless. It means that we invest each other with that power if we exchange the energy and we can do whatever we want together. We don't need daddy. There'll always be somebody that can fix the lights or [get us to] the moon. They will always be there. But 'Power To The People' means power not just physically but mentally. Invest that energy we give to Harold Wilson, Ted Heath, Richard Nixon, McGovern, for that short period, in each other.

write to John Lennon

c/o Robert Fraser Gallery
69 Duke Street
London W1

you are here

you are here

MEAT CITY

Ⓐ

Ⓐ

① WELL I BEEN MEAT CITY TO SEE FOR MYSELF

Ⓐ YES I BEEN MEAT CITY TO SEE FOR MYSELF

B♭⁺ A B♭⁺ A
BEEN MEAT CITY BEEN MEAT CITY (meat city shookdown U.S.A.)

#m 280
WELL THE PEOPLE WERE JUMPING LIKE THERES NO TOMORROW

A MEAT CITY

#m 350
FINGERLICKIN CHICKINPICKIN MEAT CITY SHOOKDOWN U.S.A

A PIG MEAT CITY°!   A A.C.D A Ⓓ
② 420
WELL I BEEN THE MOUNTAIN TO SEE FOR MYSELF

YES I BEEN THE MOUNTAIN TO SEE FOR MYSELF

50
BEEN THE MOUNTAIN BEEN THE MOUNTAIN (freak city shoo freak city shookdown U.S.A.)

590
AND THE SNAKE DOCTORS SHAKIN LIKE THERES NO TOMORROW

FREAK CITY

CHIKINSUCKIN MOTHERTRUCKIN MEAT CITY SHOOKDOWN U.S.A.

PIG MEAT CITY.

wipe   A. A.C.D.A Ⓓ
first of
2nd half USE

③ gonna china

(Jupiter)

MEAT CITY

Well…
Been Meat City to see for myself
Well I've been Meat City to see for myself
Been Meat City been Meat
Just got to give me some rock 'n' roll

Gip a kcuf

People were dancing like there's no tomorrow
Meat City
Meat City shook down
Finger-lickin' chicken-pickin' Meat City shook
down USA
Pig Meat City

Well I've been the mountain to see for myself
Well I've been the mountain to see for myself
Been the mountain, been the
Just gotta give me some rock 'n' roll

Snake doctors shakin' like there's no tomorrow
Freak City
Freak city chutzpah, well
Chicken-suckin' mother-truckin' Meat City
shookdown USA
Pig Meat City babe, yeah!

Well I'm goin' to China to see for myself
Well I'm goin' a China to see for myself

Goin' a China, Goin' a
Just got to give me some rock 'n' roll

People were jumping like there's no tomorrow
Meat City
Hey!
Finger-lickin' chicken-pickin' Meat City shook
down USA
Pig Meat City, babe!

Well I'm goin' a China
Yes I'm goin' a China (Jupiter)

Well I'm goin' a China
Yes (Right) I'm goin' a China

Come on
Yeah yeah
Come on, let's go!
Go, go, go, go, go

I'm goin' a China
Yes, I'm goin' a China

Alright, boogie!
Something's in my head!
Oh yeah, who's that, who is that, who is that?
Who is that?
And why are they doing those strange things?

MEAT CITY

John: I love New York. It's the hottest city on Earth. I haven't been everywhere in the world but it's the fastest city on Earth. The difference between New York and London is the difference between London and Liverpool.

It's more fun here. Some of the nasties think I'm here for tax reasons. But it's hardly worth explaining to people. I only decided to live here after I'd moved here. I didn't leave England with the intention…I left everything in England. I didn't even bring any clothes. I just came for a visit and stayed. If I had wanted to do it for tax I should have informed the British government; I would have gotten an amazing tax refund for one year. But I forgot to – so I just ended up paying taxes anyway, here and there. If I'd only thought of it, I would have made a million pounds or something. In America, they should stop saying I do it for the tax. I like it here! Is anywhere better?

The English tend to get a little '…you've left us!' They never say it, but you can tell it by the way they write about you. But, it's too bad. The Liverpool people were the same when I left Liverpool. Or when the Beatles left Liverpool. It was all, 'You've let us down!' You know, 'You should stay here forever and rot….' I'm not really interested. I like people to like me. But I am not going to ruin my life to please anybody.

Wherever Yoko and I lived we were going pretty fast in our lives. It was like we were a little miniature New York City in London or something, but this is the only place where everybody is going at the same speed as us, which is good. So it's like instead of going against the waves, which we'd been doing a lot of the time, in New York you go with the waves. They're all going with you.

It's that kind of inspiring thing and there's just so many great people here apart from the stars that live here – the great artists of music and of straight art, just all the people are much groovier here. It's the hippest place on Earth and that's why it's really inspiring to be here and it just makes you wanna rock like crazy.

For me New York has everything. And if I wanted to get away from it there's always New England to visit if I feel homesick for England, I feel homesick for Cornwall, or Ireland or Scotland where I went on holidays. When I think of England now, I think of my childhood or discotheques in London and in New England it's very similar with the rock and the sea and that.

I've got a little pad there where I can go to get away from the rush of New York, and I've got an apartment in the Dakota building in New York.

I also love the millions of radio stations and television channels and the piped TV movies I can get and things like that, which you can't get in England.

I can move around a bit more freely now – for meals and the odd visit to the movies. I still get recognized, though. I think it's me nose. But I can generally go to the movies. The last film I saw was *Behind the Green Door.* The first forty-five minutes were interesting, then it got a bit boring. When you've seen one cock you've seen them all.

Los Angeles is crazy – it looks so normal when you get there, but what it is, is there's all these roomfuls of crazy people moving from room to room. In New York you feel it on the streets a bit, but in LA it just looks normal and you think there's nothing happening, and then you find all this madness going on in rooms.

New York is where the music is for me. I think the farthest out I'd want to go is to have a place in Massachusetts or New England or somewhere, somewhere to escape to now and then. New York is where I live – I just don't think about it any more, I just don't think of any alternative.

I think it'd only matter if I couldn't be here when I wanted to, because I don't think I could get it on in, say Paris (which I love) or even London. You only have to look out of your window. There's just a vibe in the air that I like. I'd have liked to have lived in Rome in the days of the Roman Empire – not on the outskirts of the empire somewhere – and now I wanna live in New York. It's definitely the capital of the world, and I wanna be where that is.

When I came to New York I wasn't planning to live here, I was just visiting, maybe stay a few months…it just sort of happened. I'd probably be back in England a lot more if it didn't mean that I couldn't get back here. I'd probably be coming and going a lot more because I know it's happening in England. I hear the music coming out of there and I hear the news, or read it, so I know England has plenty of things going on, it's just…well, I know the English don't like to hear it, but it is the fifty-first state.

We were all brought up on Hollywood movies and American music, right? So going to England is just like going to San Francisco or somewhere, once you get out of that nationalistic thing – although I do revert to it still, if someone starts attacking the English I'll fight 'em, y'know, but that doesn't happen very often.

But we speak the same language and have the same culture – Heinz beans and ketchup and Doris Day and Elvis…. What the hell, it's one of the islands, just a bit farther away.

John with a meat freight truck driver, photographed by David Gahr
in Manhattan's last 1970s working-class district – Hell's Kitchen;
New York City, 24 October 1974.

Top left: *Some Time In New York City* album cover layout and photocollage by Michael C. Gross directed by Yoko Ono, 1972, featuring (top right) photocollage by Michael C. Gross directed by Yoko Ono, of President Richard Nixon and Chairman Mao Zedong dancing naked as per the lyrics of Yoko's song 'We're All Water', following Nixon's visit to The People's Republic of China, 21–28 February 1972.

Bottom: 'Goin' 'a Jupiter' – The Pioneer plaques, designed by Carl Sagan and Frank Drake, with artwork by Linda Salzman Sagan. They featured an illustration of a naked man and woman reminiscent of John & Yoko's *Two Virgins* album cover that had caused a furore only four years previously. The plaques were on board the Pioneer 10 and 11 NASA space probes that completed the first mission to Jupiter, launched from Earth on 1 March 1972 and 5 April 1973.

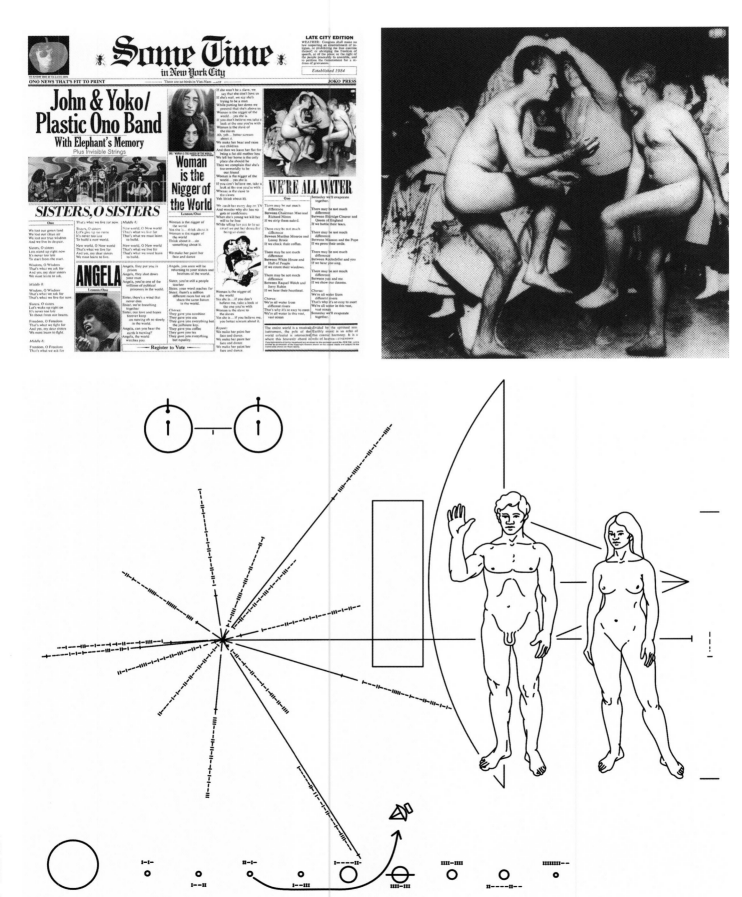

And I like the multiracial thing over here. It's like living in Europe with Britain really in the Common Market, like Europe might be in twenty years or something, people coming and going all the time, crossing borders. It's all Europeans here, and Africans, of course, but it's really like Europe, only with the main language being English.

No land, no boundaries, no passports, only people. Only people can change the world.

China – I shall go there, I will take the opportunity to try to see Mao. If he is ill or dead or refuses to see me, too bad. But if I go there I want to meet people who are doing something important. I want to take a rock band to China. That is really what I want to do. To play rock in China. They have yet [as of 1972] to see that.

Yoko: This is my city. This is where I belong.

John: I've said this many times, I have a love for [America]. Two thousand years ago, we would all have wanted to live in Rome. Not in the hills, but in Rome – and now, [New York] is Rome. This is where the action is.

People just see me. And occasionally just bother me a bit. But the most they ask for is an autograph. I don't care, I sign an autograph. Sometimes the taxi drivers, if they are young, get a little bit [star-struck]. And I say, 'Yes, it is me. Keep your eye on the road.' But apart from that it's no hassle.

In general I just walk around. I love it. People just say, 'Oh, it's him,' or, 'It isn't him,' but they don't jump on me. Because I'm not in the prime of my career, or whatever they call it. I am not Elton. He can get around, but it's pretty hard.

I was always me, all the way through it…I love motels 'cause there is no reception area. I like hotels too. But I like motels as well. Just invisible places where you check in with a credit card, in the middle of the night, anywhere. Some guys in taxis now, old guys, they recognize the voice is English, but they don't recognize me. They don't know who the hell I am. They say, 'Oh, you're English! I was over there in the war….' And they go on and on…and tell me amazing life stories…. They ask, 'What do you do?' and I say, 'I'm a musician,' and they say, 'Are you doing alright?' 'Yeah I am….'

Yoko: Around the time that I met John, I went to a palmist – John would probably laugh at this – and he said: 'You're like a very, very fast wind that goes speeding around the world.' And I had a line that signified astral projection. The only thing I didn't have was a root. But, the palmist said, 'You've met a person who's fixed like a mountain, and if you get connected with that mountain you might get materialized.' And John is

like a frail wind, too, so he understands all of these aspects. When I was in the avant-garde, at the time, I was kinda held as a high priestess or something like that. And in a way I was at the top of the mountain…and it was a lonely place to be in. And I felt like, 'Well, I don't like this. I don't want to be stuck there.' I wanted to get down and start all over again or something like that. And then, of course, John appeared.

So in a way, it was just refreshing to think of all different ideas that we think together, you see, because [I'd never had] a partnership like that. I felt that I was a lone wolf in my work. I'm just doing what I do; and here John was very much a partnership person, and he was used to that. So it was a bit difficult for me to do it – like 'Let's think together' – but it was refreshing, it was interesting.

Klaus Voormann: For me, he made it. He made it not as a star or something, he made it by being happy, being able to cope and being happy with his Yoko and with Sean. John would never be the guy who sits on the mountain and meditates for the rest of his life. That's not John. John is different. He lives where he is. He's there, with everybody, with his surroundings. He will not be just by himself. That's not John. He would never be that type of a person. And never forget, when he's happy, and he found this happiness in his life, that doesn't [mean] that he's not funny, or he's not surreal, or he's not sarcastic or whatever. All this will stay with him, even though he has found his way, you know. That's what John is, and that's what he would have been if he were still living now.

John: I still love [New York]. I've been here three-and-a-half or four years, something like that. The thing I like best about it is it's twenty-four hours. And people are always saying 'What's an American?' But there's no such thing in a place like New York. I don't know about the Midwest and all that, those kind of places, that's what is America, I suppose, but in New York it's a bit like London only more so.

I mean, everybody's a foreigner, there's no set language. You get into a cab and say 'I want to go to West 44th Street' and they go 'What you say!?' So there's all the different nationalities here and sometimes in the summer it's like being in Calcutta or something. You can cut the heat with a knife, right, and you're always hearing congas going on in the park. It's like a festival going on and I just dig it.

To me, New York is no tenser then Liverpool or London. I mean, on the streets in Liverpool, unless you're in the suburbs, you had to walk close to the wall. To get to the Cavern – for those of you who remember all that – it was no easy matter, even at lunchtime sometimes. It's a tense place and Glasgow and Newcastle [too]. London had it.

When I first got to London it was pretty nerve-wracking. We were all putting on [the] 'We're from Liverpool and we're tough' bit, but there were some hard knocks down in London, and I think that's what you feel. It's almost the difference between Liverpool and London, London and New York, and it has that tenseness but it's also…it's just going at a tremendous speed. I don't know why, but it is, so people have that kind of tenseness.

The whole music business was here, a lot of it's moved to the West Coast, because a lot of people like to go and lie out there. So a lot of the industry has gone out there, but there's still plenty of studios and musicians. There's almost cliques, which I'm not keen on, that's why I like to use a few different people from different areas.

But there's a lot of action here, a lot of good musicians, and of course all the English musicians pass through here and they cut tracks or they goof around, so there's always input coming in. And I generally stick to the same studio because I'm like that with doctors and dentists, you know: find one, stick with it.

'Profit' isn't too dirty a word here, and Madison Square is the place. I mean, when anybody tours America or comes from England, wherever they come from, they have to hit Madison Square Garden and the place in LA which I can't remember. Those are the ones that count, the rest is just travel and it's a big event with the local news makers.

There's four or five channels of news: there's three big ones and there's a couple thrown in of local stations and then the sort of BBC one – I call it WNET. There's eight news channels and they're all looking for something to say, so they always cover the big events, especially Madison Square, whether it's Muhammad Ali or Jethro Tull, and the industry is a multi-billion dollar industry – I think it's bigger than the film industry now and I think they're getting aware of that.

LA is now a rock 'n' roll town. The movies are like a side issue, almost. The movie people still live there, a lot of them, the old-time stars and that, but even the new movie stars, they hang out with the rock 'n' roll people. Rock 'n' roll people are the new stars, you know. It's great!

We're promoting peace for the whole world, but mainly aiming towards the youth. We are appealing mainly to people with violent inclinations for change. We believe violent change doesn't really accomplish anything in the long term, because in the over two-thousand-plus years we've been going, all the violent revolutions have come to an end, even if they've lasted fifty or one hundred years. The few people who have tried to do it our way, unfortunately, have been killed, i.e. Jesus, Gandhi, Kennedy and Martin Luther King. The way we might escape being killed is that we have a sense of humour and that the worst – or the least – we can do is make people laugh.

We're willing to be the world's clowns. Part of our policy is not to be taken seriously, because I think our opposition – whoever they may be in all their manifest forms – don't know how to handle humour. And we are humorous where we are. What are they…Laurel and Hardy? That's John & Yoko and we stand a better chance under that guise, because all the serious people like Martin Luther King and Kennedy and Gandhi got shot.

RECORDING MIND GAMES / FEELING THE SPACE

John: *Mind Games* to me was like an interim record between being a manic political lunatic to back to being a musician again. And *Mind Games* is like the cross between them. I was really playing mind games – mind games is what it was. I had enough of this trying to be deep and think, 'Why can't I have some fun?' And my idea of fun with music was to sing.

Yoko: In 1970 John and I had recorded and produced the *Plastic Ono Band* albums together at EMI Studios on Abbey Road, using the same musicians – Ringo Starr, Klaus Voormann and Billy Preston. In 1971, we recorded the *Imagine* and *FLY* albums at home at Tittenhurst and at the Record Plant in New York. In 1972 we made *Some Time In New York City* at Record Plant with Jim Keltner and Elephant's Memory, straight after which I made another album, *Approximately Infinite Universe*, with the same band.

In 1973, I recorded what became *Feeling The Space*. I wanted to produce it myself and for each song to have a different style, so I needed professional musicians who were versatile enough to play in different genres and rhythms. I called up Jim Keltner first and he introduced me to David Spinozza, who assembled a new Plastic Ono Band [the Plastic Ono Superband] made up of the very best New York session musicians and we recorded again at Record Plant, but this time, for the first time, without Phil Spector. Directly after those sessions, we re-hired all the same artists in the same studio to record John's album, *Mind Games*, which John produced himself.

John: I woke up and a year had gone by with no album. Yoko was bringing back tapes and acetates virtually every night and I was listening to them and said, 'Hmmm, that's good. I'll use them.' Jim Keltner, whom I've used before, on drums; Gordon Edwards on bass; David Spinozza on guitar. All New York people except Keltner. And a pianist called Ken Ascher. He's also a producer. He has just been producing Paul Williams. And a guy called Sneaky Pete [Kleinow], on steel.

Sometimes I'll want to express something, like an emotion, but that's about as far as it goes. Generally it's whatever comes out, like diarrhoea. I try to sneak up on myself so I'm not too conscious of what I'm doing. If I can just open the plug it will do itself, for good or for bad, but then I don't have to sweat over it. But I do sweat a lot. Usually over trying to do something, then I book the session and then, 'Bam!' There it is.

I've never got the lyrics done until I sing them, so I don't count them as finished. The completed ones were 'Mind Games', 'Only People', 'Aisumasen', 'Bring On The Lucie' and 'I Know'. The rest all came in the week before the start of recording. I often just have half a thing or bits and pieces in my head, but it seems when I book the time and I realize

that I have a week, that I've gotta…it suddenly starts coming out. I have to remember that next time and just book the time and make sure I do it. Otherwise I get lazy. If I book time for the studio, then I'll write. Now there isn't a manager figure around, be it Epstein or Klein, to try to tell me what to do.

With the Beatles, the songs usually happened quickly. It was just when we got into that recording 'technique' it got to be too much. So I always try to do them in as quick a time… I always did, but there were other people to deal with, right? So everybody wants to do a little perfection here and a little perfection there. I'm all for perfection as long as it doesn't take more than eight weeks because then it's a bore. What's the point of making records that come and go in two days, and that are two and three minutes long but that take you six months to make? It was good while we did it. I'm saying this right now but I just may go in next year and stay in for a year or something. I would never plan it but I'm leaving all the doors open because whenever I say something I change me mind!

I took eight weeks over it. I always record fast – I can't stand being in the studio. *Imagine* and the one before were only ten days in the studio. I can't bear taking any longer. Some of the things I'd only just finished writing when I went in.

I could have gone in with half-formed ideas, and written the rest as I went along. I have worked like that, but as it was, only a couple of lyrics needed finishing.

It's a bit personal, it's a bit political. I never make concept albums although they may sound like it. I usually try and make each track individual, but when I stick them down they form into a montage. I don't really go in for the story of Fred who met Annie. I'm more of a first-person journalist. There's no deep message about it. I very rarely consciously sit down and write a song with a deep message. Usually, whatever lyrics I write are about what I've been thinking over the past few months. I tend not to want to change an idea once it's in my mind, even if I feel differently about it later. If I stated in a song that water was the philosophy to life, then people would assume that was my philosophy forever, but it's not. It's forever changing.

It's rock at different speeds. It's not a political album, or an introspective album. Someone told me it was like *Imagine* with balls, which I liked a lot.

Pages 220–21: John sitting at the console in the control room at Record Plant while filming the TV show *Flipside*, 12 May 1973. Opposite: Bob Gruen contact sheet of Yoko and the Plastic Ono Superband (Jim Keltner, David Spinozza, Ken Ascher, Gordon Edwards, Michael Brecker and Sneaky Pete Kleinow) recording with engineer Jack Douglas at Record Plant, New York, 29 June 1973.

12A 13 13A 14 14A 15 15A 16 16A 17

→12 →12A →13 →13A →14 →14A →15 →15A →16 →16A

22A 23 23A 24 24A 25 25A 26 26A 27

7A 8 8A 9 9A 10 10A 11 11A 12

→28 →28A →29 →29A →30 →30A →31 →31A →32 →32A

→17 →17A →18 →18A →19 →19A →20 →20A →21A

John showing off his T-shirt, gifted from the four fans he nicknamed 'The Greeting Committee' – Marie Lacey, Robin Titone, Goldie Friede and Barbara McDede.

Marie Lacey: My friends Robin, Goldie, Barbara and I used to go see John every day while he was recording at Record Plant and he gave us the nickname 'The Greeting Committee'. We made up a T-shirt for

him and he surprised us by wearing it the very next day! I set up the picture (asked John to open his jacket so we could read the writing) and he asked me 'how', so I opened up his jacket for him (yes I did!!). And Robin took this picture!

Opposite: Further pictures taken by Marie Lacey.

John & Yoko working with engineer Roy Cicala at Record Plant studios,
321 W44th Street, New York, 1972.

ROY CICALA
Engineer

The Record Plant in the seventies was like the garage studios of today with the best equipment in the world and the best engineers in the world too. And [a] very campy, very down-to-earth studio; so if you walked in you didn't feel you're in a hospital, which a lot of the studios were like then. And even the new studios were like that. And we were very…wood, a lot of wood. Carpets, plush carpets. Bathrooms were all mirrors, and, you know, crazy things like that. Consoles with mirrors on the console. [laughs]

The way John liked to work was with the musicians. A lot of the writing happened in the studio. While the musicians were playing, he would be changing lyrics, making lyrics, etc. And in many cases we had the band set up and John was in the middle of the band, singing. And there was a couple of songs where John did go out of tune, and we had to fix it. So when we fixed it, all the bleed, the leakage, whatever you would call it here, would disappear from that bad note and then come back, and we used to listen to it and love it because it was almost like a mistake. So we always accented our mistakes.

He liked different things. If I would put reverb on or echo on his voice that was too much – 'Don't take it off!' We recorded with echo; recorded with all that echo. Meaning repeat echo.

His double tracking was amazing. He could sing the song twice and you would think it was one, just one voice a little wider. We used to actually put the reverb or the tape delay on the track. Nobody could touch it after. I think it was a sense of insecurity that he had, as far as the playbacks, because he was. Everybody's insecure, I guess, to a certain extent. And he loved the repeat on his voice.

In many, many cases, maybe eighty per cent, he would come

in and they would run it down, they would learn the chords, and he had the musicians that were great because they would play with him. They wouldn't try to change it in his direction. If he didn't like it he would just stop, and say 'There's too much going on, let's try it a little slower' or a little different, or we would say it to him. And on his vocals, we always did the vocals ourselves, after.

Not in all the cases though. The *Rock 'n' Roll* album, a lot of it was live. Live meaning with the musicians in the room, which they don't do nowadays because they're making perfect digital records now. But they're not selling as well, are they?

'Mind Games' was just a natural. I mean, we had the slide guitar, and then they were changed in the studio.

The studio was…very earthy and very garage sounding. Open to mistakes…. I mean, if they were really terrible mistakes like wrong chords or too many notes per bar we would fix that or redo it, but anything that might be out of tune we'd go for the actual feeling of the song, rather than the audiophile side of the song.

He definitely has the overall picture of it; didn't know how to get there. And that's one of the reasons why we recorded with a delay. I mean a lot of times, Jim Keltner, there was delay on his drums, I'm sure you heard in some of the records. The delay would inspire John to sing it that way because he was – he could accent the delay, he knew how to do it. Sibilants, accents, delay, I'm sure you people know that. And he would actually like…

What's an example? [makes sibilant sound] He would do that so the repeat would repeat after a lyric or something. He played with the delay, and that's why he liked to hear it in his head. He was quite amazing. I think it was

natural with him, though, you know, as long as he had a good headset mix it was pretty natural for him. He would hear the delay in his headsets and make it delay more. The way we used to set it up [was] if you gave it a little more volume in the microphone, the delay would last longer. That was another thing that took a few months to get it to work properly.

John would take the feeling from the drummer, from the bass player, and use them to help him with his music. He wouldn't go for the arrangement. If we had to put violins on and things like that, that would [be] an arrangement. The pureness of an arranger. But not in the rhythm sections – bass, drums, sometimes slide guitar.

He would be singing the song and then change the lyric. It just came out naturally. Some of the songs were fifteen minutes. Not the recordings, but the writing. He would write them right there. I guess he got inspired by the band and the studio atmosphere.

He had some rough times in the UK and when they came to the States. I mean, our phones were tapped, and that's – I don't know why. I think they were following John too, when he was trying to get his Green Card, but that was later on. You could hear 'em. They didn't hide tapped phones then. We were audio people, we knew what was going on. [laughs] Who tapped them I don't know, but I know that we had four lines tapped, our main lines at Record Plant New York. I mean they actually clicked; you could hear them almost talking. It was so bad. It was like Howdy Doody or whatever. It was a cartoon of tapping phones. As far as me being followed, I think I was asked that question, no, I don't remember that. But I didn't know anyone.

I think he loved New York City. The excitement, the twenty-four-hour delis, open all the time or wherever you

Opposite: (top left) Record Plant job sheet, 2 August 1973;
(top right) Record Plant work order, 12 August 1973; (bottom left)
John's sketch of Roy Cicala on a Record Plant logsheet; (bottom
right) Record Plant invoice 'for selections on album *Out The Blue*',
18 September 1973.

want to go. The Village was great then, right. A little risqué sometimes, you know, before they cleaned up New York. People on the street begging for money, and if you don't give them money, they would shoot you. [laughs] I remember that – I don't know where that happened, on 52nd Street, I think. And the guy gets out and goes into his Mercedes, right? That happens in LA a lot too. It was very exciting, New York in the late sixties, seventies.

I think the freedom in New York was much greater than England, or any other country really. I remember walking with a friend down one of the streets, and the guy lights up a joint, the police right at the back of him. And the police just came up and said, 'Put that out, will you?', and that's all they said to him.

The fans didn't know that he was ever at Record Plant. Nobody knew. We did all the major artists in the seventies, but nobody knew it. We never advertised about that. We had two entrances, freight entrance, and John used to come in the freight if there were people out in front. And nobody was allowed to come in the studio unless we knew who they were or something. I mean, the people that used to come in the studio were [people like] Jacqueline Kennedy, with her two kids, you know.

We used to go to a place called Smith's Bar. It's up the street, half a block from Record Plant. We used to walk up 44th Street – if I ate it now I would die of cholesterol. [laughs] It was amazing, the food that was in there. It's still there, I think. Right on the corner of 8th Avenue and 44th. John would go inside. And half of the people were bums in there, and the food was great. Nobody knew who he was because these people were older than I am now. [laughs] We used to go up the street on 8th Avenue, get a hamburger, or have it delivered,

or he would have sushi delivered. Was it John that wanted it out fast or was it Capitol? Because they would call us up in the middle of an album and say they needed it next week because they had their schedule.

And we used to tell them to F-off sometimes, because what are we going to do, change the creative part of John?

And in some cases we did get it ready, but we would go three days straight mixing it, and then at the end of those three days we would sleep for a week. No matter what you took, it didn't help, because you lose your power of being creative when you're… after the second day, maybe. You know, it just screws you up.

Well, you first go in and you have to get everything to work, make sure everything's working. And some of the assistants we had were great assistants and the people, you wouldn't believe who they were, what they do today. I mean, they're very well known, and they're very – they made their life very good.

Interscope Records, Jimmy Iovine was my assistant. Jack Douglas was an assistant. Shelly Yakus – he used to fall asleep…in the back of me, as an assistant. And we would set it up, not like it, set it up again. Then we would call John when we thought we were ready.

Nobody liked Yoko at the time. They just didn't like her, they thought that she broke up the Beatles, they thought she was too demanding on John.

I thought it was a love affair that was wonderful, both of them. Well, I guess I was more on the inside and saw what happened. And why they split I don't know to this day. I did understand that Yoko said go away with May, and that's how that all started.

He's writing in the studio. And the next day we'd come in, listen to the previous song that we recorded the day before. We'd love it; we went on to the next song. Only do one song a day. So I'd say in five days, five or six days, we did the basic tracks. And we had the best musicians in the world. And then from there we did vocals, and then we did like solo guitars and everything the way everybody else in world records. And I think in thirty days Capitol Records had the record.

Some Time In New York City with Elephant's Memory was an experiment with John, right? Trying to get the dirtiest sound we could get, which was easy to get.

And then *Mind Games* is more quality. We took our time getting the sounds, even though we did it fast. We got a great sound. In some cases I used to take the cymbals away from Jim and overdub the cymbals because you can get a better tom-tom sound. And the quality was better because of the way we recorded it. We were all sober. You can't drive a car right, being really drunk. Can't record being real drunk. That's the same thing. You got to focus, and we were really focused. All of us, it seemed like we were on that one track.

I think he was probably the happiest person in the world. I mean, he was walking a magic carpet. He's doing what he loves to do, and he goes home and he's doing what he loves to do. What man wouldn't love that; you know? And yeah, he had to be the happiest person in the world. The happiest days of his life, I should say.

I remember the warmth of his personality. He was just a friend that was amazing. I carry the warmth of his friendship. I mean, I remember the funny things that he did, and the positive things. A good friend, man. We had a lot of fun, yeah.

DATE: 8/2/73 STUDIO: B
TIME: 7pm-open

CLIENT: E.M.I.

Instrument			
Guitar (Reg.)	Violins	(Solo Voc.)	
(Guitar (Elec.))	Viola	Group Voc	
Guitar (Steel)			
(Piano)	Cello	Live	O/D
(Piano (Elec.))			
Honky Tonk	Harp		
Organ	Vibes		
Celeste	Marimba		
Bass (Upright)	Xylo		
(Bass (Fen.))	Bells		
(Drums)	Bell Tree		
Trumpet	Tymp		
Conga			
Bongos			
Tambourine			
Harmonica			
Trombone	Harpsichord (Single or Double)		
Fr Horn			
Tuba	Ordered by		
Clara	From		
Flute			
Sax			
Oboe			
Bassoon			

#			
1	Ac Git	John	
2	Voc	John	57
3	Guit	David	
4	Guit	John	
5	Bass	Direct & ...	
6	Pno Top	87	
7	Pno Bot	57	
8	Elec Pno	Direct	
9	Elec Pno	Direct	
10	Clavinet	Direct	
11	O.H. R	PML	
12	O.H. L	PML	
13	Lg Tom	47	
14	Sm Tom	47	
15	Snare	New Song	
16	Bass Drum	57 ...	
17	Hi Hat	C-22	
18			
19			
20			
21			
22			
23			
24			
25			
26			
27			
28			
29			
30			

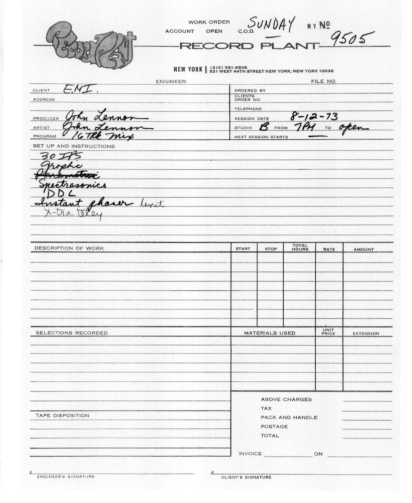

WORK ORDER   SUNDAY   N Y N⁰ 9505
ACCOUNT OPEN C.O.D.

RECORD PLANT

NEW YORK | (212) 581-6505
321 WEST 44TH STREET NEW YORK, NEW YORK 10036

CLIENT: E.M.I.
ENGINEER: FILE NO.

ADDRESS:

ORDERED BY
CLIENTS ORDER NO.

PRODUCER: John Lennon   TELEPHONE
ARTIST: John Lennon   SESSION DATE 8-12-73
PROGRAM: 16 Trk Mix   STUDIO B FROM 7PM TO open
    NEXT SESSION STARTS —

SET UP AND INSTRUCTIONS

30 IPS
Graphic
Parametric
Spectrasonics
DDL
Instant phaser limit
X-tra Delay

DESCRIPTION OF WORK	START	STOP	TOTAL HOURS	RATE	AMOUNT

SELECTIONS RECORDED	MATERIALS USED	UNIT PRICE	EXTENSION

ABOVE CHARGES
TAX
TAPE DISPOSITION   PACK AND HANDLE
POSTAGE
TOTAL
INVOICE _____ ON _____

X _____   X _____
ENGINEER'S SIGNATURE   CLIENT'S SIGNATURE

RECORD PLANT

NEW YORK | (212) 581-6505
321 WEST 44TH STREET NEW YORK, NEW YORK 10036

INVOICE # 12546
INVOICE DATE 9/18/73

THE RECORD PLANT

RECORDING STUDIO

321 West 44th Street   New York, N.Y. 10036

SOLD TO:
E.M.I. c/o CAPITOL
1750 NORTH VINE STREET
HOLLYWOOD, CALIFORNIA 90028

ARTIST: JOHN LENNON
PRODUCER: JOHN LENNON
ENGINEER: ROY CICALA

STUDIO C	YOUR P.O. NO.	SESSION DATE: SUNDAY 9-16-73	TERMS NET 30 DAYS

DESCRIPTION		UNIT PRICE	AMOUNT	TOTAL
3:00PM - 1:00AM 10 hrs.	16 trk Mix	110.00	1110.00	
1:00AM - 6:00AM 6 hrs.	2 trk Transfer	65.00	390.00	
6:00AM - 8:00AM 2 hrs.	2 trk Assemble and Edit	65.00	130.00	
6 reels ¼" tape (2400')		15.00	90.00	
Phasing Units (2) DDL		25.00	50.00 35.00	
	Tax		126.35	1931.35

Selections: All selections on Album "OUT THE BLUE"

FOR YOUR CONVENIENCE, WE PROVIDE SPACE FOR TAPE STORAGE AT OWNER'S RISK

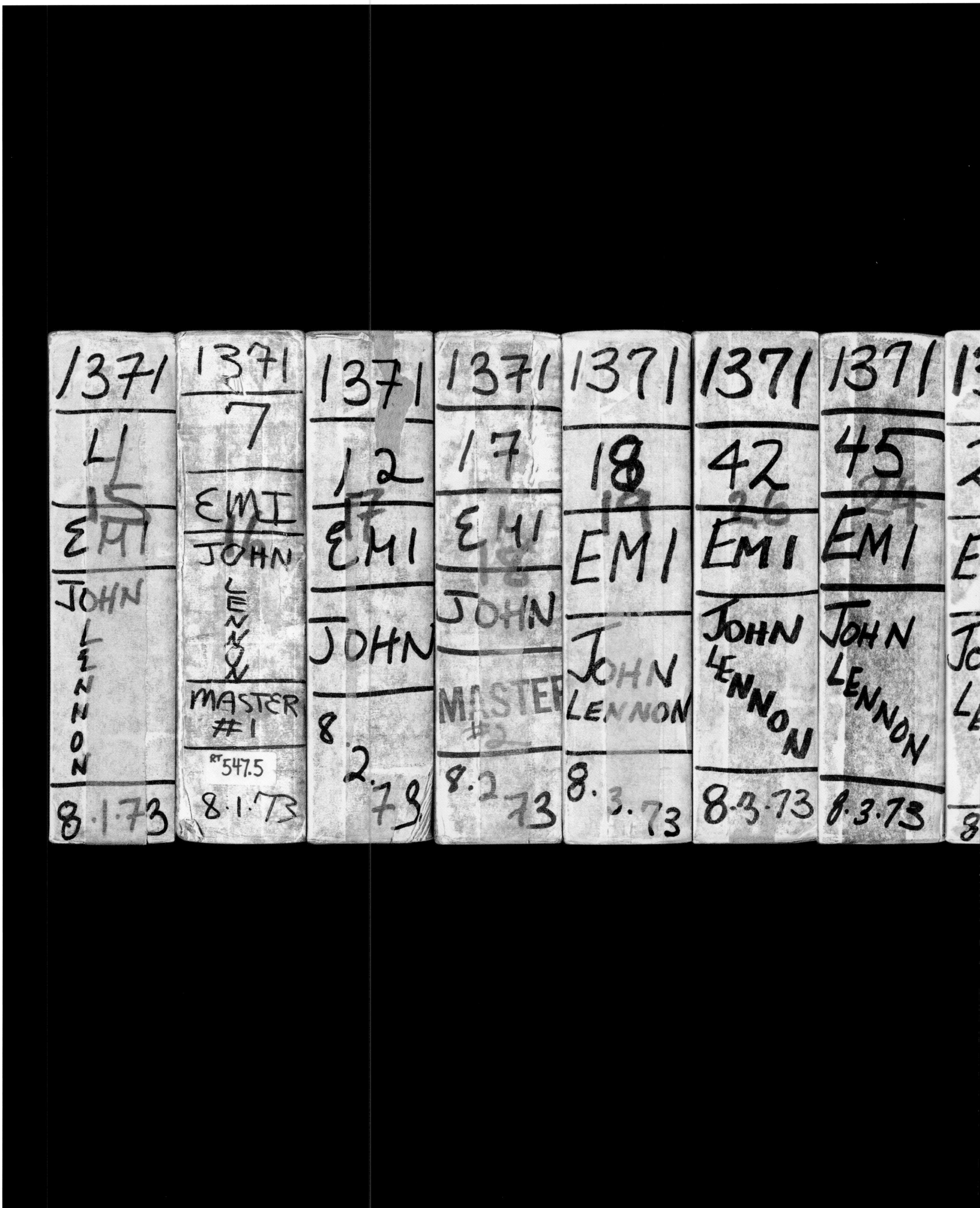
1371
4
EMI
JOHN LENNON
8.1.73
1371
7
EMI
JOHN LENNON
MASTER #1
RT 547.5
8.1.73
1371
12
EMI
JOHN
8.2.73
1371
17
EMI
JOHN
MASTER #2
8.2.73
1371
18
EMI
JOHN LENNON
8.3.73
1371
42
EMI
JOHN LENNON
8.3.73
1371
45
EMI
JOHN LENNON
8.3.73

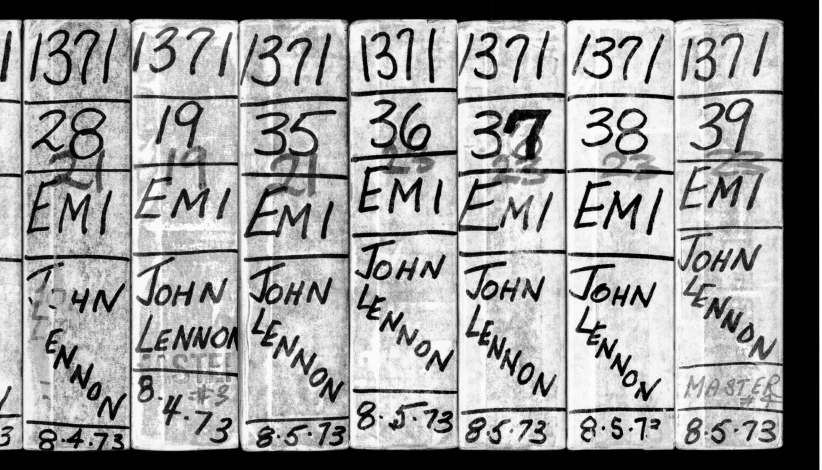

Master tapes from left to right: 1371–4 ('I Know') 8.1.73, 1371–12 ('Intuition') 8.2.73, 1371–18 ('Only People') 8.3.73, 1371–42 ('You Are Here') 8.3.73, 1371–45 ('Meat City') 8.3.73, 1371– 21 ('Mind Games') 8.4.73, 1371–28 ('Out The Blue') 8.4.73, 1371–35 ('One Day At A Time') 8.5.73, 1371–36 ('Aisumasen') 8.5.73, 1371–37 ('Bring On The Lucie') 8.5.73, 1371– 38 ('Tight A$') 8.5.73

DAN BARBIERO
Engineer

I was in music from a very young age. I was a professional choir boy at St Thomas Church in New York City on 5th Avenue and worked with Leonard Bernstein. You had to read music and be quite responsible. I went to private schools, graduated Yale, enlisted in the army and was a platoon commander in Vietnam in 1968.

I came home pretty much PTSD-ed and lived for a while in the Virgin Islands making radio commercials before returning to New York to work with my brother Michael at Media Sound Studio on 57th Street. I started in the shipping department for a couple of months, then in the studio, and after about three or four months of [my] learning really fast, Stevie Wonder came in.

Media Sound was a church that had been converted to a studio and Studio A was the church. It had a great sound to it and Stevie liked the sound, so he wanted to record there. The two guys that worked with him, Bob Margouleff and Malcolm Cecil, did all his ARP, Moog and TONTO programming and they didn't know the studio at all so they put me on the date, too, because I knew the equipment.

Stevie and I just hit it off. I loved his music, he liked me, we just hit it off. And after about a couple of sessions with him, he told the owner of the studio he wanted me to be his engineer, which was unbelievable, since I was maybe eight months in the business, something like that [laughs] and I was his engineer for *Innervisions*, which won three Grammys, one of which was for engineering.

The studio told me John called and wanted me to do his vocals. I had done a lot of vocals for Stevie, just the two of us recording vocals. I have a feeling that he called Stevie after our sessions and Stevie told him that I worked vocals with him, and so that's probably how I got to do *Mind Games*.

I had to go to the Record Plant and leave Media Sound to do that. Probably not a good idea at the time. I should have asked John to come to me, but I was too young and naive to think of that.

So I went to the Record Plant and met John and I can tell you, the first thing he said to me, was, 'Dan, I'm no Stevie Wonder, I'm just a pretty good guitarist' – for who he was, to have the humility to even make that statement

just blew me away. I mean, he was a really, really nice man. And the Beatles were gods.

Stevie's sessions had had people everywhere, he didn't care. John, it was closed, just us. The first night I remember it was John, Yoko, Roy Cicala, May Pang and me in the studio. My first wife walked in and Yoko threw her out because it was a closed session. Then they all left John and I alone. We didn't turn the machines on. We just talked the whole night. Talked! Our first session was he and I smoking dope and talking. That's all we did. All night. We didn't turn any of the equipment on.

I started singing Beatles tunes, and he said 'I didn't write that.' I sing other tunes – 'I didn't write that.' And I'd sing another tune, 'I didn't write that.' So finally I sang, 'Please don't wear red tonight.' 'I wrote that one!' I said, 'Yeah, I played that tune on the harmonica in the jungle in Vietnam till my troops went crazy.' And he got a big kick out of that.

I asked John who his big influences were, and first of all he was a huge Elvis Presley fan and he was really a rock 'n' roller. He said, 'The ballads, I do okay, but I really like rock and roll.' He liked really raucous rock 'n' roll. And obviously of course Buddy Holly and the Crickets, who were was a huge influence on their band.

Yoko was there during all the recording sessions and at the mixing for quite a few sessions, and after that she was pretty much gone.

One night we're in the studio recording and I'm doing vocals with John. The middle of the night, just the two of us. And he says, 'How's that sound?' I was tired, I'd been working ninety hours a week and said, 'That's a little out of tune, John.' The second time I said that to him he got a little mad.

He said, 'Dan, you must be a fucking choir boy!' I said, 'John, I am a choir boy.' [laughs] He got a big kick out of that.

On another tune, we had to do a back beat on a tambourine. So he says, 'Dan, take that tambourine, go in there and we'll record you.' He put me out in the studio, and I had to do the back beat, and if I missed it by a second, 'Dan, you're off!' Like, he wanted me to see what it was like to be on the other side of the glass! Which was a very cool thing to do.

We used to use a lot of different levels of John's voice. We recorded over and over, because he didn't like his voice. He was very insecure about his singing and when I criticized him, it ticked him off. But I loved the way he sang. He was far more talented than he gave himself credit for.

We used to come in early for the session, find out what was going to happen that day or if they're going to do, you know, basic tracks, set up microphones and equipment and sound check the microphones. And then, what they liked to do was set levels and mark on the console exactly what everything was, just to make it easy for the engineer to know what was going on. Roy did most of that.

Roy Cicala was great. Very calm and brilliant. And very good to me, because, again, I was so new and so green, and he was just a very, very good engineer. He was laid back. He barely spoke. He just worked and just made magic, because he knew the equipment at the Record Plant so well. I didn't, so not only did I have to work with John, but I had to learn all the equipment. And every patch bay is different. It's all different. Plus I was new anyway – you know, I had probably had a year in the business, so it was an interesting time.

The guys that worked on the *Mind Games* album did a huge amount for everybody. Spinozza did a tremendous amount of work. I knew David Spinozza because he was in Media Sound all the time doing commercials for TV and jingle music. The whole New York Philharmonic would come in.

I worked with the *Sesame Street* crew, we did all *Sesame Street*'s music. John loved to hear about that stuff, he liked the fact that I had had that kind of experience.

I remember when Sneaky Pete came in; John loved Sneaky Pete. Sneaky Pete did this – what the hell did he have again? Some tricked-up guitar sounds and John just loved the guy, because he was a real…. He looked like a Sneaky Pete, you know? John loved Sneaky Pete. He got all excited every time Sneaky Pete was in the studio.

I recorded a lot of vocals in the middle of night with just the two of us. That and a lot of mixing together. I don't remember a lot of it.

The things I remember are the conversations we had more than anything else. I asked him, 'John, why did we start at 10 o'clock at night? You can record any time you want and we're recording all night!' He said, 'Dan, there's nobody at the studio when I come. There's nobody there when we leave. I go home, it's quiet. There are crazy people out there, somebody could walk up to me and shoot me.' He had a real fear of people walking up to him on the street.

I mean, the guy was just an unbelievably kind man. There are stories about him being not kind, and it's just bullshit. My memories of him are of a very gentle, nice man. He was a man who had a charitable spirit. As you can see in the *Get Back* film,

I think he was a lot of the glue for the Beatles because he was the kindest of all of them, really.

One night I was booked in a session in the middle of the night to clean tracks, where you erase all the sections of unneeded noises off the tapes before mixing, which we usually do. It was a session without anybody, just me. And then, disaster. I accidentally erased the background vocals. So I went to another verse with the same background track, recorded it, put it on and then dropped it in. It took the whole freakin' night to get it right, and you wouldn't know it because I did it really well.

Jimmy Iovine, who was a set-up guy when I was there, walks in [in] the middle of the night and says, 'What are you doing?' I said, 'I'm just cleaning-up tracks.' He knew I was doing something weird, because I was sweating bullets. It was the Something Different girls – Jimmy had brought in those girls – they were singing background vocals on 'You Are Here'. So now you know about it, see if you can hear it!

There was a lot of technical overdubbing where we would take a vocal track and run it through the echo chamber and bring it back and add it, and so there was a lot of layering of vocals that Roy would do for him. That didn't require recording, it just required technology. Once you're mixing there wasn't much else to do.

I left the business and went into financial services. But it was one of the great high points of my life to be able to hang out with John and get to know him and talk with him, and to have been able to sit next to Stevie and sing into his ear and watch him take the harmony out and make it magic.

I have Bob Gruen's picture of John on my wall, watching over me all the time.

JIMMY IOVINE
Engineer

I have a very, very vivid memory of John Lennon and the *Mind Games* album because it was so impactful on my life. I'm telling you. I came at the very end – when Dan Barbiero was leaving the sessions. When you're in that part of your career, you're kind of doing everything. Everything from getting tea to setting up the mics to answering the phones to engineering the session. You're doing everything.

Roy [Cicala, head engineer] called me on a Sunday and asked me if I wanted to come in, just to answer the phones. I walked in, and he and John are there, and they're laughing. Roy said, 'We just wanted to see if you'd come in on a holiday to see how committed you are!' So, that was it. That was the beginning of my working with Roy and John – at the end of the mixing sessions for *Mind Games*.

Roy was the greatest recording engineer, teacher and mentor. He was a bit eccentric, but that was a great side of him. We all studied under him. He was very experimental in his

approach, which I guess is what suited John. On 'Mind Games' the song, you hear that high, high tone on it? That's an actual oscillator that they tuned with the record as they were doing it. It's a tone you use for the console to calibrate it. And that is actually what's on the record.

Roy was a taskmaster, incredible. I mean, that's how he taught you – by letting you do it and guiding you, in a way. The guy was very demanding.

Recording studios look mellow but they're very tense behind the scenes. You have an artist who is going to go out there and sing, so it's got to flow very smooth. You don't want an artist going out to the studio, putting the headphones on and they're not working, or it's the wrong mix….

In those days everything was manual and analogue. There's these two guys working together, the engineer and the second, and it's really intense. Nowadays you don't even need another person in the room

(you know, there's no tape machine to run). But then we would have four tape machines running at one time, especially with John, because he used so many vocal echoes!

Everyone that was into rock 'n' roll and was my age had the same big bang, which was [the Beatles on] *The Ed Sullivan Show*. We saw that and went right to the store and bought a guitar as soon as we could. So I was in a band from eleven years old until I was seventeen years old, playing with the same group of guys. Then I met a woman named Ellie Greenwich, who was a fabulous songwriter and she got me a couple of jobs in recording studios. And then she got me a job with Roy Cicala and Eddie Germano. And that's the one that stuck. I went there in September of '73. So, obviously, I worked with John right away.

I don't have a formal education that's applied to any business I've ever built. I only work 'feel'. I wake up in the morning and do whatever I think. I don't know how to do any of the

Pages 236–37: Studio A at Record Plant, 321 W44th St, New York, 1972.

Opposite: Jimmy Iovine (left) and John Lennon (right) at the console at Record Plant, 321 W44th St, New York, 1973. Below: Jimmy and John with John dressed up as Jimmy, on the roof of Record Plant, 321 W44th St, New York, 1974.

things that I've done. I work solely on feel, and to get indoctrinated by John was really special. It must have been somewhere around two years, something like that. It was mind-boggling to be in a room with this glorious human being. It really set the tone for my entire recording career. John would always explain things to me and teach me, and it was incredible! And he never gave me a hard time, you know what I mean? Even if it wasn't always the perfect environment. He took a lot of time with me. He was very, very kind and generous.

I remember one day, we were mixing *Rock 'n' Roll*, and we were mixing the song 'Sweet Little Sixteen' and (as usual) I set up everything for Roy, made it completely like it was done for him, how he liked it. I heard somebody saying, 'Jimmy, will you get John a coffee and me a tea?' and I said, 'Absolutely.' I stood up, and before I even turned around, John said, 'Jimmy, stay in your seat. Someone else will get the coffee. This sounds great.'

So, that was my first official mix on a record. He was like that. He didn't care how much experience you had. He was completely about feel. Either it sounded good or it didn't. I'll never forget. That was the first professional mix I ever had on an album, that song. And it was an enormous, proud moment. Mind-blowing!

I learned the basics of recording from John and Roy and I've always been able to learn really well, and like a sponge, take everything in. For the rest of my career I always recorded with a guy singing with the full band playing. Understanding how that live vocal affects everything is so important.

I was very fortunate, because it influenced me going into Springsteen, Stevie Nicks, Tom Petty and Patti Smith, who all were disciples of John. I'm sure they got some confidence in me

because John trusted me. So I just recorded exactly how I recorded with him.

John gave me a blueprint for life in recording and he created an enormous standard that I always strive for, throughout my entire career. Even when I started doing hip-hop at Interscope, I would always use that blueprint. It stayed with me my whole life. An enormous impact on how to treat artists and realize what an artist truly is, and I cherished it. I always try to protect the artists that I work with.

Bruce Springsteen had a similar sort of desire. When I went on to produce, I used John and Bruce's input and how they recorded on the production of those two albums [*Walls And Bridges* and *Born To Run*]. As a matter of fact, when Tom Petty was making his third album he wanted to take a big leap, recording-wise and I said, 'Tom, we need to make this record like it's *Walls And Bridges*.' And we did! We followed a similar tech layout.

[John] was just great to me. One day in the middle of recording, he said, 'Let's go to the movies,' and he took me to see *La Grande Bouffe*. I'm from Brooklyn. First of all, I'd never seen subtitles before. So we go in the movie theatre, it's just me and him. It's three o'clock in the afternoon, there's no one there. And we're watching this movie and I'm like, 'What's going on here?' And all of a sudden, they're eating themselves to death! That's what he was like…. He also took me to the opening of the *Sgt. Pepper* show on Broadway. He took me and told me to go get a girl. I called a girl named Toni-Ann from my neighbourhood in Brooklyn and she was my date. And then we all went in his car with him! And then we went to the Hippopotamus with Robert Stigwood. And that night he introduced me to Ronnie Spector. And then I helped her make a record with Springsteen, 'Say Goodbye To Hollywood'.

We'd walk around Manhattan, just me and him, no security. We'd go to Downey's Steakhouse (next door on 8th and West 44th Street). He was just really kind to me, what can I say? What a gift all of us have had.

You know what's crazy? There aren't that many of us. Because after he left the Beatles, in the five years and seven albums he recorded from 1970 to 1975, I worked on four of them! (*Mind Games*, *Walls And Bridges*, *Pussycats* and *Rock 'n' Roll*). I was very fortunate, I really was. I learned everything! After that it was all adding on to it and I've always recorded like that. There's a little bit they did in *The Defiant Ones* documentary they did on me and Dre where you see me recording with Stevie Nicks. It's exactly the set-up that I used to use with John.

Hey, by the way there's a great picture of me and John in 'Brooklyn' T-shirts. Would ya like it? This is very indicative of our relationship. You know when you were a kid you had like five shirts? [laughs] I was living with my mother and she would clean 'em. John went out and found the exact same 'Brooklyn' T-shirt I used to wear and came into work dressed exactly like me. [laughs] It was so good we went outside and took a photo.

THE PLASTIC U.F.ONO BAND

Jim Keltner: Drums & Percussion

Gordon Edwards: Bass

Rick Marotta: Drums & Percussion

Yoko Ono: Wind

David Spinozza: Guitar

Sneaky Pete Kleinow: Pedal Steel Guitar

Ken Ascher: Piano

Photographed by Bob Gruen, San Diego,
California, 17 September 1973.

JIM KELTNER
Drums & Percussion

When you're with people who are really funny and fun to be around, the conversation flows easily. And the same is true when you're playing with great musicians – you start to feel the connection and energy with everyone listening and playing together, as you lock into the groove. That's how my favourite records were made. For me, hearing the playback is always the most fun. Listening to Spinozza playing that rhythm and those leads and big brother Gordon on bass, with that beautiful tone. He's such a sweet soulful man and so funny. All those things are reflected in the music of each take, and you can hear how much we're all enjoying playing together in all these mixes.

The guitar bass and drums are not there just for the pocket. It's about the conversation between us. And if you're hearing John Lennon's voice in your headphones and the great Kenny Ascher playing John's chords on the keys, there's just no question of where you're going and how you're going to get there. Between Gordon and David, we were just laughing all the time. And then when my brother drummer Rick Marotta, who always makes me laugh, came to play with us on a couple of tracks ('Bring On The Lucie (Freda Peeple)' and 'Meat City'), it became even more like a party.

To me, the musicians on this album are like the East Coast version of the Wrecking Crew. When the band was originally put together for Yoko, John & Yoko had previously worked with Elephant's Memory who were a real New York jamming party-rock band. For her next album, which became *Feeling The Space*, Yoko had wanted to spread her wings and explore songwriting in ways she hadn't tried before, so she needed musicians who were experienced in playing a lot of diverse styles.

For *Mind Games*, John, of course, was the reason we were all together. And we all knew what a special thing it was to be playing his music with him in New York City, in the city that he loved so much. All of us having spent so much time in the studio were accustomed to being given explicit instructions for the tracking. John would pick up on the feel from us, the vibe, and we would just go from there.

I've been so blessed in my career to play with some of the greatest singers in the world and every time I was working with John, I couldn't help finding myself naturally focusing intently on his voice because it was so great. When I caught myself doing it, I would try and shift my attention elsewhere because I had been taught as a drummer you're not supposed to ever play to the vocal.

I was concerned about it until I had a conversation with Ringo, way back when I first met him, and asked him, 'I was told that when you're recording with a singer, don't play to the vocal, because that will always be the first thing to be redone. But it was really hard for me not to.' And he said to me, 'Hey, I've always played to the vocal!' [laughs] And that was a huge relief. So I never worried about it again.

John was crazy about Yoko, and she was always there at the sessions. She was producing this with John, in a way. She was always looking out for him, managing things for him and helping keep things on track. She would get on the talkback and say, 'It's too heavy' or something like that, and we would all be sensitive enough to make an appropriate adjustment.

Being in the studio with John, the time went by so fast and so easily because he knew what he wanted and he knew it when he heard it. Musicians need something to rise to. John brought it to the table and it was like a feast. His singing was effortless and perfect imperfection, which we're all striving for as players.

Mind Games – what a real gift. The record was recorded in only five days. It speaks to the proficiency of the great engineering by Roy Cicala and the soulful Record Plant staff. At Record Plant in New York, they would record the drums in what we used to call a 'tree house' – I was up a few feet from the floor in a semi-enclosed baffle. There might have been an umbrella on top – that was quite a common thing – with the microphones everywhere. I was right next to the wall, looking out into the room, and able to see everybody. Roy Cicala was a really sweet-natured guy. He was always very calm and so adept at finding John the sounds he wanted.

Jimmy Iovine had just started working there. He was moving microphones around and sweeping the floors. He had such a great vibe about him. I still remind him once in a while that he used to be 'Little Jimmy'. He was the first one to come up to me every morning at the studio when my eyes were barely open – I'd hear this voice calling me, 'Hey Jimmy, you want coffee? How 'bout cigarettes?' And I would say, 'Yeah, Jimmy. Thank you.' He'd bring me coffee and cigarettes, man. Little Jimmy. It's so amazing to think of all he went on to achieve.

DAVID SPINOZZA
Guitars

You know, I don't know why these musicians got chosen for the *Mind Games* sessions, particularly. Maybe Roy Cicala recommended us. I do remember the funniest thing. The first phone call that I got was from Yoko.

One day I came home and on the answering machine it just said 'Hi, this is Yoko Ono, Y-O-K-O,' she spelt her name, and I thought that was hysterical! 'This is Yoko, Y-O-K-O. I'd like to hire you for a record. Please call me back.'

I thought somebody was playing a joke on me at first. Yoko called me herself. I don't remember how she got my number. And when I walked in, there was Gordon Edwards, there was Kenny Ascher.

At the time I was in a rhythm section playing a lot with Rick Marotta and with Gordon. I played with Gordon on a lot of sessions. Kenny and I did a lot of stuff. Kenny, Rick and I, especially – the three of us did a lot of sessions together. And I might have recommended them.

But Jim, I didn't even know. He was a Californian drummer. I only met him on those sessions. We did Yoko's record first, so I think she then told John about us. I certainly didn't know him and I think Yoko had to have put that together.

I think there was a drum room and then Kenny was to the right of me, I remember, piano. I think John and I sat next to each other. He was playing acoustic and singing pilot vocals. I can see Gordon up to my left, in front of me, but we'd all sort of see each other. And Yoko was in the console room with Roy and Dan helping to advise John.

It was a lot to record in five days. I think the sessions were midday or maybe at two in the afternoon. Like a typical booking group, it'd be two till five and seven till ten. They usually wouldn't be from ten in the morning. Ten to noon was jingle time for commercials. And then the record days would start at two. It's funny, you never knew if you were going to walk into a session whether there was going to be four songs in three hours with a lot of sight reading and everything written out beforehand, or whether you were going to be doing one song for three hours and working it out in the room.

John definitely worked fast. He liked to just show you the song and he kind of wanted to get it over with. He didn't really ever dictate a part. He never sang notes and said, 'Play this.' He just had a way of getting the best out of everyone.

On 'Mind Games', I always thought that was a clever line, that repeated slide over all the changes. John found the three notes that worked on all the chord changes. It was great. I remember we wound up playing something like Cuban reggae when it got to the chorus. The bass player in my band when I was a kid was from Jamaica. I had visited before the seventies and had heard reggae bands. I already was very hip to it. I love that music.

There's a thing that always surprised me – in the second verse, when Gordon goes an octave down, he does this half-step bass passing tone. The IV chord that nobody really plays. It always sort of stuck out to me as like, 'Why did he do that?' But it actually kind of works, I don't know what key we're in, but if, say, it was in the key of C, he goes G flat to the F chords, but John didn't really write it that way. It makes it sound so interesting.

The other thing that stands out for me is that I love Jim Keltner's jalopy-sounding press-rolls on the snare drum. I always love them! He kinda plays a fresh one, like you don't know what it's going to be, but he's got the time going in his head so it comes out right. But it sounds like a jalopy! [laughs]

There are two guitar solos in my life where I felt like I wanted to do it again. And they were 'Right Place Wrong Time' by Doctor John, where they were like 'No, no, it's magic, get out of here,' and I felt so like dejected and like, 'Oh my God, I could have played so much better.' And on 'Aisumasen' I wanted to do another guitar solo on that. I just remember John hitting the talkback and saying, 'That's the best guitar solo you ever played on anything!' I was like, 'Can I try one more?' [laughs]

When I first met Gordon and he heard me play, he said, 'There's no way you're white! Don't tell me you're Italian!' He said, 'On my deathbed I'm going to be saying, "What the hell is Spinozza?"' [laughs]

I would have loved to have played this live. Back in the day, a lot of us studio guys, we didn't go on the road that much because we were so busy, you know, going to the next session and stuff. I had very little time playing live.

I was joking with my girlfriend the other day, I said, 'My autobiography would be called *My Life in Headphones*. I spent more time in headphones than I ever did on a stage. [laughs]

Opposite top: David Spinozza (guitar). Opposite bottom: Ken Ascher (keyboards). Below top: Jim Keltner (drums). Below bottom: Gordon Edwards (bass) and Rick Marotta (drums), rehearsing as the Plastic Ono Superband, New York, 1973.

KEN ASCHER
Piano, Organ, Mellotron

David Spinozza called me and said Yoko wanted to do an album, and that Keltner was coming in to play drums, and he was going to get Gordon.

Yoko came up to me after one of our sessions and said John would like to meet me. I went over to meet John and we stayed up, just talked for the evening. And then *Mind Games* began. It was mind-blowing, Jim and David and Gordon and I are playing on these tracks with John Lennon!

John could be very specific when he told me what he wanted me to do. One time, he just had me play very simply and at one point I added an eighth note under the quarter and he said, 'Kenny don't do that.' He told me what he wanted but I was never locked up. It's just trusting what's in the room, so to speak, just go for it and if it doesn't work, you go back and do take two, you know? John was not a bossy person at all but once he got to the studio, he was always keen to get to work.

He hears things immediately, and he'll say something humorous that kept him from being bossy. He would say something, 'Come on girls!' [laughs]; if there was a couple of downbeats that obviously weren't together, he stopped immediately.

Why go on? It's not right. That's a good impatience. It's being in the moment.

John's manner as artist and producer in the studio, singer and guitar player, whatever he was playing, was done with a lightness of mind. If he stops a take, it's not, 'That was awful.' He never said that! He definitely had a lightness about his manner, which made it a pleasure to do what we were doing. It never got heavy. I don't remember ever leaving the session exhausted. This was making music, this was making a record with John Lennon. And humour was part of it.

The interesting thing about John is that he is singing, he's playing a guitar, and he's producing, all at the same time. He did this naturally but it's not as easy as one would think! His instincts were immediate and his basic musicality was really deep.

John would be writing in 4/4 time, and then he'll do those interesting bars that are odd. It's always so fascinating to me; there's just like this conception of 'OK, two, three, four, and one, two, three…'. Then it turns around on itself, and it never feels wrong.

It never feels uncomfortable. It's another part of his style. Every time John does it, it feels like that's just the inevitable thing that's supposed to happen and it's comfortable, compared to awkward and, you know, 'What's happening here? What happened?'

There's a lot of lyrics besides the notes and the harmonies, and I'm sitting here, thinking, 'Where did all these words come from?' This endless fountain of well put-together words. The specificity of what he says, put together as a lyric, one after another, and the ideas, thoughts, concepts. It's an unselfconscious presence. It is being in the moment.

Having your feet securely in your art, on the floor, and being who you are.

John is totally in there, he's just totally doing what he's doing. It's not selfconscious. It's just happening and it doesn't feel forced at all. John was comfortable to be around because I wasn't expecting anything; I didn't know what to expect. I was a bit in awe. I mean, here I am talking to John Lennon! The gift for me was that I just went and said, 'OK, I'm going over to John & Yoko's apartment, we're going to talk. We'll meet, I'll be there for fifteen minutes.' And it turned out we spent quite a few hours talking.

I feel my eyes tearing up a little bit listening to *Mind Games*. The total experience of it. It's good to see how powerful a writer and performer John was. Thank goodness that we have these recordings. It makes me appreciate the company that we were in and what I was feeling then.

Music comes through us, you know? There are moments when I feel at one with the universe. They're not static, they're moving. There's an energy field about it. I think we all have these moments. It's all personal. But it is magical. It's a unification of life. Everything is happening.

And I have felt, during those moments, just completely connected. That feeling of growth and energy is really terrific. We're lucky, those of us who have experienced this. When I get excited about stuff, I want to play the piano. I would like to get together and play this music again with these [people].

Intuition. That's another perfect word for this. Letting it be. Letting it grow. Letting it move yourself where you need to be if you aren't in the right place, that's nature. It's fantastic! It's the wind and the air. He knows where to move it around.

GORDON EDWARDS
Bass

I am West Indian. My mother was from Saint Catherine in Jamaica and my father was from Saint Vincent, and they met on the boat coming over here [to the USA]. I was born in 1938 and I grew up in Bed-Stuy, Brooklyn, New York, listening to the radio. In New York they had radio shows that would play the same music every day at the same time. My mother used to like Rudy Vallée and people like that, and we would play and sing calypso music. My favourite calypso artists were Sparrow, Lord Macbeth and Lord Kitchener.

Early in the new year of 1964, you'd be just riding places, and you'd see stickers all over New York saying 'The Beatles are coming.' You ride a cab, 'The Beatles are coming.' They had people riding the buses who would stick 'em behind seats, 'The Beatles are coming.' And no one knew what the Beatles were. And then they were on *The Ed Sullivan Show* and then everyone coast-to-coast knew who the Beatles were. And they wiped American music out. They were the first English group that, because of their Liverpool accents, we could understand what they were singing about. [laughs]

I've got gold records on my wall – Paul Simon, Carly Simon, Van McCoy;

everybody steals from everybody in the music business, so when I made one person a hit, they said, 'Shit, I'm going to get him so he can make me a hit!' And if the Lord blessed, I'd make them a hit and I was on my way.

James Brown! You know James Brown? I was his regular bass player in the studio. And I always tell people this – that no one knows, when I went to play in the studio, I was the only black man in the studio recording. The Godfather of Soul – he got nothing but white musicians out there. The drummer, the guitar player, the horn player. And here I came. I broke down a lot of doors.

We were a rat pack. Kenny Ascher, he played with Van McCoy and all these other guys – we were interchangeable! We'd see each other like two or three times a day on sessions. And at night time, I started working a little bit with David Spinozza and his band. I'm telling you, we were all busy for like twenty-four hours straight. Except when we went to the bathroom! [laughs]

Kenny Ascher is not a piano player. He's a pianist. He sits down and he can play Chopin, he can sight-read music, he can play [by] ear, he can just play, man. In other words, if somebody asked me to recommend them a pianist for a job, I wouldn't hesitate in sending them Kenny Ascher. Would not hesitate in the least.

Jim Keltner is the most unique drummer I've ever played with. In other words, there's things that he does that other drummers try to do but can't do because they'd be wrong. He makes it right. That's the best way I can explain it. The last letter in the alphabet is the letter Z; well, Jim Keltner plays as if the last letter in the alphabet is A! He switches the whole show around, and after a while, you say, 'You know, he's right, it is A!' He can play. I don't know how he does it. Don't find out, listening

very carefully to each other – they know what kind of bass line I'm gonna play, I know the kind of guitar line he's gonna play and we play it and get a groove going.

Although there's four or five individuals, we're all playing as one. And I don't know anybody that would change that. The way Keltner give me that open road – who gets a chance to play like that? So we would try it, just go with the flow. Oh man, long before I even met Jim I knew how he rolls into different strokes. People would say, 'He's crazy, man. You gotta watch out for him. He'll start going on three.' And I was thinking, 'If he's crazy, I'm crazy, because I'm feeling the same thing he's feeling!' When he makes that roll, oh man!

And John's voice doesn't hurt – you would think we had been practising for months to try and achieve this. Good luck trying to find someone who could play this live!

The whole rhythm section tracked their parts together, and I think they added a few parts like Sneaky Pete and the background vocals later.

I used a '58 Fender Precision bass and we had one line going directly into the board as well as a mic-ed up amp for that external sound and feeling; I think it was a tube-type Ampeg B-15.

I had a man, Pasquale, who was my bass doctor – the only man I would let work mechanically on my bass. I play La Bella flatwound steel strings. I don't like that scraping or popping sound from round wound strings; it's gotta be smooth. I try to imitate as well as I can the sound of an upright without it being an upright.

My mother always said the only thing you can do with a groove is mess it up. And I've used that as a principle throughout my life. [laughs]

SNEAKY PETE KLEINOW
Pedal Steel Guitar

I didn't create the name. People started using that when I had an old band where everyone had a nickname of sorts and I got that name hung on me, and I'm sorry I did. I tried to shake it off but they won't let me so I still have it. I was never sneaky. I was very forthcoming and spoke my mind. I wasn't sneaky at all.

The steel guitar was virtually my first love and that relationship remains intact. Actually I loved it long before I could play it. I was brought to the steel guitar by hearing some lap players, people that had lap guitars, and I started off doing that but I was very amateurish and I just gradually got to the point where I had my own steel guitar. They didn't call it steel guitar then – they called it electric slide guitar. So my grandmother rented a single neck for me. I met my wife, Ernesteen, in that class. She's still pretty cute.

It was quite a long time ago that I started to reach out and try to develop some style of my own. I think we kind of succeeded in that, we learned how to create better sounding music. My very first ear-opener was an old 78 rpm record I found in Mom's collection. It was Bing Crosby singing 'Sweet Leilani' and 'Blue Hawaii'. There was a steel guitar on it that made my eyes misty and I couldn't stop playing that record.

Then I started hearing someone called Jerry Byrd on the *Grand Ole Opry*. What a fantastic virtuoso! This player more than anyone else gave me the incentive to buy my first steel. To this day I believe Jerry is the most clever and emotional player to ever touch a steel guitar.

When I began playing professionally I somehow seemed to end up working with trios – usually guitar, bass and steel. I guess that's how I evolved such a crazy approach to the instrument.

I think it was actually some small degree of boredom that made me attempt to get a guitar sound or an organ sound or whatever out of that old axe.

I was playing all the solos and all the fills and I desperately looked for variety. So all the while I was learning to play the steel I was unconsciously learning the techniques of other instruments through the medium of the steel guitar. Somehow all of this confusion developed into a unique style and right or wrong, you've got to admit it's different!

I recorded with John Lennon in New York and also did various sessions with him in Los Angeles. It's great when somebody [like Lennon] says, 'Here's the track, what would you like to do?', but most of the time they have exactly what they want you to do all worked out, and even though you can think of half-a-dozen phrases which would sound better, they don't want to know.

Most steel players live around Nashville and the South. They're country musicians – and I come from a different background. So I fell into playing a lot of different types of styles of steel, and that's partly why I appear on so many sessions. The other reason is, there aren't too many steel players around LA. Everyone's doing it. But progress is slow. It takes years of experimenting to become fluid and easy on pedal steel guitar.

I try to adopt a different approach in everything I do. When I play with a person I try to adapt my style to fit what I think they are trying to achieve. I don't let technique interfere. I play what I think sounds right. It's mostly technique. I really don't use any gimmicks or gadgets or special tunings although I do have a tuning that people don't use too much. But that's not what it is. I think it's technique.

I taught myself to play cables, and I have my own method and my own pedal changes. I wouldn't recommend my system. I do a lot of things the hard way. Most steel players prefer the rod system. I just happen to prefer the old cables. If you want to learn badly enough you'll pick it out. There aren't many tutors about and not really anyone to give you advice. I just sat down and listened to records and kept improvising and adding. Whenever I do a session I'm not thinking 'steel guitar', I'm thinking 'What kind of sound will fit here?'

I just play one string at a time. I don't put two strings together in unison, as is done in Nashville and other places. And don't use the Boss Tone. I have my own fuzz tone that I had designed for me. It has a really mellow sound. You've got to be sure that one string stops ringing before you jump to the next one. That is the only secret of it. Of course, the technique is getting your vibrato right and picking it with the right pressure. Good equalizing, when you are mixing, helps a heck of a lot.

I use an envelope filter, octave divider and chorus. The chorus is a signal splitter made by Roland. One output is a straight signal, and the other output is signal that bends itself up and down in pitch. The speed of that can be altered, and the blend of the two gives a chorus. It is like two things playing along together. Now, if you control that down to the point where it is not too obvious, it produces a nice, fat sound. Instead of doubling by digital delay, you double by pitch variation. I also use an Echoplex [tape delay]. I do not use reverb because I don't like its sound. I have always used a tape echo of some kind or other. Built my first one out of a tape recorder, before anybody else was using them.

My belief is that no instrument should be limited by what it is.

SOMETHING DIFFERENT: CHRISTINE WILTSHIRE, JOCELYN BROWN, ANGEL COAKLEY & KATHY MULL
Backing Vocals

Jocelyn Brown: I'm from a religious, gospel, black-oriented farming family. We lived in North Carolina, in the woods. It was cotton and tobacco and stuff. We lived the country way. My grandmother had sixteen children altogether. My mother was one of them and my aunty, they put the music in my love and in my life.

My mum's morning avenue was 'sing'. So I sang making breakfast. I sang cleaning up. My aunt Barbara helped me to become better with my voice, and my cousin Brenda helped me to be able to harmonize with two other voices. So I got my lessons there, from my own.

We lived in the South and the Ku Klux Klan were on the horizon. They were doing what they did. But we were in the country and we were living away from the violence. We were blessed that we didn't live it like that. We knew it existed, you know, and we knew we were black, there was no question about that.

We migrated from North Carolina to Brooklyn. Brooklyn was beautiful. It allowed you to see the difference in culture. In Brooklyn, we had an opportunity to live another kind of life.

My first great friend was Christine Wiltshire. We were eight and six or something in there. She was my partner. My godmother lived next door to her and we used to play in the backyard all the time. Up and down the alley in the back, and ride our bikes. [laughs] We were such silly little girls. She was my best friend.

Christine Wiltshire: My mother knew I wanted to sing. I studied voice lessons and I auditioned for the High School of Music and Art and I got into that. I auditioned for the All City Chorus, and I got into that. I always wanted to sing. I went to this school called the Brooklyn Ethical Culture School, and I was the only black person in my class, from kindergarten until eighth grade. There were only two of us in the whole school!

I had a teacher named Cesar Longo. He used to be on 85th Street in Manhattan and I would go to him after school. I was singing theatre tunes and arias and I was singing in German, Italian and a little French.

There were so many things that my parents were denied that I was exposed to – the Philharmonic, and ballet, and the opera, and we went to

the theatre. I loved those things. I just ate it up. And that's what I wanted to do. Now, after they pushed all this on me and introduced me to all that, my father says, 'What do you want to do when you get out of school?' I said, 'I want to be a singer.' He said, 'Well, singing's not a job!' [laughs]

This was a black man who put himself through John Jay Law School because he had applied to Harvard, he had the grades, he was accepted. And our last name is Wiltshire, which is an English name, so they just assumed that he was white. Of course, when he had to send his picture in, they sent him a letter saying, 'We're very sorry, but we don't accept coloureds.' Back then, we hadn't even become negroes! [laughs] So my parents had a completely different plan for me and running around the country being an entertainer was not it. I never wanted to do anything else. Nothing inspired me like music did.

Jocelyn Brown: Me and Angel was in church together. Her mother and my mother knew each other and we were in the choir together. We learned the basics of being together and harmonizing.

The last person that I met was Kathy Mull. She came to Brooklyn and we hooked up because she met some friends of ours and we all intertwined and began to sing together. And me, Christine, Kathy and Angel Coakley became Something Different. We had a friend named Richard Cummings. He was the keyboard player we knew at that time and he used to work with us. But we hadn't stepped out yet. I stepped out when I met with my friend, Howie Wyatt, and he knew that we could get some work together if we tried; and we did! He offered us some gigs with Zulema. This was live and studio, and as life began to go on, we worked with Monti Rock III, Disco-Tex and the Sex-O-Lettes.

Page 249: Sneaky Pete Kleinow plays his steel guitar at Record Plant, 321 W44th St, New York, 1973.
Opposite: Something Different: Angel Coakley, Jocelyn Brown and Christine Wiltshire singing background chorus for Zulema on the *Soul!* TV show on Channel 13, New York, 29 November 1972.

Christine Wiltshire: We were young and we had this energy and we wanted to have this message when we sang. There used to be an engineer, upstairs on the second floor of the studios, we used to call him 'Jimmy Shoes'. He let us make a little tape of ourselves; and we recorded a song, 'Thank You, Love'.

Jocelyn Brown: Jimmy Shoes, baby! [laughs] John Lennon came into the office, and he was beaming all over the place about the record, and he gave us the job! We had an opportunity to do something that nobody else was doing. It was like, 'Yo! Are you ready for this!?'

Christine Wiltshire: It was like a fairytale. Jesus, I knew every Beatle song in school! I almost had a notebook with their pictures on it – Dr Kildare won out on that one! [laughs] That was a big deal, man. It was scary and fun and fabulous!

Jocelyn Brown: John was phenomenal. He was special, baby. He would wrap a song up with feeling with his voice and then he'd include the girls on developing the background part. He'd work with us individually with the guitar. He would say it to me, 'That groove that you got there, Jocelyn, I want that. I want that, Jocie!'

It was so incredible to feel a guy from [England] the way we did, because we were from America. We were black Americans, you know what I'm saying? And he was allowing us to share, and we allowed him to share with us. That was such a union which knocks anything under racism out of the pocket. Music is universal. It has no face. It has no colour. But it has love. And we got there with him.

He knew what to say, when to say it, and if he saw us struggling he could make it right – to be as perfect as possible on what he was giving us

to do. He would ask us to be ballsy when he felt it should have been that way. He opened the door to us doing different kinds of harmonies, which was the real deal. That was an experience of experiences. He didn't sing what he didn't feel. He sang what he felt and what he had in his heart. His whole being allows you to understand that he needed to be able to say what he felt. He was delivering a message of himself and it tripped me out. We were all in love with John.

When I'm singing, a feeling comes within me that's almost like as if you just had a drink, and there's a warmness, the warmth of the drink just began to go from your throat all the way down your body, and you begin to feel this tingling all over yourself; it's a drink of the Spirit. That's what he was doing. I admire that so much, because that tells you, what's there to hold back for? Nothing! Let it go. You let it go and let it talk. Let it be the preacher, let it be the message.

After the sessions our conversation on the train was so quiet and intense, because we couldn't wait till we'd get to a place where we could really talk! So when we got to the house, we lost it! We just bounced off all the walls and just lost our minds! [laughs]

'We got to finish working with John Lennon!!! Oh my God!!!' you know? And it was something that didn't nobody take our place! He believed in us! He gave me my future and I'm so thankful.

Christine Wiltshire: I remember when Yoko came, after we finished, she says, 'I want them to do my album too!' We were so young, and it came time to eat. We're all ordering hamburgers, French fries, and she ordered sushi. I'd never had sushi in my life. She let me taste it, and I've been eating sushi ever since. She was my introduction to sushi, and I always was thankful to her for that!

Not only was Yoko handling so much back then, she was getting all kinds of flak from people who resented her because they didn't know who she was and they didn't understand what she was trying to do. This woman stepped in and was like, 'No, you're not going to be the clown of today. No, you do shit that matters.' She gave John organization in his life.

As an entertainer sometimes it's very easy to lose focus of who you are and what you want to be about because you're on this 'fun' train. Everybody's saying 'yes' to everything you do. She gave him boundaries. He didn't even know he was ready for it. That's what people resented, she was taking the party animal away and they wanted him to continue to be that.

She was a stand-out, 'she's in our way' kind of thing to these people and they hated her for it. But she's a very strong woman. She didn't let that fluster her. She put them glasses on, honey, put that hat on and said, 'Come on, let's go!' And just kept it right on moving! Let's give her credit for the shit that she really did and the stuff that she held together. A lot of people don't know. She was pretty essential in terms of just putting men in their place.

When I grew up, we didn't have women doctors, women electricians, women who were CEOs of any companies. Women were nurses and housekeepers and librarians and teachers. They didn't have assertive roles. I don't think a lot is really known about how assertive a woman she was. And that story should be told. She didn't take no shit! She sat over there quiet, but she didn't take no shit! [laughs] Women-to-women, we can tell that, for most of us who have a head on our shoulders, that's the reason we've survived in this business this long. It's a battle, but we do it because we love it.

Top: Yoko with Michael Brecker at Record Plant, 321 W44th St, New York, 1973. Bottom: Gordon Edwards (bass) and Rick Marotta (drums) rehearsing in New York, 1973.

MICHAEL BRECKER
Saxophone

I'd always been playing rock 'n' roll and R&B. I grew up listening to Ray Charles and AM radio and really got into rock music in college. I was very serious about it and listened to a lot of guitar players (to mimic them and distort the hell out of them) and by the time I moved to NY there was a need for horn players to play something on record other than bebop. So I started to get some work on saxophone with my brother Randy on trumpet and Barry Rogers on trombone, and we got a good reputation as a horn section. My brother and I formed a group called the Brecker Brothers and made a bunch of albums for Arista, and I play on *Saturday Night Live* every week, which is a lot of fun.

I use a Selmer saxophone and a La Voz Medium Reed and the mouthpiece is presently the Dukoff D9. I'm not suggesting that all saxophone players use this, this is what works for me. Everyone is different. Everyone hears differently. The only suggestion I can make is – go for what you hear and if possible try not to let anyone sway you. If you're looking for a sound, stick with it unless it's obviously not working.

Music for me is largely intuitive. I'm not a real intellectual kind of player. My mind doesn't work that way. I think fairly quickly, I'm aware of the chords when I'm playing, most of the time. I'm not real tuned into that.

Lately I've been more tuned into shapes and pivot points and melodies particularly when I'm recording I've been trying to concentrate on playing melodically and less mechanical, playing looser and just let what naturally happens happen, without trying to colour it.

For me I think the most important thing is time. Without that, it doesn't matter what notes you play. Notes are important too for me but if I'm not somehow really connected in a meaningful way to what's happening in the rhythm section it really is pointless in jazz or jazz-related music. I practise with a metronome. I get depressed when I do it because I rush. [laughs] It does help.

RICK MAROTTA
Drums & Percussion

I never hit a drum until I was nineteen. As far as I'm concerned that was a great advantage! I just took these drumsticks the size of baseball bats and started hitting the drums as hard as I could. I still believe that just flailing away is a great way to start out on a instrument. If you have any talent at all, it will come out. After that you can go back and learn the rudiments. If you play simply, you can even play freakier, more imaginative stuff in a tasteful way.

When I first walked into Record Plant, John Lennon was sitting at the console talking to Jack Douglas. I got there early because I wanted to make sure everything was going to be perfect, and I wanted to go in and say hello to John first. And I was wearing – do you remember SIR? Studio Instrumental

Rental? So, I was wearing an SIR T-shirt. And I walked in and John was really deep in this conversation about something to do with the recording.

I have my sticks and my cymbal bag, and my snare drum in my hands, and that was it. And I'm just standing there and I have this SIR T-shirt on, and they're talking, and John kind of looks up at me and he goes, 'What? Whatever it is, just drop it. You can just leave it in there and go,' thinking I was from SIR!

And Jack turned to him and said, 'John, this is Rick Marotta, he's going to be on drums.' And he did a complete one-eighty, he was like, 'Oh, Rick! I'm so sorry!' But I remember thinking, 'I gotta be careful what I wear into the

studio next time I go someplace where I don't know the guy!' [laughs]

John was very open. As you can imagine, it was hard to be John Lennon, and it was hard to be Yoko Ono but they were always inclusive with us. There was never a 'You're you and we're us,' it was always 'We're all one.' Yoko would say, 'Oh, Rick, John and I are going to go to dinner, you guys want to come?' And John would never say, 'Well, can't we have a night to ourselves?' He would go, 'Yeah, yeah, we're going; you guys wanna come?'

It was a really interesting time in my life and in the history of music, I feel honoured to be even part of it, in whatever little way I was.

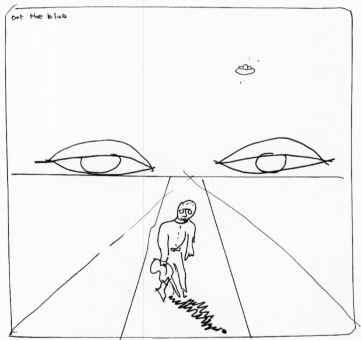

Pages 254–55: Original John Lennon *Mind Games* album front and back covers, released 29 October 1973. Above and opposite: Five of John's sketches – a storyboard of photocollages – experimenting with the possible album titles 'you are here' and 'out the blue'; July 1973.

out the blue.

John: I made that cover by hand like a montage. It's sort-of like a prediction. There is Yoko lying down like that and there's me walking away with the briefcase. And after that is when we split. So it's sort of apparent in the *Mind Games* period, although it wasn't apparent on a conscious level. It wasn't intentional. They made a nice logo at Capitol and combined the shots, front and back, so he comes and goes like that, right? I planned it to be like a movement, but I didn't plan to do that. I was seeing it as two frames from a movie, that it would be a movement. I didn't actually think of the physical idea of doing that [putting one on the front cover and one on the back cover], which is a very good idea.

Opposite: 'The High Plains, New Mexico' photographed by David Plowden, east of Las Vegas, New Mexico, 1972, taken from his book *Floor of the Sky* (1972), and used by John as the background image for his *Mind Games* album artwork.

Top: The original Polaroid of John holding an attaché case, photographed by Yoko in front of a US Army recruitment poster at the airport on the way to Washington, DC, on 27 June 1973, used as the cutout on the covers.

Bottom: Yoko photographed by Bob Gruen at Record Plant, 1973, used by John for 'the mountain'.

John Lennon's chop mark or 'hanko'. Popular in Asia, it is used as an artist's unique, individual signature, stamped in red. It is a patented, registered trademark and – like a fingerprint – no two are the same. Designed by John and custom-made in Tokyo in January 1971, the Japanese kanji characters read 'like a cloud, beautiful sound'.

DECLARATION OF NUTOPIA
We announce the birth of a
conceptual country, NUTOPIA.
Citizenship of the country can be
obtained by declaration of your
awareness of NUTOPIA.
NUTOPIA has no land, no boundaries,
no passports, only people.
NUTOPIA has no laws other
than cosmic.
All people of NUTOPIA are
ambassadors of the country.
As two ambassadors of NUTOPIA, we
ask for diplomatic immunity and
recognition in the United Nations of
our country and its people.

YOKO ONO LENNON

JOHN ONO LENNON

Nutopian Embassy
One White Street
New York, New York 10013
April 1st, 1973

MIND GAMES Produced
& Arranged by JOHN LENNON
THE PLASTIC U.F.ONO BAND
Vocals: John Lennon
Piano, Organ, Mellotron: Ken Ascher
Guitar: David Spinozza
Bass: Gordon Edwards
Drums: Jim Keltner
(plus Rick Marotta on "Meat City"
& "Bring On The Lucie")
Sax: Michael Brecker
Pedal Steel: Sneaky Pete
Background Chorus:
Something Different
Extra Sensory Percussion, Guitar,
Clavichord: Dr. Winston O'Boogie
A Los Paranoias
Engineers: Roy Cicala & Dan Barbiero
Mastering: Tom Rabstanek
Special Thanks To:
Shelley, Jimmy, Greg, Kevin,
May, Jon and all at 321.

Disease by Dennis
Space by Yoko
Cover by John Lennon
Mountain from Bob Gruen
Recorded and Mastered at
Record Plant, N.Y., N.Y.

"Madness is the first sign of dandruff."
Dr. Winston O'Boogie

"Only people can change the world."
y.o.

Side One

MIND GAMES
We're playing those mind games
together
Pushing the barriers planting seeds
Playing the mind guerrilla
Chanting the Mantra peace on earth
We all been playing those mind
games forever
Some kinda druid dudes lifting the
veil
Doing the mind guerrilla
Some call it magic the search for
the grail
Love is the answer and you know that
for sure
Love is a flower you got to let it, you
got to let it grow
So keep on playing those mind games
together
Faith in the future outta the now
You just can't beat on those mind
guerrillas
Absolute elsewhere in the stones of
your mind
Yeah we're playing those mind games
forever
Projecting our images in space and
in time
Yes is the answer and you know that
Yes is surrender you got to let it, you
got to let it go
So Keep on playing those mind games
together
Doing the ritual dance in the sun
Millions of mind guerrillas
Putting their soul power to the karmic
wheel
Keep on playing those mind games
forever
Raising the spirit of peace and love
(I want you to make love, not war,
I know you've heard it before)*

TIGHT AS
Just as tight as you can make it
Hard and slow ain't hard enough
Just as tight as you can shake it girl
Git it on and do your stuff
Tight as you can git it
Tight as got it made
Uptight's alright but if ya can't stand
the heat you better get back in
the shade
Just as tight as an Indian rope trick
Long and tough ain't hard enough
Just as tight as a dope fiend's fix
my friend
Git it up and do your stuff
Tight as you can boogie
Tight as got it made
Uptight's alright but if ya can't stand
the heat you better back in
the shade
Well tight as got me cornered
Tight as got me laid
Tight as strut your stuff so tough
Just a sweating in the midnight shade*

AISUMASEN
When I'm down really yin
And I don't know what I'm doing
Aisumasen aisumasen Yoko
All I had to do was call your name
And when I hurt you and cause you
pain
Darlin I promise I won't do it again
Aisumasen aisumasen Yoko
It's hard enough I know just to feel
your own pain
It's hard enough I know to feel your
own pain
All that I know is just what you tell me
All that I know is just what you show
me
When I'm down real sankpaku
And I don't know what to do
Aisumasen aisumasen Yoko san
All I had to do was call your name
Yes, all I had to do was call your
name*

ONE DAY (AT A TIME)
You are my weakness, you are my
strength
Nothing I have in the world makes
better sense
Cause I'm the fish and you're the sea
When we're together or when we're
apart
There's never a space in between the
beat of our hearts
Cause I'm the apple and you're the
tree
One day at a time is all we do
One day at a time is good for you
You are my woman, I am your man
Nothing else matters at all, now
I understand
That I'm the door and you're the key
And every morning I wake in your
smile
Feeling your breath on my face and
the love in your eyes
Cause you're the honey and I'm
the bee
One day at a time is all we do
One day at a time is good for us two
(you too)*

BRING ON THE LUCIE
(FREDA PEEPLE)
We don't care what flag you're waving
We don't even want to know your
name
We don't care where you're from or
where you're going
All we know is that you came
You're making all our decisions
We have just one request of you
That while you're thinking things over
Here's something you just better do
Free the people now
Do it do it do it do it do it now
Well we were caught with our hands
in the air
Don't despair paranoia is everywhere
We can shake it with love when
we're scared
So let's shout it aloud like a prayer
Free the people now
Do it do it do it do it do it now
We understand your paranoia
But we don't want to play your game
You think you're cool and know what
you are doing
666 is your name
So while you're jerking off each other
You better bear this thought in mind
Your time is up you better know it
But maybe you don't read the signs
Free the people now
Do it do it do it do it do it now
Well you were caught with your
hands in the kill
And you still got to swallow your pill
As you slip and you slide down the hill
On the blood of the people you killed
Stop the killing now
Do it do it do it do it do it now
Bring on the lucie*

SW-3414

Side Two

INTUITION
My intentions are good, I use my
intuition
It takes me for a ride
But I never understood other people's
superstitions
It seemed like suicide
And I play the game of life
I try to make it better each and
every day
And when I struggle in the night
The magic of the music seems to
light the way
Intuition takes me there
Intuition takes me everywhere
Well my instincts are fine
I had to learn to use them in order
to survive
And time after time confirmed an old
suspicion
It's good to be alive
And when I'm deep down and out and
lose communication
With nothing left to say
It's then I realize it's only a condition
Of seeing things that way
Intuition takes me there
Intuition takes me anywhere*

OUT THE BLUE
Out the blue you came to me
And blew away life's misery
Out the blue life's energy
Out the blue you came to me
Every day I thank the Lord and Lady
For the way that you came to me
Anyway it had to be two minds
one destiny
Out the blue you came to me
And blew away life's misery
Out the blue life's energy
Out the blue you came to me
All my life is been a long slow knife
I was born just to get to you
Anyway I survived long enough to
make you my wife
Out the blue you came to me
And blew away life's misery
Out the blue life's energy
Out the blue you came to me
Like a U.F.O. you came to me
And blew away life's misery
Out the blue life's energy
Out the blue you came to me*

ONLY PEOPLE
Only people know just how to talk
to people
Only people know just how to change
the world
Only people realize the power of
people
A million heads are better than one,
so come on, get it on!
Well I know how we tried and the
millions of tears that we cried
Now we are hipper we been thru the
trip
And we can't be denied with woman
and man side by side
Make no mistake it's our future we're
making, bake the cake and eat
it too!
We don't want no pig brother scene!
Only people know just how to talk
to people
Only people know just how to change
the world
Only people realize the power of
people
A million heads are better than one,
so come on, get it on!
Well it's long overdue there ain't
nothing better to do
Now we are hipper we been thru
the trip
We can fly right on thru, there's
nothing on earth we can't do
Fish or cut bait it's our future we're
making all together now pull the
chain!
We don't want no pig brother scene!
Only people know just how to talk
to people
Only people know just how to change
the world
Only people realize the power of
people
A million heads are better than one,
so come on, get it on!*

I KNOW (I KNOW)
The years have passed so quickly
One thing I've understood
I am only learning
To tell the trees from wood
I know what's coming down
And I know where it's coming from
And I know and I'm sorry (yes I am)
But I never could speak my mind
And I know just how you feel
And I know what I have done
And I know and I'm guilty (yes I am)
But I never could speak my mind
I know what I was missing
But now my eyes can see
I put myself in your place
As you did for me
Today I love you more than
yesterday
Right now I love you more right now
Now I know what's coming down
I can feel where it's coming from
And I know it's getting better (all
the time)
As we share in each other's minds
Today I love you more than
yesterday
Right now I love you more right now
Ooh hoo no more crying
Ooh hoo no more crying*

YOU ARE HERE
From Liverpool to Tokyo
What a way to go
From distant lands one woman one
man
Let the four winds blow
Three thousand miles over the ocean
Three thousand light years from the
land of the rising sun
Love has opened up my eyes
Love has blown right through
Wherever you are, you are here
Wherever you are, you are here
Three thousand miles over the ocean
Three thousand light years from the
land of surprising sun
East is east and west is west
The twain shall meet
East is west and west is east
Let it be complete
Three thousand miles over the ocean
Three thousand light years from the
land of the morning star*

MEAT CITY
Well I been Meat City to see for
myself
Yes I been Meat City to see for
myself
Been Meat City been Meat City
Just got to give me some rock 'n roll
People were dancing like there's no
tomorrow
Meat City
Fingerlickin chickinpickin Meat City
shookdown U.S.A.
Pig Meat City
Well I been the mountain to see for
myself
Yes I been the mountain to see for
myself
Been the mountain been the mountain
Just got to give me some rock 'n roll
Snake doctors shakin like there's no
tomorrow
Freak City
Chickinsuckin mothertruckin Meat
City shookdown U.S.A.
Pig Meat City
Well I'm gonna China to see for
myself
Well I'm gonna China to see for
myself
Gonna China gonna China
Just got to give me some rock 'n roll
Wolf the people were jumping like
there's no tomorrow
Meat City
Chickinsuckin mothertruckin Meat
City shookdown U.S.A.*

*All Selections Composed by
JOHN LENNON
Copyright ©1973 John Lennon
All Rights Reserved.

Original inner sleeve with lyrics
and credits (left) and vinyl labels
(opposite) for the *Mind Games*
album, 1973.

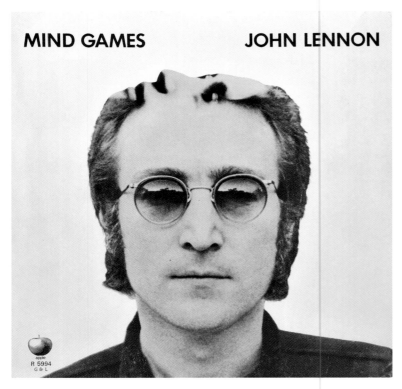

MIND GAMES   JOHN LENNON

apple
R 5994
G & L

Apple
R 5994

MIND GAMES
MEAT CITY
JOHN LENNON

2 C 008-05494

stéréo

john lennon
mind games

STEREO EAR-10474

MIND GAMES   JOHN LENNON
マインド・ゲームス   歌とギター ジョン・レノン
ミート・シティ MEAT CITY

apple
Ⓗ ¥500

Opposite: Cover artwork for the 'Mind Games' single release in October and November 1973. United Kingdom (top left); Sweden (top right); France (bottom left); Japan (bottom right).
Below: Original single labels for 'Mind Games' (left) and 'Meat City' (right) for the UK (16 November 1973, top) and USA (29 October 1973, bottom).

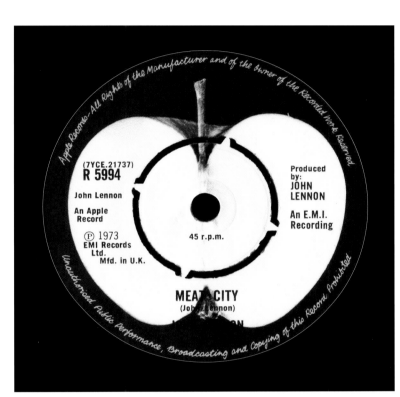

Pages 264–65: John photographed by Michael Brennan relaxing by the pool with a paperback, a mug of English breakfast tea, a pack of Gitanes, his Martin D28 acoustic guitar, panama hat and a portable radio, while staying at Lou Adler's house, 800 Stone Canyon Road, Bel Air, Los Angeles, California, 14 November 1973.

Below and pages 268–69: John Lennon with Tony King (Promotions Manager of Apple Records) dressed as the Queen, having fun filming a TV commercial for *Mind Games*, Capitol Records, 24 October 1973.

Mind Games TV Commercial
24 October 1973

John: Did I tell you about the commercial we've done for the new album? Hah! It's great! We have the Queen plugging the record for us. It starts inside a house with a door swinging open, over a red carpet and then inside. It's all done in very good taste, Your Majesty!

It's a friend of mine in drag, as it were. There's 'Land Of Hope And Glory' and someone says [in a posh soprano voice] 'I've been asked to do this commercial. It relates to a gramophone record…' and it goes on like that. I'm hoping Her Majesty will be able to laugh at it. A few vodkas and it was all over. His identity will be revealed by himself. I'm not sure how much he wants people to know about it!

Tony King: The first of John's albums I worked on was *Mind Games*. The campaign for it featured a somewhat unusual TV commercial. The idea came when Mike Hazlewood and I got stoned one night at his house in LA, and for reasons I can't remember I began doing an impersonation of the Queen telling people to go and buy the album. Mike laughed his head off, and then he recorded it. Afterwards, I had an idea. 'Let's play it to John as a surprise,' I said. We carried the tape machine out to the car and put it on the back seat. We picked John up and were driving down Sunset Boulevard, when Mike pressed play on the tape player. Suddenly, there was my impersonation of the Queen booming out. John was hysterical with laughter.

I thought no more about it, but then the next day John rang me up. 'I want to do a TV commercial, with you as the Queen advertising *Mind Games*,' he said. 'OK,' I said, shocked. 'Fine, sure, if that's what you want.' It got more surreal when I realized I had to find a costume to wear as the Queen. I went down to Western Costume, a store used by Hollywood, but my visit coincided with Halloween. Back then,

hardly anyone in the UK bothered with Halloween, and I had no idea how big a deal it was in the US. Rather than being able to slip in and out quietly, the store was packed.

'Which one of you is the Queen?' the woman behind the counter shouted. Everyone turned to look at me as I raised my hand. I must have annoyed the people queuing because I kept on rejecting the dresses they sent out for me to try on. 'No,' I said, turning down yet another. 'Her Majesty wouldn't be seen dead in that.' Eventually, they found one that had enough of a ballgown look to it.

The recording took place at a studio in Santa Monica. Elton was in town, and I'd talked to John about him quite a lot. 'You'd like him,' I'd said. So when I suggested that Elton come along to the recording, John said he'd really like to meet him. It was quite a weird introduction, as Elton turned up in the middle of my getting changed. I stood there wearing a crown and make-up, but still in my jeans: 'Elton, John… John, Elton.'

There was a great atmosphere in the studio. May [Pang, John & Yoko's PA] was there, as were Roy Cicala, who ran the Record Plant studio in New York, and Jimmy Iovine. I sat resplendent on a throne, a bottle of vodka stashed underneath it. The crew were hilarious. One guy, who was particularly attractive, came up to me and said, 'Do you want to fool around, Your Majesty?' I gave him a regal look and said, 'Later, baby.'

The advert itself opened with 'Land Of Hope And Glory' playing and a pair of doors opening to reveal me sat on the throne, sceptre in one hand and a copy of *Mind Games* in the other. 'Good evening,' I said, doing my best impersonation of Her Majesty. 'I have been asked to do this commercial. It relates to a gramophone record called

Mind Games by John Lennon.' Then the music cut to the title song of the album, and the camera zoomed in on the sleeve. You can hear John sniggering in the background. In the offcuts, there's footage of John and me dancing, and of Elton taking Polaroids from behind the cameras. It was a really fun day. We did a lot of TV spots for the album and loads of press promotion.

Elton John: I first met John Lennon through Tony King, who had moved to LA to become Apple Records' general manager in the US. In fact, the first time I met John Lennon, he was dancing with Tony King. Nothing unusual in that, other than the fact that they weren't in a nightclub, there was no music playing and Tony was in full drag as Queen Elizabeth II. They were at Capitol Records in Hollywood, where Tony's new office was, shooting a TV advert for John's forthcoming album *Mind Games*, and, for reasons best known to John, this was the big concept.

I took to him straight away. It wasn't just that he was a Beatle and therefore one of my idols. He was a Beatle who thought it was a good idea to promote his new album by dancing around with a man dragged up as the Queen, for fuck's sake. I thought: 'We're going to get on like a house on fire.' And I was right. As soon as we started talking, it felt like I'd known him my entire life.

All I ever saw from him was kindness and gentleness and fun, so much so that I took my mum and Derf [Elton's stepfather] to meet him. We went out to dinner, and when John went to the toilet, Derf thought it would be a great joke to take his false teeth out and put them in John's drink; there was something infectious about John's sense of humour that made people do things like that. Jesus, he was so funny. Whenever I was with him, or even better, him and Ringo, I just laughed and laughed and laughed.

PROD. NO CAPITOL Records-323
SCENE
TAKE
SOUND
DIRECTOR DOLLINGER
CAMERAMAN PORTER
DATE 10-24-73
INT.
PRODUCED BY W/O TAPE

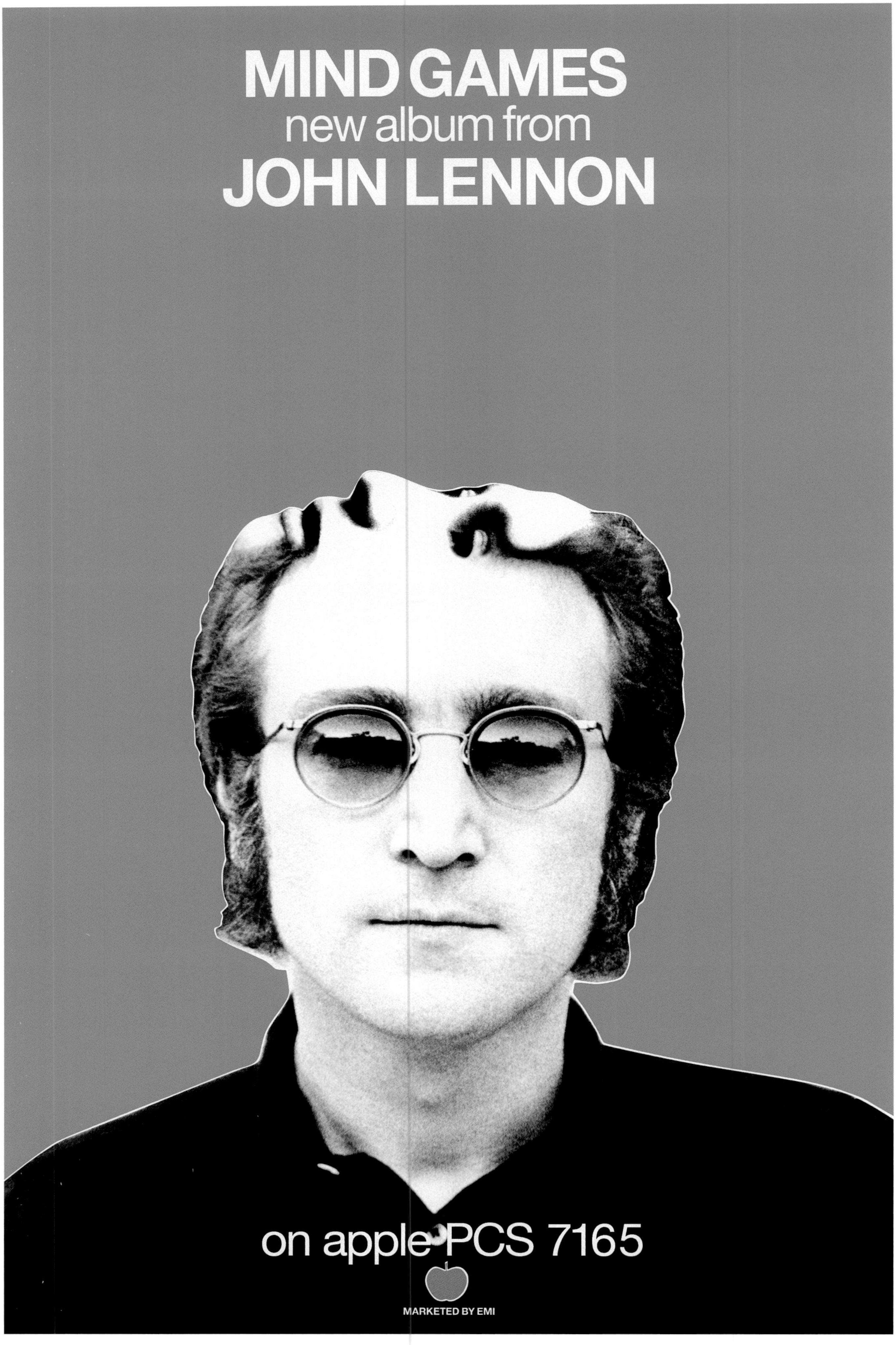
MIND GAMES
new album from
JOHN LENNON
on apple PCS 7165
MARKETED BY EMI

Opposite and below: *Mind Games* album press adverts.

Pages 272–73: 'Mind Games' single advertisement paste-up (left) and as published (right) in *Melody Maker*, 17 November 1973.

MIND GAMES
JOHN LENNON

apple

Apple Album SW-3414

MIND GAMES

JOHN LENNON

Apple Single 1868

Interview with Elliot Mintz, Malibu Beach, CA
1 November 1973

Elliot: The new album, *Mind Games*, on Apple has just come out this week. Do you ever like to talk about what the music means, what it represents to you, or what led up to *Mind Games*? You have any thoughts about the song itself?

John: Well, Elliot, I was sitting at home one year….

Elliot: I mean, really.

John: Have thoughts about what? The music. The music is music, and the words are poetry that you sing and sometimes it fits the music, sometimes it doesn't. It's just so complicated to talk about.

Elliot: The phrase. What does the phrase 'mind games' mean to you?

John: Well, *Mind Games* was actually a book that somebody sent me, which I wrote an intro to. And it was an interesting book, I enjoyed it. And it just came out as a song. The lyrics have nothing to do with the book except for it's a mind game itself, the lyrics.

Elliot: It's the kind of thing that people are constantly playing with each other in a search for finding out who each other really is.

John: Whether we're searching or not is not the point, it's just the fact that the games are going on; so, we can choose what kind of games we want to play or which side we want to play on.

Elliot: Do you think that most people are always playing mind games with each other? Do you think that life has some semblance of reality to it, or is it all just games?

John: I don't know; I'm just a singer-songwriter, you know. Don't ask me about it. I just sing, right? And write.

Elliot: You have recorded and naturally promoted dozens of albums by now. Is it a drag after the record is out to be concerned about whether or not it's being played, and whether or not it's a hit? Do you care about that?

John: Yeah, I do care. I think I care more about making the record and how it sounds. Does it please me? And then, after that, I have to deal with, 'Oh, are they going to play it?' 'Did I say some word they don't like?'

Elliot: There's a great song on the album, one of my particular favourites, 'Freda Peeple'. And, in that, you never seem to ever really get away from your political experiences. Do you find you're becoming more and more political as life goes on, in your music and your personal life, or less political?

John: I just change every five days.

Elliot: What about today?

John: Today it's beach and fish heads, right? You know, in a way, everything's political, like everything's a game, ha ha.

Elliot: But do you actively participate or take any interest in, like, Watergate affairs, stuff like that?

John: Well, I'm not going to buy the record, if that's what you mean. [laughs] Sam Ervin [chair of the Senate Watergate Committee] – shouldn't have done it, Sam!

Elliot: I'll ask the question again.

John: Am I getting more political? I don't know. I don't think about how I'm getting. I'm only thinking about how I am now.

Elliot: How are you now?

John: Now I'm fine and dandy. We've got our table here. We're eating well. The sun's out.

Elliot: So, politics, at the moment, anyway, does not seem to be a major issue?

John: At this precise second, no. No, I'm not – I'm not into anything, you know.

Elliot: Do you feel better about *Mind Games* than you do *Imagine*? Are all the records pretty much the same to you? Do you have a favourite? A preference? Is one more indicative of where you are than another?

John: I'm always the same. You know, I'm always on whatever I've just done. And so I'm on *Mind Games*. I don't like it better or worse than *Imagine* or *A Hard Day's Night*, you know; they're all…as I was telling you in the car on the way here, my calendar is which record was out at the time – that's how I remember what was going on.

I don't remember what year anything was, just 'Oh, that was "Instant Karma!", oh, that was "A Hard Day's Night", oh, this is "Mind Games".'

The only difference is on 'Mind Games' it's a Mellotron, on 'Imagine', it's an orchestra. No, I'm kidding. What's the difference?

Elliot: The difference is that 'Imagine' seems to be kind of a fantasy, wish-fulfilment, dreamy type.

John: So is 'Mind Games'. The song is almost the same story backwards. Well, you know, I mean, it's the same!

Elliot: What about the future? Do you have any thoughts in your head now about what you want to do after this?

John: Well, I'm already working on the next one with Phil Spector. It started out as *Oldies But Mouldies*, but I seem to be writing a few songs, so, it'll be a bit of everything, I think.

Below and page 276: John being interviewed by his friend Elliot Mintz for ABC Channel 7 *Eyewitness News* while walking on Malibu Beach between the Malibu Beach Inn and Malibu Pier, 1 November 1973.

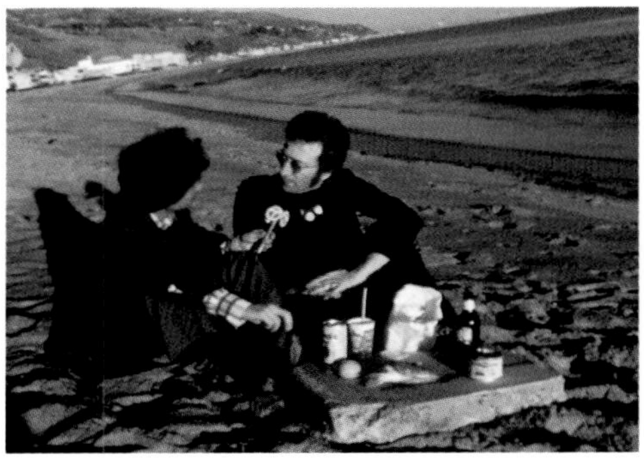
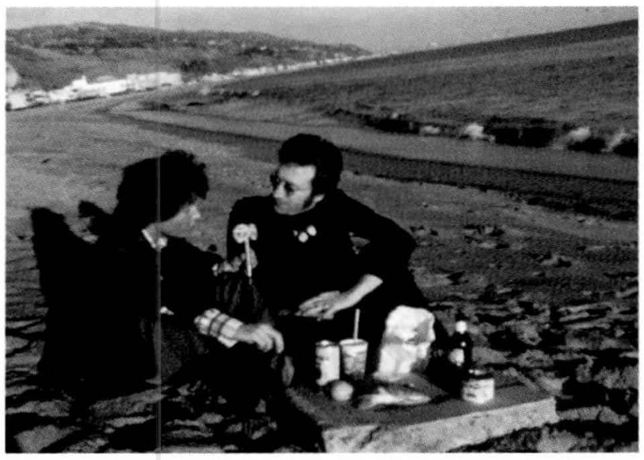
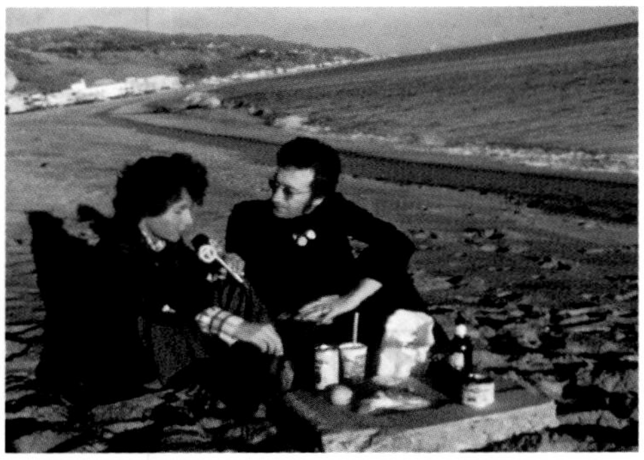
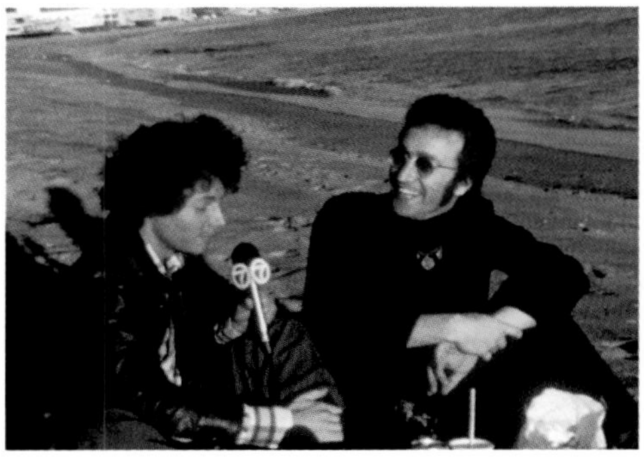
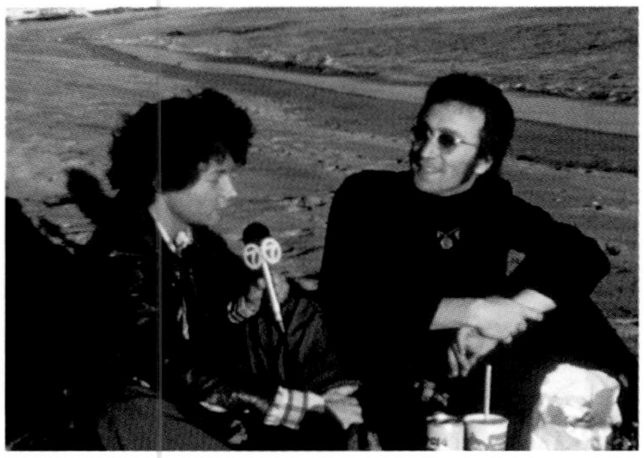
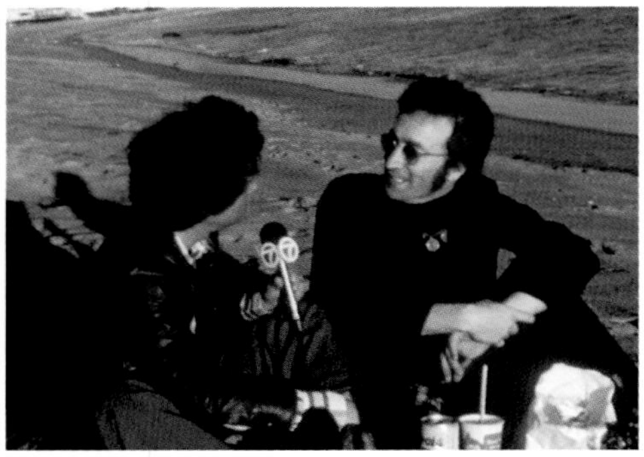
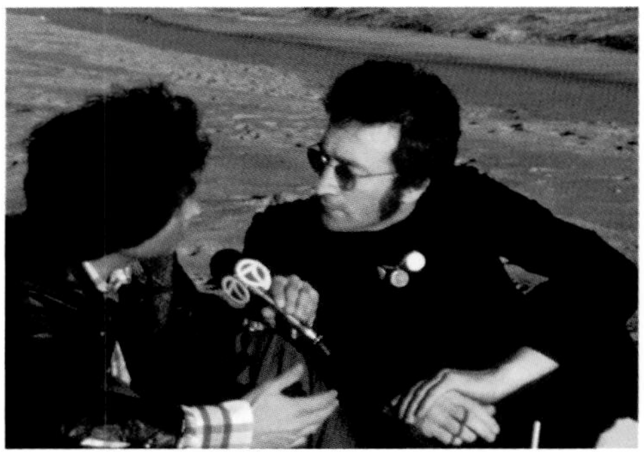
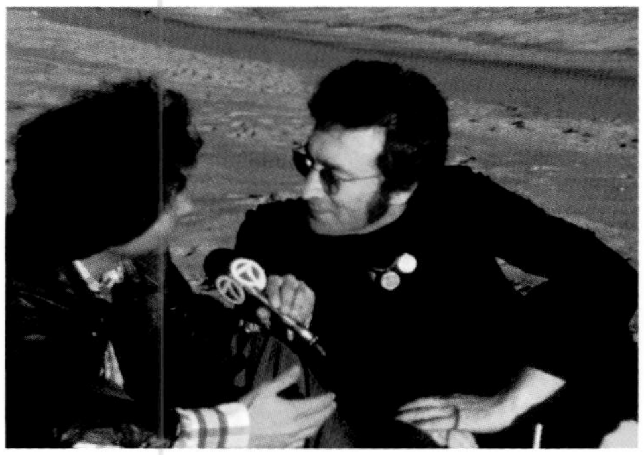
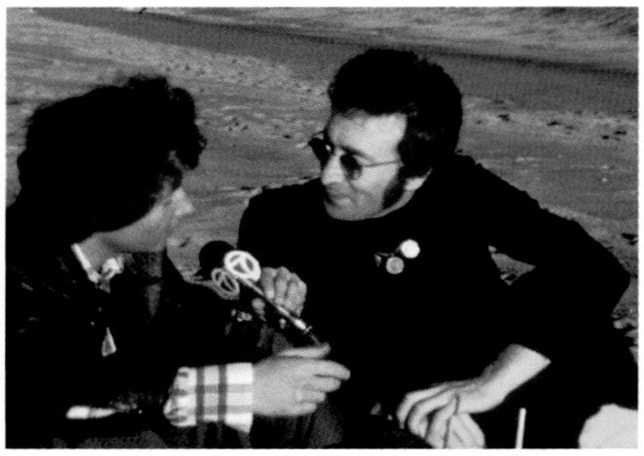
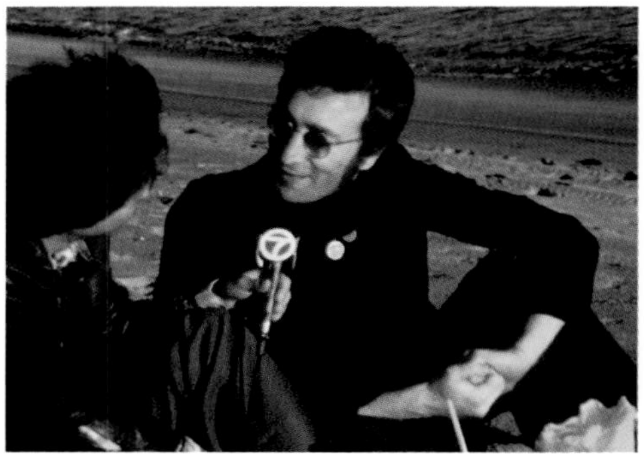
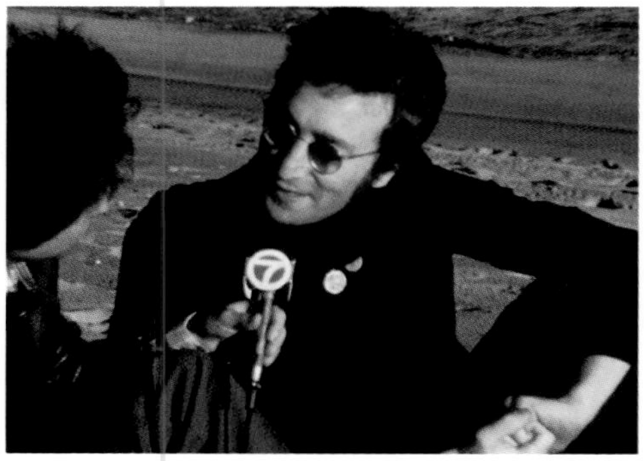
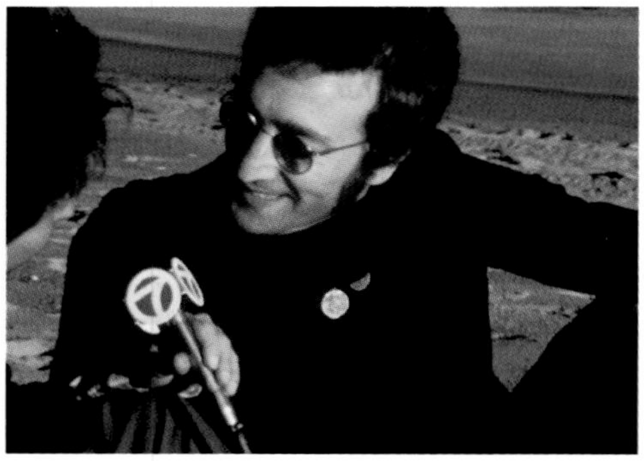
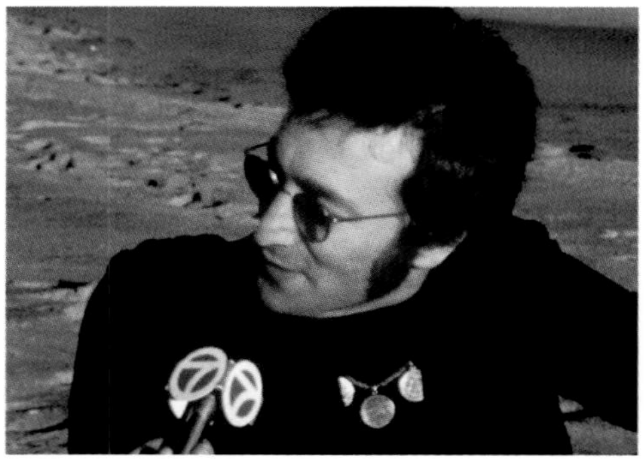
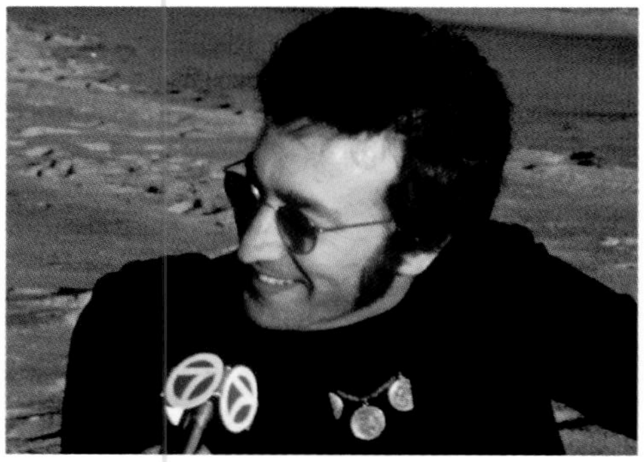
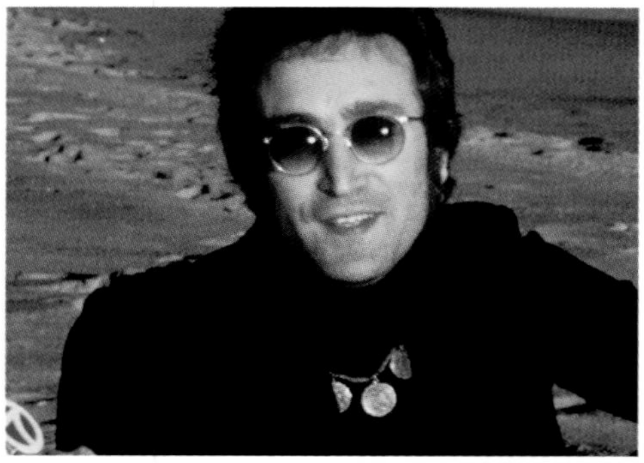

Elliot: You cannot do an interview with John Lennon without asking the inevitable question, 'Will the Fab Four ever get together again?' You've been asked it a million times, but you don't consider that a better period of time in your life, a happier, more elated time?

John: No, no, no. Maybe, when I'm sixty, I might think, 'Oh, that was it,' but I doubt it. I do try and live for today. It was painful, but it's done, you know. But most people don't know why it started either. Neither do we.

Elliot: When you think back during that period of time known as Beatlemania, are the thoughts happy ones?

John: Yeah, yeah. Most of them are good, you know, I've even forgotten what touring was like. I mean the bad side of it.

I just remember the laughs, you know. And the funny bits. I don't remember the lousy food and that. Mind you, now I talk about it, yes, I think I do! [laughs]

Elliot: In the long run, would you consider them happy recollections?

John: Sure, sure, you know, it was a great experience at twenty-four or -five, whenever it was, to do all that instead of something else. I couldn't think of anything better to do besides be a fisherman.

Elliot: Do you miss it?

John: No, I don't miss it. I've done it, that's enough. I'd have hated to wait all my life till I was fifty to 'make it', as they say.

Elliot: Do you think you got out of it at a good time, or looking back do you think maybe you should have gotten out of it earlier, or…?

John: I think if we'd left any later it would have been…. It was getting nearly too late, you know.

Elliot: I'd like to know the highest moment and the lowest moment, when it was its best and when it was its worst?

John: A couple of high moments like first time in America, you know, hearing us on every channel, and ten records in the charts or whatever it was. Another high moment was Australia. You know, it's funny, but there was more people came to see us there than anywhere. I mean, it looked like, I think, the whole of Australia was there.

Low moments are those moments like when Brian died, you know? Things like that, which are just, you know…. We weren't ready for it. And they were the real low moments, suddenly finding ourselves on our own, you know?

Elliot: Are you happier now, do you think, than during all those years?

John: I'm basically the same, I just have a bit more experience, so maybe I can deal with it maybe one per cent better, but I'm pretty much the same, just older.

Elliot: A lot of people in America still don't really understand why it all ended. A million and one rumours, conflicting stories…if you had to make one statement as to what busted up the Beatles, what ended it, what would you say?

John: Because we all had basically had enough. And nobody knew how to say it. We mightn't even have been aware that we'd had enough, ourselves. You know, that's why I say maybe we should have finished it a bit sooner.

Elliot: Since the split, each one of the Beatles has gone his own way and has enjoyed a tremendous amount of popularity. But still the question: will they ever team up again?

John: It's quite possible, yes. I don't know why the hell we'd do it, but it's possible.

Elliot: Would you like that to happen?

John: If it happens, I'll enjoy it.

Elliot: Would you want to initiate that happening?

John: Well, I couldn't say.

Elliot: If you could…is it something you would like to see yourself doing?

John: If I could…I don't know Elliot, because you know me, I go on instinct, and if the idea hit me tomorrow, I might call them and say, 'Come on, let's do something.' And so, I couldn't really tell you. If it happens, it'll happen.

Elliot: So, it is not something that you would totally rule out as never taking place again?

John: No, no. My memories are now all fond, and the wounds are healed. And if we do it, we do it; if we record, we record. I don't know. As long as we make music.

Elliot: And there's no hard feelings to any member of the group or anything?

John: No, nobody in particular. [laughs] No, nobody.

Elliot: I wish you all the luck with *Mind Games*.

John: Thanks.

Elliot: It's a great record. I like it.

John: Thank you.

Elliot: And you.

John: I quite like yourself, actually. Back to you, Barney. *Mind Games*, folks! Out now!

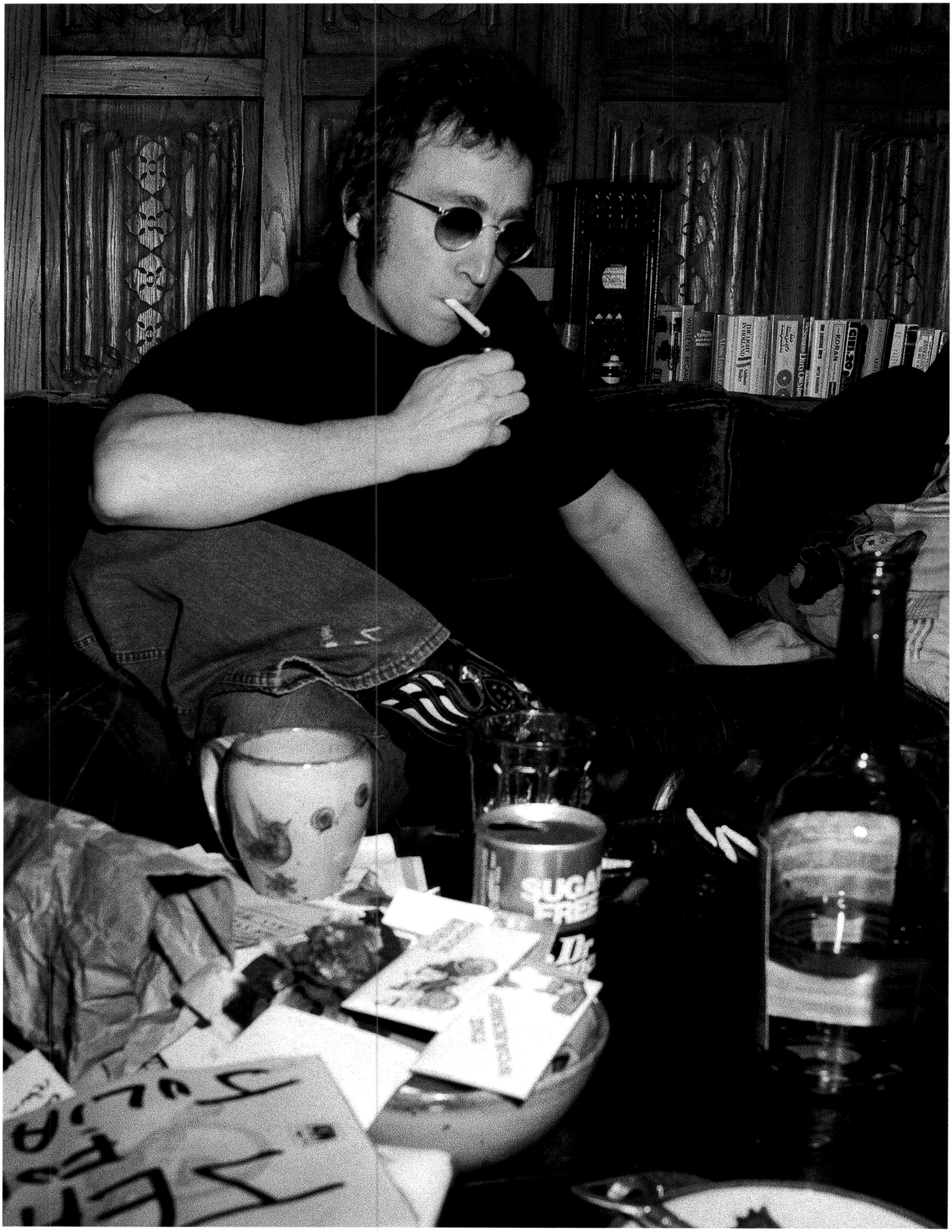

Opposite: John in the living room of Lou Adler's house in LA being interviewed by Patrick Snyder-Scumpy for *Crawdaddy* magazine, 15 November 1973. A reminder to buy jeans for Julian Lennon sits on the table along with the remnants of celebrations the previous evening.

John sitting on the kitchen worktop at Lou Adler's house in LA. The *Crawdaddy* magazine article written by Patrick Snyder-Scumpy from the interview conducted on 15 November 1973 to promote *Mind Games* was published in March 1974. John's portrait graced the cover.

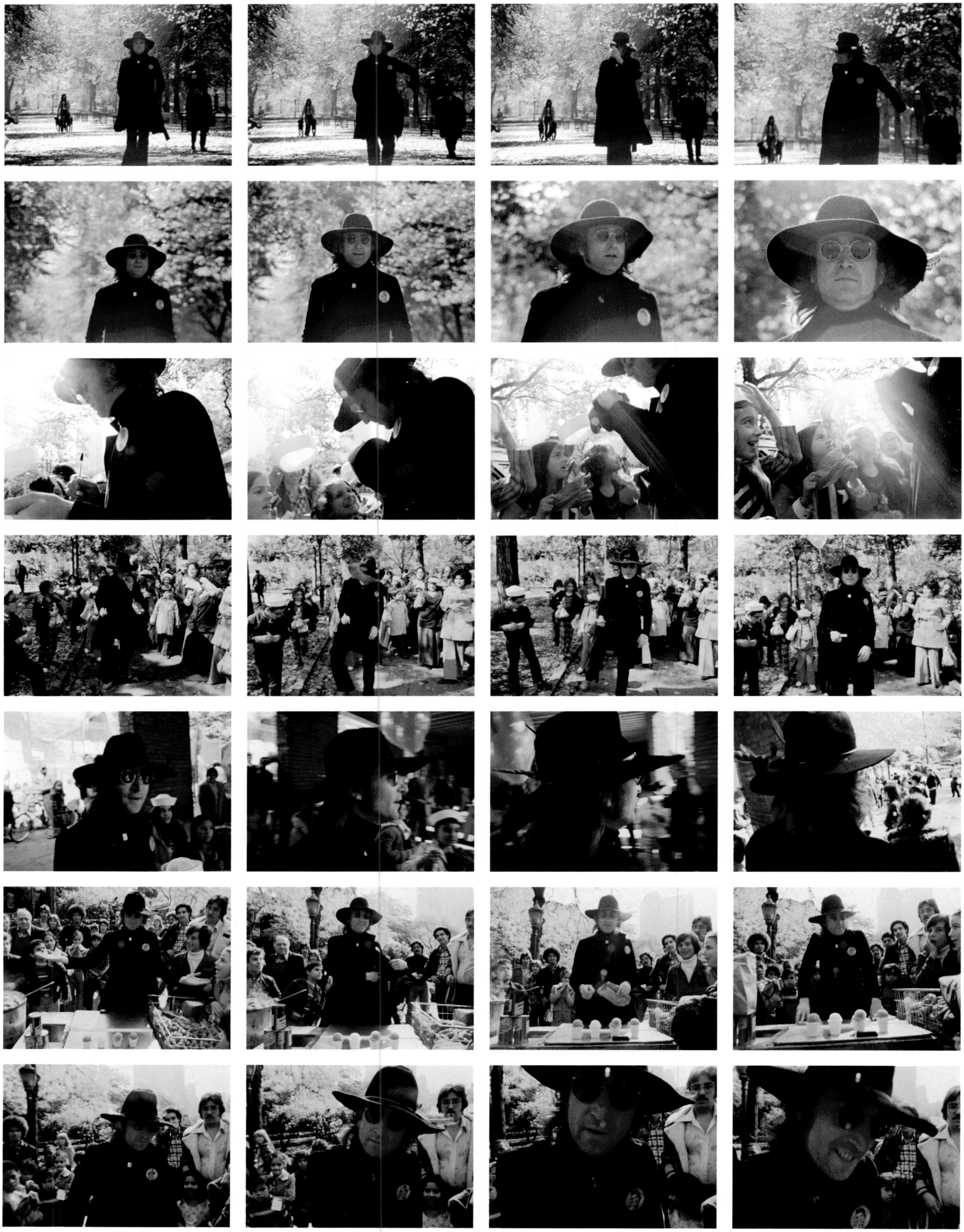

SOURCES OF ILLUSTRATIONS

Every effort has been made to locate and credit copyright holders of the material reproduced in this book. The author and publisher apologise for any omissions or errors, which can be corrected in future editions.

a = above, b = below, c = centre, l = left, r = right

1 Photograph by Yoko Ono, © Yoko Ono Lennon; 4–5 Photograph by Brian Hamill; 6–7 Photograph by Brian Hamill; 8–9 © Bob Gruen/www.bobgruen.com; 10 Handwritten notes by John Lennon, © Yoko Ono Lennon; 12 © Bob Gruen/www.bobgruen.com; 14 Typewritten lyrics by John Lennon with handwritten annotations, © Yoko Ono Lennon; 17 'Mind Games' Advert © Yoko Ono Lennon; 18 Handwritten lyrics by John Lennon, © Yoko Ono Lennon; 19 Illustrations by John Lennon, © Yoko Ono Lennon; 20 Stills from home video of John Lennon writing and practising 'Make Love Not War', © Yoko Ono Lennon; 21 Typewritten lyrics by John Lennon, © Yoko Ono Lennon; 22 *Make Love Not War* poster by Wilfred Weisser, courtesy of the Centre for the Study of Political Graphics; 23a, 23c Handwritten notes by John Lennon, © Yoko Ono Lennon; 23bl *Make Love Not War* badge designed by Penelope and Franklin Rosemont from Solidarity Bookshop, Chicago, Illinois, March 1965; 23br Illustration by A.S. Eddington for *The Nature of the Physical World* by A. S. Eddington (Cambridge University Press, 1929); 24–25 Rider–Waite tarot deck illustrated by Pamela Colman Smith, first published 1909; 26 John Lennon portfolio including: postcard © Yoko Ono Lennon, album cover Vertigo Records, illustration by Aleister Crowley for *The Equinox* Volume III, No. 1 by Aleister Crowley (Universal Publishing Company, 1919); 27 John Lennon portfolio including: photocollage by John Lennon, © Yoko Ono Lennon, photocollage by Yoko Ono and John Lennon, © Yoko Ono Lennon, Great Seal of Nutopia stamp designed by John Lennon, © Yoko Ono Lennon, logo and postcard artwork by Yoko Ono, © Yoko Ono Lennon, Rider–Waite tarot card illustrated by Pamela Colman Smith, first published 1909; 28 John Lennon portfolio including The Good Samaritan postcard © The Estate of Marc Chagall, John Holding a Pig postcard photo by Dan Richter, © Yoko Ono Lennon, cover art from *The Art and Practice of the Occult* by Ophiel (Peach Publishing Co., 1972); 30 Stills from *The Beatles in Retreat* TV special, © Rai Uno; 33 Photo by Clay Perry, © Yoko Ono Lennon; 35 Handwritten annotations by John Lennon in *Cheiro's Book of Numbers*, by William John Warner (London Publishing Company, 1926), © Yoko Ono Lennon; 37 Handwritten notes by Yoko Ono and John Lennon, © Yoko Ono Lennon; 38 Hand prints and handwritten notes by John Lennon, © Yoko Ono Lennon; 39 Hand prints and handwritten notes by John Lennon, © Yoko Ono Lennon; 40 *I Ching* coins Private Collection; 41a © Yoko Ono Lennon; 41b Artwork by Yoko Ono, © Yoko Ono Lennon; 42–43 Polaroid by Yoko Ono, handwritten notes by John Lennon, © Yoko Ono Lennon; 44al Photograph by Bob. Courtesy http://www.meetthebeatlesforreal.com/2013/12/greek-treat.html; 44ar Photograph by Bob. Courtesy http://www.meetthebeatlesforreal.com/2013/12/greek-treat.html; 44b, 45c © The Trustees of the British Museum; 45 Illustrations by Planet Illustrations; 46–49 Courtesy Yoko Ono Lennon; 50–51 © Bob Gruen/www.bobgruen.com; 52 Photograph by Brian Hamill; 54–55 Photograph by Brian Hamill; 57 Photograph by Brian Hamill; 58 Typewritten lyrics by John Lennon with handwritten annotations, © Yoko Ono Lennon; 61 Photograph by Brian Hamill; 62a Photograph by Anita Hoffman; 62b Photograph by Anita Hoffman; 64 Photograph by © Giles Larrain; 65 Photograph by David Fenton/Getty Images; 66–67 Photograph by Andrew Sacks/Getty Images; 68 Film stills from *Ten for Two* concert film, © Yoko Ono Lennon; 69 Typewritten essay with handwritten annotations by Jerry Rubin, © Jerry Rubin, courtesy Yoko Ono Lennon; 70a Photograph by Anthony Camerano/Alamy Stock Photo; 70b Photograph by Anthony Camerano/Alamy Stock Photo; 71 Film stills from *The Dick Cavett Show*, courtesy Daphne Productions; 72al US Government memorandum, 12 January 1972, courtesy US Government; 72ar FBI memorandum with annotations, 28 January 1972, courtesy FBI Department; 72bl US Government memorandum, 4 February 1972, courtesy US Government; 72br US Senate letter, 4 February 1972, courtesy US Senate; 74al US President letter, 6 March 1972, courtesy US Government; 74ar John Lennon FBI airtel, courtesy FBI Department; 74bl FBI memorandum with annotations, 21 April 1972, courtesy FBI Department; 74br US Government memorandum, 21 April 1972, courtesy US Government; 75al US Government memorandum, May 1972, courtesy US Government; 75ar FBI memorandum with annotations, 25 April 1972, courtesy US Government; 75bl FBI airtel, 5 June 1972, courtesy US Government; 75br FBI airtel, 27 July 1972, courtesy US Government; 76al John Lennon information sheet with illustration, courtesy FBI Department; 76bl US Government memorandum, 30 August 1972, courtesy US Government/FBI Department; 76ar US Government memorandum, 24 October 1972, courtesy US Government/FBI Department; 76br FBI airtel, 8 December 1972, courtesy US Government; 78 Typewritten lyrics by John Lennon with handwritten annotations, © Yoko Ono Lennon; 80 © Bob Gruen/www.bobgruen.com; 83 © Bob Gruen/www.bobgruen.com; 84 Typewritten lyrics by John Lennon with handwritten annotations,

© Yoko Ono Lennon; 87 Photograph by Art Fein, courtesy Capitol Records; 88 Photograph by Art Fein, courtesy Capitol Records; 89 Photograph by Art Fein, courtesy Capitol Records; 90 Illustrations by John Lennon, © Yoko Ono Lennon; 91 Photograph by Art Fein, courtesy Capitol Records; 92 Photograph by Mark Sennet; 93 American Airline receipts and tickets courtesy Yoko Ono Lennon; 94–95 © Bob Gruen/www.bobgruen.com; 96–97 Photograph by Koh Hasebe/Shinko Music/Getty Images; 98 © Bob Gruen/www.bobgruen.com; 100–101a Floorplan illustration by Planet Illustrations; 101b Illustration by Yoko Ono, © Yoko Ono Lennon; 102–103 Photographs by Sibyl Bender, © Yoko Ono Lennon; 104–105 Stills from home video filmed by John Lennon, © Yoko Ono Lennon; 106–107 Photograph by Koh Hasebe/Shinko Music/Getty Images; 108a Photograph by Koh Hasebe/Shinko Music/Getty Images; 108b Photograph by Koh Hasebe/Shinko Music/Getty Images; 109a Photograph by Koh Hasebe/Shinko Music/Getty Images; 109b Photograph by Koh Hasebe/Shinko Music/Getty Images; 110–111 Photograph by Koh Hasebe/Shinko Music/Getty Images; 112 Typewritten lyrics by John Lennon with handwritten annotations, © Yoko Ono Lennon; 115al Photograph by Garth Eliassen/Getty Images; 115ar Photograph by Declan Haun/Chicago History Museum/Getty Images; 115b Photograph by Garth Eliassen/Getty Images; 116–117 Peter Simon Collection (PH 009). Special Collections and University Archives, University of Massachusetts Amherst Libraries; 119 © Fred J. Maroon; 120a Photograph by Bettmann/Getty Images; 120b © Globe Photos/ZUMAPRESS.com ZUMA Press, Inc./Alamy Stock Photo; 121 Handwritten memo by John Lennon, © Yoko Ono Lennon; 122 Illustration and photocollage by John Lennon courtesy Yoko Ono Lennon; 123a, 123b postcard by Mitock and Sons postcards, photograph by Mark Rader, modified by John Lennon, courtesy Yoko Ono Lennon; 124–125 Watergate Hotel stationery and folder courtesy Yoko Ono Lennon; 126 Photograph by Christopher Li/*The Washington Post*; 127 Photograph by Christopher Li/*The Washington Post* via Getty Images; 128 Declaration of Nutopia typewritten document, © Yoko Ono Lennon; 130 Typewritten document, © Yoko Ono Lennon; 131a © Bob Gruen/www.bobgruen.com; 131b © Bob Gruen/www.bobgruen.com; 132–133 Photograph by Popperfoto via Getty Images/Getty Images; 134 © Bob Gruen/www.bobgruen.com; 135 Nutopia press conference clipping mounted on board and signed, © Yoko Ono Lennon; 136 Great Seal of Nutopia designed by John Lennon, © Yoko Ono Lennon; 137 Typewritten letters and Great Seal of Nutopia stamp by John Lennon, © Yoko Ono Lennon; 138–139 Stamps designed by John Lennon, photographs by Karla Merrifield, © Yoko Ono Lennon; 140–141 Illustrations and stamps by John Lennon, © Yoko Ono Lennon; 142–143 Film stills from the First International Feminist Planning Conference video filmed by John Lennon, Yoko Ono, Jon Hendricks and Nadja Gruen, © Yoko Ono Lennon; 145 Photographs by Agnese De Donato; 147a Photograph by Agnese De Donato; 147b Photograph by Karla Merrifield, © Yoko Ono Lennon; 148 Photograph by Agnese De Donato; 149 Typewritten page from booklet made by Yoko Ono and John Lennon, © Yoko Ono Lennon; 150–151 Typewritten pages and illustrations by Yoko Ono and John Lennon, © Yoko Ono Lennon; 152–153 Film stills from the First International Feminist Planning Conference video filmed by John Lennon, Yoko Ono, Jon Hendricks and Nadja Gruen, © Yoko Ono Lennon; 155 Photograph by Bettmann/Getty Images; 156 Photograph © Press International, courtesy Yoko Ono Lennon; 157 Photo courtesy of the National Organization for Women, Seattle-King County Chapter/Prints and Photographs Division, Library of Congress, Washington, DC (LC-USZC4-6626); 158–159 © Ann-Victoria Phillips 58W72nd St NY/Smith College Special Collections; 160–161 Michael Brennan/Iconic Images; 163 Typewritten essay by John Lennon, © Yoko Ono Lennon; 164 Typewritten essay by John Lennon, © Yoko Ono Lennon; 165 Typewritten essay by John Lennon, © Yoko Ono Lennon; 166 Photograph courtesy Arbeiderbladet/Arbeiderbevegelsens Archive and Library; 167 Typewritten letter by John Lennon, © Yoko Ono Lennon; 168 Typewritten letter by John Lennon, © Yoko Ono Lennon; 169 Typewritten letter by John Lennon ,© Yoko Ono Lennon; 170 Typewritten letter by John Lennon, © Yoko Ono Lennon; 171a Typewritten letter by Elliot Mintz, © Elliot Mintz; 171b Typewritten letter by Elliot Mintz, © Elliot Mintz; 172 Typewritten lyrics by John Lennon with handwritten annotations, © Yoko Ono Lennon; 175 Michael Brennan/Iconic Images; 176a Handwritten notes and drawings by John Lennon, © Yoko Ono Lennon; 176b Handwritten notes and drawings by John Lennon, © Yoko Ono Lennon; 177 Front cover *Jet* magazine, 26 October 1972, Private Collection; 178 Handwritten notes and drawings by John Lennon, © Yoko Ono Lennon; 181 Illustration by John Lennon, © Yoko Ono Lennon; 183 © Bob Gruen/www.bobgruen.com; 184a © Bob Gruen/www.bobgruen.com; 184b © Bob Gruen/www.bobgruen.com; 185 © Bob Gruen/www.bobgruen.com; 186 Typewritten lyrics by John Lennon with handwritten annotations, © Yoko Ono Lennon; 189a AP Photo/Alamy Stock Photo; 189b Photograph by Bettmann/Getty Images; 190 Photographs © CBS News; 192 Typewritten lyrics with handwritten annotations by John Lennon, © Yoko Ono Lennon; 195 Typewritten letter with handwritten annotations by John Lennon, © Yoko Ono Lennon; 196 Handwritten lyrics by John Lennon, © Yoko Ono Lennon; 197a Photograph courtesy Capitol Records; 197b Photograph courtesy Capitol Records; 198 Photograph by Ethan Russell/© Apple Corps

Ltd.; 200 Handwritten letter by John Lennon, © Yoko Ono Lennon; 201 Handwritten letter by John Lennon, © Yoko Ono Lennon; 202 Handwritten letter by John Lennon, © Yoko Ono Lennon; 203 Typewritten letters with handwritten annotations by John Lennon, © Yoko Ono Lennon; 204 Typewritten lyrics with handwritten annotations, © Yoko Ono Lennon; 207 © Bob Gruen/www.bobgruen.com; 208 Courtesy Yoko Ono; 209 Photographs by Iain Macmillan, © Yoko Ono Lennon; 210 Typewritten lyrics with handwritten annotations by John Lennon, © Yoko Ono Lennon; 213 Photograph by David Gahr/Getty Images; 214al Album cover art © Yoko Ono Lennon; 214ar Photocollage by Yoko Ono, © Yoko Ono Lennon; 214b Pioneer Plaques designed by Carl Sagan and Frank Drake, artwork by Linda Salzman Sagan, courtesy NASA/Ames; 216 Photograph by David Gahr/Getty Images; 217 Photograph by David Gahr/Getty Images; 218–219 Photograph by David Gahr/Getty Images; 220–221 Photograph by Richard Rosen; 223 © Bob Gruen/www.bobgruen.com; 224 Photograph by Robin Titone; 225 Photographs by Marie Lacey; 226a © Bob Gruen/www.bobgruen.com; 226b © Bob Gruen/www.bobgruen.com; 229 Handwritten and typewritten documents from Record Plant including portrait by John Lennon, © Yoko Ono Lennon; 230–231 Master tape boxes © Yoko Ono Lennon; 232 Courtesy Dan Barbiero; 234–235 Master tape boxes © Yoko Ono Lennon; 236–237 Photograph by Richard Rosen; 238 © Bob Gruen/www. bobgruen.com; 239 Courtesy Jimmy Iovine; 240–247, 249 © Bob Gruen/www.bobgruen. com; 250 Still from Soul! TV show on Channel 13; 252 © Bob Gruen/www.bobgruen. com; 254–255 Artwork by John Lennon containing photos by Yoko Ono, Bob Gruen and David Plowden, © Yoko Ono Lennon; 256–257 Artworks by John Lennon, © Yoko Ono Lennon; 258 Photograph by David Plowden, © David Plowden; 259a Polaroid by Yoko Ono, © Yoko Ono Lennon; 259br © Bob Gruen/www.bobgruen.com; 259bl Chop mark by John Lennon, © Yoko Ono Lennon; 260 Mind Games album sleeve © Yoko Ono Lennon; 261 Mind Games album labels © Yoko Ono Lennon; 262 'Mind Games' single cover artwork © Yoko Ono Lennon; 263 'Mind Games' single labels © Yoko Ono Lennon; 264-265 Michael Brennan/Iconic Images; 266a Photograph © Yoko Ono Lennon; 266b Photograph © Yoko Ono Lennon; 268-269 Stills from the Mind Games advert © Yoko Ono Lennon; 270 Mind Games press advert © Yoko Ono Lennon; 271 Mind Games press advert © Yoko Ono Lennon; 272 'Mind Games' press advert © Yoko Ono Lennon; 273 'Mind Games' press advert © Yoko Ono Lennon; 275 Stills from interview with John Lennon and Elliot Mintz, courtesy Elliot Mintz; 276 Stills from interview with John Lennon and Elliot Mintz, courtesy Elliot Mintz; 278 Tom Zimberoff/Iconic Images; 279 Michael Brennan/Iconic Images; 280–281 Stills from 'Mind Games' music video © Yoko Ono Lennon; 288 WAR IS OVER! artwork poster by John Lennon & Yoko Ono, © Yoko Ono Lennon

Front cover
John Lennon in LA, California, November 1973
© Michael Brennan/Getty Images.

Back cover
Cover artwork for Mind Games by John Lennon, containing photographs by Yoko Ono, Bob Gruen and David Plowden © Yoko Ono Lennon.

Pages 4–5: John & Yoko photographed by Brian Hamill standing on Bank Street pier, New York, looking out over the Hudson River, 13 October 1972.
Pages 6–7: John & Yoko photographed by Brian Hamill strolling past a prime meat market in the West Village, New York, 13 October 1972.
Pages 8–9: John & Yoko photographed by Bob Gruen, walking up Central Park West, New York, 2 April 1973, after the Declaration of Nutopia press conference and before viewing their Dakota apartment for the first time.
Pages 280–281: Stills from the 'Mind Games' music video, directed by John, showing him strolling through Central Park and other locations in New York; filmed on 15 November 1974.

10   Notes (handwritten): John Lennon, on mixing the Mind Games album, 1973.
13   Print interview: Uncut, 2016.
14–15   Lyrics: 'Mind Games' written by John Lennon © 1973 Lenono Music administered by Downtown Publishing Ltd.
16   Radio interview: BBC Radio, 6 December 1980.
        Audio interview: David Sheff, 10–28 September 1980.
        Press interviews: Peter Goddard, Toronto Star, 22 February 1973; Patrick Snyder-Scumpy with Jack Breschard, Crawdaddy, March 1974; Beverly Magid, Record World, 17 November 1973; Ron Skoler, Rock, 14 August 1972.
        TV interview: Elliot Mintz, Channel 7 Eyewitness News, 1 November 1973.
18   Lyrics: 'Mind Games' written by John Lennon © 1973 Lenono Music administered by Downtown Publishing Ltd.
19   Press interviews: Beverly Magid, Record World, 17 November 1973; Ron Skoler, Rock, 14 August 1972.
21   Lyrics: 'Make Love Not War' written by John Lennon © 1970 Lenono Music administered by Downtown Publishing Ltd.
23   Notes (handwritten): John Lennon, 1970 and 1973.
29   Essay: John Lennon, 1978, published in Skywriting by Word of Mouth, Pan Books, 1986.
30   Essay: John Lennon, 1978, published in Skywriting by Word of Mouth, Pan Books, 1986.
        Audio interview: David Sheff, 10–28 September 1980.
        Press interview: Petticoat, March 1971.
        Audio interview: Tom Donahue, KSAN-FM, 21 September 1974.
31   Video interview: Maharishi Mahesh Yogi, Mantra and Transcendental Meditation, 22 July 2009.
        Essay: Maharishi Mahesh Yogi.
32   Audio interview: David Sheff, 18 July 1980.
        Books: Richard DiLello, The Longest Cocktail Party, Charisma, 1972; Derek Taylor, Fifty Years Adrift (In an Open Necked Shirt), Genesis Publications, 1984; Jonathan Cott, Days That I'll Remember, Omnibus Press, 2013.
        Press interview: Sunday People, September 1968.
33   Audio interviews: David Sheff, 10–28 September 1980 and 18 July 1989.
        Press interview: John Blake, Liverpool Echo, 27 April 1979.
35   Book: Cheiro (William John Warner), Cheiro's Book of Numbers, London Publishing Company, 1926, with handwritten annotations by John Lennon, 1968.
36   Essay: Yoko Ono, 'On Numbers', 3 May 1971, first published in This Is Not Here exhibition catalogue (Everson Museum of Art, Syracuse, 1971).
37   Essay: Yoko Ono, 'On Numbers', 3 May 1971, first published in This Is Not Here exhibition catalogue (Everson Museum of Art, Syracuse, 1971).
        Notes (handwritten): Yoko Ono and John Lennon, numerological calculations.
38–9   Notes (handwritten): John Lennon, left and right hand prints and handwriting in ink.
42–3   Notes (handwritten): John Lennon, I Ching diary, 1973, including lyric fragments of 'Mind Games', 'You Are Here', 'One Day (At A Time)' and 'Aisumasen (I'm Sorry)' written by John Lennon © 1973 Lenono Music administered by Downtown Publishing Ltd. and The Serenity Prayer variously attributed to Winnifred Crane Wygal and Reinhold Niebuhr, 1930s.
53   Essay: Yoko Ono, 'Sometime In NYC or Why We Would Love To Live In New York', March 1972.
56   Essay: Yoko Ono, 'Sometime In NYC or Why We Would Love To Live In New York', March 1972.
58–9   Lyrics: 'Tight A$' written by John Lennon © 1973 Lenono Music administered by Downtown Publishing Ltd.
60   Radio interviews: Capital Radio, 12 November 1973; Tony Prince, Radio Luxembourg, 12 December 1973.
        Press conference: Bed-In for Peace Event, Room 702, Hilton Hotel, Amsterdam, Holland, 26 March 1969.
        Press interviews: Roy Carr, New Musical Express, 7 October 1972; Bill Jobes, Washington Star, 6 February 1975.
63–4   Essay: John Lennon, 'The Price of Fun', 1978, published in Skywriting by Word of Mouth, Pan Books, 1986.
        TV interviews: Bob Harris, Old Grey Whistle Test, BBC TV, 17 March 1975; Jon Wiener with Amy Goodman, Democracy Now, 8 December 2005; Yoko with Amy Goodman, Democracy Now, 17 October 2007.
        Press interviews: Andrew Tyler, New Musical Express, 19 January 1974; Lisa Robinson, Hit Parader, December 1975.
69   Essay: Jerry Rubin (typewritten with handwritten annotations by Rubin): 'A Report on Ann Arbor and the Freeing of John Sinclair', 10 December 1971, first published in Berkeley Barb, 24–30 December 1971.
71   Essay: John Lennon, published in Skywriting by Word of Mouth, Pan Books, 1986.

Film interview: *The US vs John Lennon*, Lionsgate, 2006.

73   Essay: Tom Hayden, 'Enemy of the State: The Secret War Against John Lennon', published in *Memories of John Lennon* edited by Yoko Ono, 2005.

77   Essay: Tom Hayden, 'Enemy of the State: The Secret War Against John Lennon', published in *Memories of John Lennon* edited by Yoko Ono, 2005.

78–9   Lyrics: 'Aisumasen (I'm Sorry)' written by John Lennon © 1973 Lenono Music administered by Downtown Publishing Ltd.

81   TV interviews: Bob Harris, *Old Grey Whistle Test*, BBC TV, 17 March 1975.
Film interview: *American Masters*, PBS, 2010.
Essay: Yoko Ono, *John Lennon Anthology*, 1998.
Audio interviews: David Sheff, 29 June 1989; Simon Hilton, 2018.

82   Essay: Yoko Ono, *John Lennon Anthology*, 1998.
Press Interview: Jolyon Wilde, *Sunday People*, 16 December 1973; Francis Schoenberger, *Spin*, 1975 (published October 1988); Pete Hamill, *Rolling Stone*, 5 July 1975.
Radio interview: Dave Sholin, RKO, 8 December 1980.
Audio interview: David Sheff, 10–28 September 1980.

84–5   Lyrics: 'One Day At A Time' written by John Lennon © 1973 Lenono Music administered by Downtown Publishing Ltd.

86   Audio interviews: David Sheff, 10–28 September 1980; Maurice Hindle, 2 December 1968; Hans Ulrich Obrist, April 2009; Simon Hilton, 9 September 2009.
Press interviews: *Beat*, September 1971; Alan Smith, *New Musical Express*, 31 July 1971; Jann S. Wenner, *Rolling Stone*, 4 February 1971; Barbara Graustark, *Rolling Stone*, 1 October 1981; Henry Edwards, *Crawdaddy*, 9 August 1971.
Essay: Yoko Ono, *Weight Object No 5 / Mind Scale*, 1990.
Online: Yoko Ono, Facebook and Twitter Q&As, imaginepeace.com, 2009–16.

99   Press Interview: Francis Schoenberger, *Spin*, 1975 (published October 1988); Chris Charlesworth, *Melody Maker*, November 1973.
Audio interviews: Simon Hilton, 2023; Philip Norman, 2008; David Sheff, 14 July 1989.
Book: Bob Gruen, *John Lennon: The New York Years*, Stewart, Tabori & Chang, 2005.

101   Handwritten notes: Yoko Ono.

112–13   Lyrics: 'Bring On The Lucie' written by John Lennon © 1973 Lenono Music administered by Downtown Publishing Ltd.

114   Press interviews: Chris Charlesworth, *Melody Maker*, November 1973; Andrew Tyler, *New Musical Express*, January 1974; Patrick Snyder-Scumpy with Jack Breschard, *Crawdaddy*, March 1974; Jann S. Wenner, *Rolling Stone*, January 1971.
Film interview: Gloria Emerson, *24 Hours with John & Yoko*, BBC TV, 1969.
Book: Jon Weiner, *Come Together*, University of Illinois Press, 1991.

118   Press interviews: Chris Charlesworth, *Melody Maker*, November 1973; *Daily Express*, June 1973; Steve Peacock, *Rock*, March 1973; Andrew Tyler, *New Musical Express*, January 1974; Lisa Robinson, *Hit Parader*, December 1975; Francis Schoenberger, *Spin*, 1975 (published October 1988); Ivor David, *Daily Express*, November 1973.

121   Letter (handwritten): John Lennon to Hall Smith.

128   Essay: John Lennon & Yoko Ono: 'Declaration of Nutopia', 1 April 1973.

129   Essay: Yoko Ono, 'Surrender to Peace', *New York Times*, December 1982.
Audio interview: Daniel Schecter, June 1973.
Press interviews: Ivor David, *Daily Express*, November 1973; Steve Peacock, *Sounds*, November 1973; Steve Peacock, *Rock*, March 1973; Peter Occhiogrosso, *Soho News*, December 1980.
Essay: Yoko Ono, 'On This Day of the Birth of Nutopia', imaginepeace.com, 1 April 2008.

130   Announcement by the National Committee for John and Yoko for a press conference at the Association of the Bar of the City of New York, 42 W44th Street, New York on 2 April 1973.

137   Letters (typewritten): John Lennon, to Elephant's Memory, his father Freddie Lennon and Harold and David.

144   Essays: Yoko Ono, *Onobox*, 1992 and 'Memoirs', 1992.

146   Press interview: Betty Danfield, *The Detroit News*, June 1973.

148   Audio recording: Yoko Ono, NOW Feminist Conference, June 1973.

149   Lyrics: 'Coffin Car' written by Yoko Ono © 1973 Ono Music administered by Downtown Publishing Ltd.

150   Booklet: Yoko Ono, *To My Sisters with Love*, 1973, containing lyrics to: 'O Sisters O Sisters' written by Yoko Ono © 1972 Ono Music administered by Downtown Publishing Ltd.; 'Looking Over From My Hotel Window' written by Yoko Ono © 1973 Ono Music administered by Downtown Publishing Ltd.; 'Woman Is The Nigger Of The World' written by John Lennon © 1972 Lenono Music administered by Downtown Publishing Ltd.; and essays: Yoko Ono, 'What Is the Relationship Between the World and the Artist', Cannes Film

Festival, May 1971, first published in *This Is Not Here* exhibition catalogue (Everson Museum of Art, Syracuse, 1971); and poems: Yoko Ono, 'Air Talk', 1967, from 'Some Notes On The Lisson Gallery Show' published in Yoko Ono at *Yoko Ono: Half-A-Wind Show* (London Lisson Gallery, 1967) reprinted in *Grapefruit*, Sphere, 1971; 'Sense Piece', 1968, published in *Grapefruit*, 1971 ; 'Water Talk', 1967, for *Half-A-Wind Show*, Lisson Gallery, London 1967, reprinted in *Grapefruit*, 1971; 'Let's Piece I', 1960, published in *Grapefruit*, 1971.

151   Booklet: Yoko Ono, *To My Sisters with Love*, 1973, containing lyrics to: 'Approximately Infinite Universe' written by Yoko Ono © 1972 Ono Music administered by Downtown Publishing Ltd.; 'Coffin Car' written by Yoko Ono © 1972 Ono Music administered by Downtown Publishing Ltd.; 'Warrior Women' written by Yoko Ono © 1972 Ono Music administered by Downtown Publishing Ltd.; and essay: 'Victims of the Phantom Society', 15 March 1973, first published in *The Staff*, vol, 3, no. 10 (issue 79), 23–29 March 1973.

154–6   Essay: Yoko Ono, 'The Feminization of Society', February 1972, abridged version first published in the *New York Times*, February 1972; first published as an unabridged version in *Sundance*, May 1972.

162   Essays: Yoko Ono, *Onobox*, 1992 and 'Memoirs', 1992.
Audio interviews: BBC Radio, 6 December 1980; David Sheff, 14 July 1989.

163   Essay: John Lennon, 'This Could Be the Start of Something, Pig', 1973.

164–5   Essay: John Lennon, 'A Tale of Two Titties', 1973.

166   Essay: Berit Ås, 'As Good as Swimming', 2003.

167   Letter (typewritten): John Lennon to Bitten Modal, 1973.

168   Essay (typewritten): John Lennon, 'On Being Inclined But Not Having the Wherewithall', 1973.

169   Letter (typewritten): John Lennon to R. P. Bagguley, *Sun Time*, 27 May 1973.

170–1   Letters (typewritten): John Lennon, to Elliot Mintz, June 1973 and Elliot Mintz, to John Lennon, 25 June 1973.

172–3   Lyrics: 'Intuition' written by John Lennon © 1973 Lenono Music administered by Downtown Publishing Ltd.

174–7   Audio interview: David Sheff, 10–28 September 1980.
Online: Yoko Ono, Facebook and Twitter Q&As, imaginepeacecom, 2009–16.
Press interviews: Ivor David, *Daily Express*, November 1973; Lisa Robinson, *Hit Parader*, December 197; Peter Occhiogrosso, *Soho News*, December 1980; Robert Hilburn, *LA Times*, December 1973; Francis Shoenberger, *Spin*, 1975 (published October 1988); Beverly Magid, *Record World*, 17 November 1973.
Essay: John Lennon, 'The Ballad of John and Yoko', 1978, published in *Skywriting by Word of Mouth*, Pan Books, 1986.

176   Notes (handwritten): John Lennon, 1972–73.

178–9   Lyrics: 'Out The Blue' written by John Lennon © 1973 Lenono Music administered by Downtown Publishing Ltd.

180   Essay (verbatim transcription from typewritten pages with handwritten annotations): John Lennon, 'Memoirs', 1970s.

182   Press interviews: Ivor David, *Daily Express*, November 1973; Beverly Magid, *Record World*, November 1973; Roy Carr, *New Musical Express*, October 1972; Tom Doyle, *Q*, October 2010; Barbara Graustark, *Newsweek*, December 1980.
Audio interview: David Sheff, 10–28 September 1980, BBC Radio, 6 December 1980.
Film interview: *24 Hours with John & Yoko*, BBC TV, 1969.

186–7   Lyrics: 'Only People' written by John Lennon © 1973 Lenono Music administered by Downtown Publishing Ltd.

188   Essay: Yoko Ono, *Mind Games* LP liner notes, November 1973.
Radio interview: Dave Sholin, RKO, 8 December 1980.
TV interview: *The Mike Douglas Show*, Westinghouse, 14–18 February 1973; David Frost, 19 June 1969.

189   Audio recording: Troops out of SE Asia rally, Times Square, New York, 22 April 1972.

191   Press conference: *Bed-In for Peace Event*, Room 702, Hilton Hotel, Amsterdam, Holland, 26 March 1969.
Film Interview: Abram De Swaan, *Rood Wit Blau*, Nederland 2, 12 December 1968.
Essay: John Lennon & Yoko Ono, 'Declaration of Nutopia', 1 April 1973.

192–3   Lyrics: 'I Know (I Know)' written by John Lennon © 1973 Lenono Music administered by Downtown Publishing Ltd.

194   Press interviews: Patrick Snyder-Scumpy, *Crawdaddy*, March 1974; Robert Hilburn, *LA Times*, 23 January 1973; Chris Charlesworth, *Melody Maker*, 8 March 1975; *Rolling Stone*, 19 July 1973; Peter Goddard, *Toronto Star*, 22 February 1973; Ron Skoler, *Rock*, 14 August 1972; Ivor David, *Daily Express*, 17 November 1973.

195   Letter (typewritten with handwritten annotations): John Lennon, to Paul McCartney and Linda from Sonny and Cher O'Lennon.

196   Lyrics: 'I'm The Greatest' written by John Lennon © 1973 Lenono Music administered by Downtown Publishing Ltd.

ACKNOWLEDGMENTS

199 Press interviews: Robert Hilburn, *LA Times*, December 1973; Andrew Tyler, *New Musical Express*, January 1974; Chris Charlesworth, *Melody Maker*, March 1975; Peter Occhiogrosso, *Soho News*, December 1980; Andrew Tyler, *New Musical Express*, September 1973; Martin Kirkup, *Sounds*, September 1973; Faye Levine, *Ms. Magazine*, October 1973; Dave Marsh, *Newsday*, October 1973. Audio interview with Elliot Mintz, Beverly Hills Hotel, 16 April 1973.

200–1 Letter (handwritten): John Lennon, 'Newsweakanalldowithout', 23 March 1973.

202 Memorandum (handwritten): John Lennon, 'Imagine no possessions', May/June 1973.

203 Letters (typewritten): John Lennon, to ABKCO, 29 May 1973; Allen Klein, May 1973; John Lennon; and Jack, 30 July 1973.

204–5 Lyrics: 'You Are Here' written by John Lennon © 1973 Lenono Music administered by Downtown Publishing Ltd.

206 Audio interviews: Howard Smith, September 1971; Elliot Mintz, Beverly Hills Hotel, 16 April 1973; David Wigg, June 1969. TV interview: *Frost on Sunday*, BBC, August 1968. Press interview: David Bailey, *GQ*, March 2014.

209 Audio interview: Elliot Mintz, Beverly Hills Hotel, 16 April 1973.

210–11 Lyrics: 'Meat City' written by John Lennon © 1973 Lenono Music administered by Downtown Publishing Ltd.

213 Press interviews: Chris Charlesworth, *Melody Maker*, November 1973; Francis Shoenberger, *Spin*, 1975 (published October 1988); Ron Skoler, *Rock*, August 1972; Andrew Tyler, *New Musical Express*, January 1974; Steve Peacock, *Rock*, March 1974; Jean-François Vallée, *Record Mirror*, April 1972; Barbara Lewis, *Ohio Gazette*, October 1973; Jonathan Cott, *Rolling Stone*, March 1971. TV interviews: Bob Harris, *Old Grey Whistle Test*, BBC, April 1975; John Lennon speaking to reporters after receiving his green card, US Immigration and Naturalisation Services offices, 26 Federal Plaza, New York, 27 July 1976; interview with Yoko Ono, 2005; *American Masters*, PBS, 2010.

215 Press interviews: Andrew Tyler, *New Musical Express*, January 1974; Jean-François Vallée, *Record Mirror*, April 1972; Jonathan Cott, *Rolling Stone*, March 1971. Audio interview: David Wigg, BBC, May 1969. TV interview: Bob Harris, *Old Grey Whistle Test*, BBC, April 1975; John Lennon speaking to reporters after receiving his green card, 27 July 1976; interview with Yoko Ono, 2005; *American Masters*, PBS, 2010. Press conference: *Bed-In for Peace Event*, Room 702, Hilton Hotel, Amsterdam, Holland, 26 March 1969.

217 TV interview: Bob Harris, *Old Grey Whistle Test*, BBC, April 1975. Audio interview: David Wigg, BBC, May 1969. Press conference: *Bed-In for Peace Event*, Room 702, Hilton Hotel, Amsterdam, Holland, 26 March 1969.

222 Press interview: Francis Schoenberger, *Spin*, 1975 (published October 1988); Patrick Snyder-Scumpy, *Crawdaddy*, March 1974; Beverly Magid, *Record World*, November 1973; Caroline Boucher, *Disc*, November 1973; Chris Charlesworth, *Melody Maker*, November 1973. Audio interview: Simon Hilton, 2019.

224 Online interview: meetthebeatlesforreal.com, 2012.

227–8 TV interview: *American Masters*, PBS, 2010.

232 Audio interview: Simon Hilton (Dan Barbiero), 2023.

238–9 Audio interview: Simon Hilton (Jimmy Iovine), 2023.

242 Audio interview: Simon Hilton (Jim Keltner), 2023.

243 Audio interview: Simon Hilton (David Spinozza), 2023.

246 Audio interview: Simon Hilton (Ken Ascher), 2023.

247 Audio interview: Simon Hilton (Gordon Edwards), 2023.

248 Online interview: acousticstorm.com, October 2004. Essay: Sneaky Pete Kleinow, album liner notes, 1979. Press interviews: Rex Anderson, *New Musical Express*; Mick Houghton, *ZigZag*, March 1975; Joe Goldmark, *Steel Guitarist Magazine #2*, May 1979; *Steel Guitar Forum*.

250–1 Audio interviews: Simon Hilton (Christine Wiltshire & Jocelyn Brown), 2023.

253 Video interview: *Michael Brecker Q&A at The University of North Texas*, 1984. Audio interview: Simon Hilton (Rick Marotta), 2023.

256 Audio interview: BBC Radio, 6 December 1980; David Sheff, 10–28 September 1980.

267 Press interview: Andrew Tyler, *New Musical Express*, 19 January 1974. Books: Tony King, *The Tastemaker*, Faber & Faber, 2023; Elton John, *Me*, Macmillan, 2019.

274 TV interview: Elliot Mintz, Malibu Beach, CA, *Channel 7 Eyewitness News*, 1 November 1973.

277 TV interview: Elliot Mintz, Malibu Beach, CA, *Channel 7 Eyewitness News*, 1 November 1973.

A dream you dream alone is only a dream;
A dream you dream together is a reality.
y.o.

Producer and Creative Direction: Yoko Ono Lennon & Sean Ono Lennon

Editor: Simon Hilton

Publisher: Tristan de Lancey
Designer: Nick Jakins
Managing Editor: Jane Laing
Associate Editor: Georgina Kyriacou
Senior Production Controller: Sadie Butler

Lenono Photo Archive: Karla Merrifield, Sari Henry and Gina Devincenzi

Lenono Art Archive: Connor Monahan, Marcia Bassett, Michael Sirianni and Nick Lalla

Lenono Audio Archive: Rob Stevens

Lenono Film Archive: Simon Hilton

Studio One: Helen Barden, Sibyl Bender and Bob Deeb

Legal: Jonas Herbsman

PR: Murray Chalmers at MCPR

Initial photo restoration and Photoshop work: Simon Hilton and Sam Gannon

Additional research: Sam Gannon and Grace Davyd

Film and video archive transfers: Dave Northrop, Bruce W. Goldstein, Scott Delaney, Jack Serrani, Stephen Walsh, Rob DeSaro, Beth Simon, Elle Crowley and André Macaluso at Deluxe Northvale

Special thanks:
Sean Ono Lennon, Julian Lennon, Kyoko Ono, Charlotte Kemp Muhl, Corrie Deeb, Casady Gifford, Chanda Misevis, Jonas Herbsman, Jim and Cynthia Keltner, Gordon Edwards and Bridget St. John, Rick Marotta, David Spinozza, Ken Ascher, Christine Wiltshire, Jocelyn Brown, Dan Barbiero, Jimmy Iovine, Cary Jones at Not Today, Bob and Elizabeth Gruen and Richelle DeLora at Bob Gruen Studio, Nadya Gruen, Elliot Mintz, Jann S. Wenner, Jon Hendricks, Sara Seagull, Dick Cavett, Berit Ås, Inge Ås, Marie Lacey, Robin Titone, Goldie Friede, Barbara McDede, Paul Hicks, Matthew Cocker, Richard Perry, Pat Thomas, Dan and Jill Richter, Peter Bendrey, Paul McGhie, Guy Hayden, Hannah Neaves, Azi Eftekhari, Adam Barker, Alex Doherty, Jonathan Richman, Haris Abbey, Bruno Morelli, Sujata Murthy, Tim Plumley, Darren Evans, Faye Fanneran, Graham Simpson, Emita Meetarbhan, James Swindells, Dan London, Alex Aiken, Chris Ramsay, Alexander Crowe, David Plowden, Mary Ellen Budney, Stephen Goeman and David Driscoll at Beinecke Rare Book & Manuscript Library Yale University, Lucienne Powell, Diana Hilton, Peter and Jenny Powell, Mayra Acosta Martinez, Megan Maher and Christy Barnes

Websites:
johnlennon.com
imaginepeace.com
citizenofnutopia.com

INDEX

Overleaf: John Lennon & Yoko Ono – *War Is Over! If You Want It Love and Peace from John & Yoko*, 1969/1971; offset lithograph, 76 × 50.8 cm.

WAR IS OVER!

IF YOU WANT IT

Love and Peace from John & Yoko